Autobiography in Indian Writing in English

Autobiography in Indian Writing in English

Lawrence D'Souza

CYBER TECH PUBLICATIONS
4264/3, Ansari Road, Daryaganj, New Delhi-110002 (India)
Ph.: 011-23244078. Fax: 011-23280028
E-Mail: cyberpublicationsdelhi@yahoo.com

AUTOBIOGRAPHY IN INDIAN WRITING IN ENGLISH

Lawrence D'Souza

First Edition 2009

Published by :

G.S. Rawat for **Cyber Tech Publications**
4264/3, Ansari Road, Daryaganj, New Delhi-110002 (India)
Ph.: 011-23244078. Fax: 011-23280028
E-Mail: cyberpublicationsdelhi@yahoo.com

Preface

"Autobiography in Indian Writing in English" is very humble endeavour to present Indian critical responses to Indian poetry, prose fiction, drama and autobiography. The contributors are from various Indian Universities. They have enriched this book with their research findings.

The book highlight different aspects of Indian life and literature in English in simple and understandable style which is a veritable literary feast to the students, researchers and teachers of Indian writing in English.

Though foreign in its origin, English has been adopted in India as a language of education and literary expression besides being an important medium of communication amongst the people of various regions. The beginning of Indian literature in English is traced to the end of the 18th century and the beginning of the 19th, by which time English education was more or less firmly established in the three major centers of British power in India - Calcutta, Madras and Bombay. Ram Mohan Roy (1774-1833), a social reformist from Bengal who fought for widow remarriage and voting rights for women, was the pioneer of Indian writing in English. Roy insisted that for India to be included among the world's nations, education in English was essential. He, therefore, campaigned for introduction of scientific education in India through the English medium.

The freedom struggle resulted in a revolutionary brand of writing that voiced sentiments against the British Empire. Several political leaders from different parts of the country emerged as literary figures such as Bal Gangadhar Tilak, Lala Lajpath Rai, Kasturi Ranga Iyengar and T. Prakasham. The English language became a sharp and strong instrument in the hands of Gandhiji, who edited and wrote for papers like 'Young India' and 'Harijan'. He also wrote his autobiography, 'My Experiments With Truth', which is known for its literary flair. Jawaharlal Nehru (1889-1964) stands out as another prominent leader who excelled in writing prose. He is particularly remembered for his Glimpses of World History, Discovery of India and An Autobiography (1936).

—Author

CONTENTS

1

Indian English Literature

Indian English Literature (IEL) refers to the body of work by writers in India who write in the English language and whose native or co-native language could be one of the numerous languages of India. It is also associated with the works of members of the Indian diaspora, especially people like Salman Rushdie who was born in India. It is frequently referred to as Indo-Anglian literature. (Indo-Anglian is a specific term in the sole context of writing that should not be confused with the term Anglo-Indian). As a category, this production comes under the broader realm of postcolonial literature- the production from previously colonised countries such as India.

Indian English Literature has a relatively recent history, it is only one and a half centuries old. The first book written by an Indian in English was by Sake Dean Mahomet, titled Travels of Dean Mahomet; Mahomet's travel narrative was published in 1793 in England. In its early stages it was influenced by the Western art form of the novel. Early Indian writers used English unadulterated by Indian words to convey an experience which was essentially Indian. Raja Rao's Kanthapura is Indian in terms of its storytelling qualities. Rabindranath Tagore wrote in Bengali and English and was responsible for the translations of his own work into English. Dhan Gopal Mukerji was the first Indian author to win a literary award in the United States. Nirad C. Chaudhuri, a writer of non-fiction, is best known for his The Autobiography of an Unknown Indian where he relates his life experiences and influences. P. Lal, a poet, translator, publisher and essayist, founded a press in the 1950's for Indian English writing, Writers Workshop.

R.K. Narayan is a writer who contributed over many decades and who continued to write till his death recently. He was discovered by Graham Greene in the sense that the latter helped him find a publisher in England. Graham Greene and Narayan remained close friends till the end. Similar to Thomas Hardy's Wessex, Narayan created the fictitious town of Malgudi where he set his novels.

Some criticise Narayan for the parochial, detached and closed world that he created in the face of the changing conditions in India at the times in which the stories are set. Others, such as Graham Greene, however, feel that through Malgudi they could vividly understand the Indian experience. Narayan's evocation of small town life and its experiences through the eyes of the endearing child protagonist Swaminathan in Swami and Friends is a good sample of his writing style.

Simultaneous with Narayan's pastoral idylls, a very different writer, Mulk Raj Anand, was similarly gaining recognition for his writing set in rural India; but his stories were harsher, and engaged, sometimes brutally, with divisions of caste, class and religion.

LATER HISTORY

Among the later writers, the most notable is Salman Rushdie, born in India, now living in the United Kingdom. Rushdie with his famous work Midnight's Children (Booker Prize 1981, Booker of Bookers 1992) ushered in a new trend of writing. He used a hybrid language - English generously peppered with Indian terms - to convey a theme that could be seen as representing the vast canvas of India. He is usually categorised under the magic realism mode of writing most famously associated with Gabriel García Márquez.

Bharati Mukherjee, author of Jasmine (1989), has spent much of her career exploring issues involving immigration and identity with a particular focus upon the United States and Canada.

Vikram Seth, author of A Suitable Boy (1994) is a writer who uses a purer English and more realistic themes. Being a self-confessed fan of Jane Austen, his attention is on the story, its details and its twists and turns.

Shashi Tharoor, in his The Great Indian Novel (1989), follows a story-telling (though in a satirical) mode as in the Mahabharata drawing his ideas by going back and forth in time. His work as UN official living outside India has given him a vantage point that helps construct an objective Indianness.

Other authors include Anita Desai, Kiran Desai, Arundhati Roy, Chitra Banerjee Divakaruni, Raj Kamal Jha, Jhumpa Lahiri, Bharti Kirchner, Khushwant Singh, Amit Chaudhuri, Amitav Ghosh, Vikas Swarup, Rohinton Mistry, Kiran Nagarkar and C R Krishnan.

DEBATES

It would be useful at this point to bring in the recent debates on Indian Writing in English ("IWE").

One of the key issues raised in this context is the superiority/ inferiority of IWE as opposed to the literary production in the various languages of India. Key polar concepts bandied in this context are superficial/authentic, imitative/creative, shallow/ deep, critical/uncritical, elitist/parochial and so on.

The views of Rushdie and Amit Chaudhuri expressed through their books The Vintage Book of Indian Writing and The Picador Book of Modern Indian Literature respectively essentialise this battle.

Rushdie's statement in his book - "the ironic proposition that India's best writing since independence may have been done in the language of the departed imperialists is simply too much for some folks to bear" - created a lot of resentment among many writers, including writers in English. In his book, Amit Chaudhuri questions - "Can it be true that Indian writing, that endlessly rich, complex and problematic entity, is to be represented by a handful of writers who write in English, who live in England or America and whom one might have met at a party?"

Chaudhuri feels that after Rushdie, IWE started employing magical realism, bagginess, non-linear narrative and hybrid language to sustain themes seen as microcosms of India and supposedly reflecting Indian conditions. He contrasts this with the works of earlier writers such as Narayan where the use of English is pure, but the deciphering of meaning needs cultural familiarity. He also feels that Indianness is a theme constructed only in IWE and does not articulate itself in the vernacular literatures. (It is probable that the level of Indianness constructed is directly proportional to the distance between the writer and India.) He further adds "the post-colonial novel, becomes a trope for an ideal hybridity by which the West celebrates not so much Indianness, whatever that infinitely complex thing is, but its own historical quest, its reinterpretation of itself".

Some of these arguments form an integral part of what is called postcolonial theory. The very categorisation of IWE - as IWE or under post-colonial literature - is seen by some as limiting. Amitav Ghosh made his views on this very clear by refusing to accept the Eurasian Commonwealth Writers Prize for his book The Glass Palace in 2001 and withdrawing it from the subsequent stage.

The renowned writer V. S. Naipaul, a third generation Indian from Trinidad and Tobago and a Nobel prize laureate, is a person who belongs to the world and usually not classified under IWE. Naipaul evokes ideas of homeland, rootlessness and his own personal feelings towards India in many of his books.

Jhumpa Lahiri, a Pulitzer prize winner from the U.S., is a writer uncomfortable under the label of IWE.

Recent writers in India such as Arundhati Roy and David Davidar show a direction towards contextuality and rootedness in their works. Arundhati Roy, a trained architect and the 1997 Booker prize winner for her The God of Small Things, calls herself a "home grown" writer. Her award winning book is set in the immensely physical landscape of Kerala. Davidar sets his The House of Blue Mangoes in Southern Tamil Nadu. In both the books, geography and politics are integral to the narrative. In his novel Lament of Mohini (2000), Shreekumar Varma touches upon the unique matriarchal system and the sammandham system of marriage as he writes about the Namboodiris and the aristocrats of Kerala.

As the number of Indian writers in English keeps increasing, with everyone with a story to tell trying to tell a story, and as publishing houses in India vie among themselves to discover the next new whiz-kid who will land up with world fame, it could become increasingly difficult to separate the wheat from the chaff. Research, debates and seminars on IWE continue with increasing frequency. However,it might be too early a stage in the history of Indian writing in English to pass any final judgement.

POETRY

A much over-looked category of Indian writing in English is poetry. As stated above, Rabindranath Tagore wrote in Bengali and English and was responsible for the translations of his own work into English. Other early notable poets in English include Derozio, Michael Madhusudan Dutt, Joseph Furtado, Armando Menezes, Toru Dutt, Romesh Chandra Dutt, Sarojini Naidu and her brother Harendranath Chattopadhyaya.

In modern times, Indian poetry in English was typified by two very different poets. Dom Moraes, winner of the Hawthornden Prize at the precocious age of 19 for his first book of poems "A Beginning" went on to occupy a pre-eminent position among Indian poets writing in English. Nissim Ezekiel, who came from India's tiny Bene Israel Jewish community, created a voice and place for Indian poets writing in English and championed their work.

Their contemporaries in English poetry in India were Arvind Mehrotra, Jayanta Mahapatra, Gieve Patel, A. K. Ramanujan, Rajagopal Parthasarathy, Keki Daruwala, Adil Jussawala, Arun Kolatkar, Dilip Chitre, Eunice De Souza, Kersi Katrak, P. Lal and Kamala Das among several others. A generation of exiles also sprang from the Indian diaspora. Among these are names like Agha Shahid Ali, Sujata Bhatt, Melanie Silgardo and Vikram Seth.

The current generation of Indian poets writing in English includes Ranjit Hoskote, Smita Agarwal, Gopi Kottoor, Jeet Thayil, Tishani Doshi, Tabish Khair, Vijay Nambisan, H. Masud Taj, Rukmini Bhaya Nair, C.P. Surendran,Imtiaz Dharker, Vivek Narayanan, Samartha Vashishtha, Meena Kandasamy, Gavin Barrett, Anjum Hasan, Jerry Pinto, Shreekumar Varma, Arundhathi Subramaniam, Anand Thakore, Meena Alexander, Gayatri Majumdar, A J Thomas, Kumar Vikram and Thachom Poyil Rajeevan.

INDO-NOSTALGIC WRITING

Indo-Nostalgic writing is a somewhat loosely defined term encompassing writings, in the English language, wherein nostalgia regarding the Indian subcontinent, typically regarding India, represent a dominant theme or strong undercurrent. The writings may be memoirs, or quasi-fictionalized memoirs, travelogues, or inspired in part by real-life experiences and in part by the writer's imagination. This would include both mass-distributed "Indo-Anglian" literature put out by major publishing houses and also much shorter articles (e.g. feature pieces in mainstream or literary magazines) or poetry, including material published initially or solely in webzines.

Certainly, Indo-Nostalgic writings have much overlap with post-colonial literature but are generally not about 'heavy' topics such as cultural identity, conflicted identities, multilingualism or rootlessness. The writings are often less self-conscious and more light-hearted, perhaps dealing with impressionistic memories of places, people, cuisines, Only-in-India situations, or simply vignettes of "the way things were". Of late, a few Indo-nostalgic writers are beginning to show signs of "long-distance nationalism", concomitant with the rise of nationalism within India against the backdrop of a booming economy.

In addition to focusing on nationalism or any universal themes, many writers emerged out with innovative ideas and techniques in writing poetry. It is a pity that there are many writers whose writings still remain unnoticed either due to lack of source to get their works recoganised or less oppurtunities does not knock the doors of the right person. Writers like Krishna Srinivas, M.K.Gopinathan, etc have contributed enormous poetry collection to the growth of Indian English Literature. Krishna Srinivas concentrated on all sorts of social aspects in his poetry, and M.K.Gopinathan poetic mission is to spread peace in the minds of the readers. M.K.Gopinathan's anthologies includes, "I go on for ever", "A Fresh Rose" and "It is not my fault" which contained interesting subjects of day to day life.

Typically, the authors are either Western-based writers of Indian origin (e.g. Salman Rushdie, Rohinton Mistry), or Western writers who have spent long periods of time in the subcontinent, possibly having been born or raised in India, perhaps as the children of British Raj-era European expatriates or missionaries (e.g. Jim Corbett, Stephen Alter). Or, they may even be Anglo-Indians who have emigrated from the subcontinent to the West. Third Culture Kids (TCKs) often grow up to produce Indo-Nostalgic writings that exhibit palpably deep (and perhaps somewhat romanticized) feelings for their childhoods in the subcontinent. Accordingly, another common theme in Indo-Nostalgic writing is "rediscovery" or its cousin, "reconnection".

Of course, for mass-distributed authors, Indo-Nostalgic writings may not necessarily represent all of their literary output, but certainly would represent a high percentage; it is their sweet spot, after all. Finally, it is worth noting that the markets for such writers are almost entirely in the West; despite the rapid growth in the incomes of urban Indians, the sales of English-language literature within India (other than books required for educational degrees or professional purposes) are minuscule compared to sales in the West, even if one includes pirated copies.

2

AUTOBIOGRAPHY OF GANDHI

Gandhi's autobiography, which he had titled 'My experiments with Truth' can be rated as one of the most popular and the most influential books in the recent history. It was written at the instance of Swami Anand. It appeared in the Weekly 'Navjivan' during 1925-28. It covers Gandhi's life up to 1920. He did not cover the period after that as it was well known to the people and most of the concerned persons were alive. Besides he felt that his experiments in that period were yet to yield definite conclusions.

Gandhi's autobiography is very different from other autobiographies. The autobiographies normally contain self-praise by the authors. They want to criticize their opponents and boost their own image in the people's eyes. Gandhi's autobiography is completely free from all this. It is marked with humility and truthfulness. He had not hidden anything. In fact, he is rather too harsh on himself. He did not want to show to the world how good he was. He only wanted to tell the people the story of his experiments with Truth.

Truth, for Gandhi, was the supreme principle, which includes many other principles. Realization of the Truth is the purpose of human life. Gandhi always strove to realize the Truth. He continuously tried to remove impurities in himself. He always tried to stick to the Truth as he knew and to apply the knowledge of the Truth to everyday life. He tried to apply the spiritual principles to the practical situations. He did it in the scientific spirit. Sticking to the truth means Satyagraha. Gandhi therefore called his experiments as 'Experiments with

Truth' or 'Experiments in the science of Satyagraha.' Gandhi also requested the readers to treat those experiments as illustrative and to carry out their own experiments in that light.

AN INTRODUCTION

Mohandas Karamchand Gandhi was a man considered one of the great sages and prophets. He was held as another Buddha, another Jesus, Indians called him the 'Father of the Nation'. They showered their love, respect and devotion on him in an unprecedented measure. They thronged his way to have a glimpse of him, to hear one world from his lips.

They applied on their foreheads the dust on the path he had trodden. For them, he was almost an incarnation of God, who had come to break the chains of their slavery. The whole world bowed to him in reverence. Even his opponents held him in great respect.

Mohandas Gandhi was, however, not a great scholar, nor was he a great warrior. He was not born with exceptional faculties. Neither was he a good orator, nor a great writer. He did not claim anything exclusively divine in him. He did not claim being a prophet or having superhuman powers. He considered himself an average man with average abilities. Born in a middle class Bania family in an obscure princely State in a corner of India, he was a mediocre student, shy and nervous. He could not muster courage to speak in public. His first attempt at legal practice miserably failed.

But he was a humble seeker of Truth. He was a man with exceptional sincerity, honesty and truthfulness. For him, understanding meant action. Once any principle appealed to him, he immediately began to translate that in practice. He did not flinch from taking risks and did not mind confessing mistakes. No opposition, scorn or ridicule could affect him. Truth was his sole guiding star. He was ever-growing; hence he was often found inconsistent. He was not concerned with appearing to be consistent. He preferred to be consistent only with the light within.

He sacrificed his all and identified himself with the poorest of the poor. He dressed like them, lived like them. In the oppressed and the depressed people, he saw God. For him, they too were sparks of the divine light. They might not have anything else, but they too had a soul. For Gandhi, soul-force was the source of the greatest power. He strove to awaken the soul-force within himself and within his fellowmen. He was convinced that the potentialities of the soul-force have no limit. He himself was a living example of this conviction. That is why this tiny and fragile man could mobilise the masses and defeat the mighty British empire. His eleven vows, his technique of Satyagraha, his constructive programme - all were meant to awaken and strengthen the soul-force. He awakened and aroused a nation from semi-consciousness. It was a Herculean task. For, India was not a united country, it was a sub-continent. It was a society divided in different classes, castes and races, in people with different languages, religions and cultures.

It was a society where almost half of the population i.e., women, was behind purdah or confined to the four walls of houses, where one-fourth of the population - the depressed classes - was living marginalised life, where many did not have a single full meal every day. Gandhi made the oppressed sections wake up and break their chains. He mobilised the people and united them to work for the cause of Swaraj, which gave them a sense of belonging, a sense of purpose. Gandhi wanted to win Swaraj for the masses. For him, Swaraj did not mean replacement of White masters by brown masters. Swaraj meant self-rule by all. He said: "Real Swaraj will come, not by the acquisition of the authority by a few, but by the acquisition of the capacity by all to resist authority when it is abused." He worked to develop such a capacity. Development of such a capacity involved transformation of the individual.

Transformation of the individual and transformation of the society - they were not separate, unrelated things for Gandhi. Revolutionary social philosophies had concentrated on changing the society. On the other hand, spiritual seekers had concentrated on the inner change. Gandhi not only bridged the gap between these extremes, he fused them together. Gandhi was thus both a saint and a social revolutionary. For Gandhi, unity of life was great truth. His principle of non-violence stemmed from this conviction. Non-violence was not a matter of policy for him; it was a matter of faith. He applied the doctrine to all the departments of individual and social life and in so doing revolutionized the doctrine, made it dynamic and creative. He believed that a true civilization could be built on the basis of such non-violence only.

He rejected the modern civilization. For him, it was a disease and a curse. This civilization leads to violence, conflicts, corruption, injustices, exploitation, oppression, mistrust and a process of dehumanisation. It has led the world to a deep crisis. The earth's resources are being cornered by a handful of people without any concern for others and for the coming generations. The conventional energy sources are getting depleted. Forests are being destroyed. Air, water, soil-everything has been polluted.

We are living under the shadow of nuclear war and environmental disasters. Thinking men the world over are looking to Gandhi to find a way out of this crisis and to build an alternative model of sustainable development. Gandhi knew that the earth has enough to satisfy everybody's need but not anybody's greed. He had called for the replacement of greed with love. Gandhi is, therefore, now a source of inspiration and a reference book for all those fighting against racial discrimination, oppression, domination, wars, nuclear energy, environmental degradation, lack of freedom and human rights-for all those who are fighting for a better world, a better quality of life. Gandhi is, therefore, no longer an individual. He is a symbol of all that is the best and the most enduring in the human tradition. And he is also a symbol of the alternative in all areas of life-agriculture, industry, technology, education, health, economy, political organisations, etc. He is a man of the future - a future that has to be shaped if the human race has to survive and progress on the path of evolution.

We hereby give a short version compiled from his Autobiography. We cover the period of his life from 1869 to 1922.

BIRTH AND PARENTAGE

Mohandas Karamchand Gandhi was born at Porbandar, a coastal city in Kathiawad (now a part of the Gujarat State) on the 2nd October 1869. He was the youngest child of his parents, Karamchand and Putlibai.

Gandhis belonged to the Modh Bania community. They were originally grocers. However, Uttamchand, Mohan's grandfather, rose to become Dewan of the Porbandar State. Mohan's father. Karamchand, also served as the Dewan of Porbandar, Rajkot and Vankaner States. Kathiawar then had about 300 small States.

Court intrigues were the order of the day. At times, Gandhis became their victim. Uttamchand's house wasonce surrounded and shelled by the State troops. Karamchand was once arrested. However, their courage and wisdom earned them respect. Karamchand even became a member of the Rajashanik Court, a powerful agency to solve disputes among the States.

Karamchand had little education, but had shrewdness of judgment and practical knowledge acquired through experience. He had little inclination to amass wealth and left little for his children. He used to say that "My children are my wealth'. He married four times, had two daughters by the first two marriages and one daughter and three sons by his fourth marriage. Putlibai, his fourth wife, was younger to him by 25 years. She was not much educated but was well-informed about practical matters.

Ladies at the palace used to value her advice. She was deeply religious and superstitious and had strong will-power. She used to visit the temple daily and regularly kept difficult vows. Mohan loved his mother. He used to accompany her to the Haveli (Vaishnav temple).

Mohan had a great devotion for his father and he often used to be present at the discussions about the State problems. Gandhis had Parsi and Muslim friends and Jain monks used to make regular visit. Mohan thus had occasion to hear discussions about religious matters also. Being the youngest, he was the darling of the household.

Childhood

Mohan attended Primary School at Porbandar. When he was seven, his family moved to Rajkot. He was a mediocre student, was shy and avoided any company. He read little besides the text books and had no love for outdoor games. He had no love for outdoor games. However, he was truthful, honest, sensitive and was alert about his character. Plays about Shravan and Harishchandra made a deep impression on him. They taught him to be truthful at any cost and to serve his parents with devotion.

He was married along with his brother and cousin for the sake of economy and convenience. He was only 13 then. He enjoyed the festivities of the marriage. Kasturbai, his wife, was of the same age. She was illiterate but strong-willed. His jealousy and immature efforts to make her an ideal wife led to many quarrels. He wanted to teach her but found no time. His experience later made him a strong critic of child-marriages.

Mohan joined High School at Rajkot. He was liked by the teachers and often received prizes. But he neglected physical training and hand-writing. Habit of taking long walks made up for the first neglect, but he had to repent later for the neglect of handwriting. He was devoted to his father and considered it his duty to nurse him during his illness. In the High-School, he made friends with one Sheikh Mehtab, a bad character. He stuck to the friendship despite warnings from family-members. He wanted to reform Mehtab but failed. Mehtab induced him to meat-eating, saying that it made one strong and that the British were ruling India because they were meat-eaters. Mohan was frail and used to be afraid even to go out alone in the dark. The argument appealed to him. Later, he realized that lying to his parents was worse than not eating meat, and abandoned the experiment.

Mehtab once sent him to a brothel, but God's grace saved him. He induced Mohan to smoking. This once led to stealing. But all this became unbearable for Mohan. He confessed his guilt to his father, who did not rebuke him but wept silently. Those tears cleaned Mohan's heart and taught him a lesson in nonviolence. Mohan's father died when Mohan was 16. He had nursed him daily. But at the time of his death, Mohan was with his wife. He always felt ashamed for this lapse. Mohan passed the matriculation examination in 1887. He attended the College at Bhavnagar, but left after the first term. At that time, the idea of his going to England for studying law came up. Mohan was fascinated. He made up his mind and overcame resistance from the family-members. He took the vow not to touch wine, women and meat at the instance of his mother to remove her fears. He then sailed from Bombay in September 1888, leaving behind his wife and a son. The caste elders were against his going to England. They excommunicated him from the caste.

Gandhi in England

Gandhi reached England by the end of September 1888. Everything was strange to him. He was shy and diffident, could not speak English fluently and was ignorant of British manners. Naturally, loneliness and homesickness gripped him. Gandhi became a vegetarian for life. It was difficult to get vegetarian food. Friends persuaded him to break the vow of vegetarianism but he stuck to it. He began searching vegetarian restaurants and found one ultimately. He purchased Salt's book 'Plea for Vegetarianism', read it and became vegetarian out of conviction. He studied other literature and joined the Vegetarian Society. He came in contact with the leaders of that radical cult, became a member of the Society's Executive Committee and contributed articles to the Society's paper. He even started a Vegetarian club in his locality and became its Secretary. This experience gave him some training in organising and conducting Institutions. Experiments about diet became a life-long passion for him.

Gandhi Tries to Play the 'English Gentleman'

For a brief period, Gandhi tried to become 'The English Gentleman' to overcome lack of confidence and to make up for the 'fad' of vegetarianism. He wanted to become fit for the British elite society. He got clothes stitched from an expensive and fashionable firm, purchased an expensive hat and an evening suit and learnt to wear the tie. He became very careful about his appearance. He even joined a dancing class, but could not go on for more than three weeks. He purchased a violin and started learning to play it. He engaged a tutor to give lessons in elocution. But all this was for a brief period of three months only. His conscience awakened him. He realised that he was not going to spend his whole life in England; he should rather concentrate on his studies and not waste his brother's money. He then became very careful about his expenses.

Study of Religions

Gandhi also started the study of religions. Before that, he had not even read the Gita. Now he read it in the English translation. He also read Edwin Arnold's 'The Light of Asia,' Blavatsky's 'Key to Theosophy' and the Bible. Gita and The New Testament made a deep impression on him. The principles of renunciation and non-violence appealed to him greatly. He continued the study of religions throughout his life.

Gandhi becomes a Barrister

Bar examinations were easy. He therefore studied for and passed the London matriculation examination. Becoming a Barrister meant attending at least six dinners in each of the twelve terms and giving an easy examination. Gandhi, however, studied sincerely, read all the prescribed books, passed his examination and was called to the bar in June 1891. He then sailed for home.

A Period of Turmoil

Gandhi's three year's stay in England was a period of deep turmoil for him. Before that, he knew little of the world. Now he was exposed to the fast-changing world and to several radical movements like Socialism, Anarchism, Atheism etc. through the Vegetarian Society. He started taking part in public work. Many of his ideas germinated during this period.

Gandhi in South Africa

Gandhi returned to India as a Barrister, but he knew nothing about the Indian law. Lawyers used to pay commissions to touts to get cases. Gandhi did not like this. Besides, he was shy and an occasion to argue in the Court unnerved him. He became a disappointed and dejected 'Bridles Barrister'. At that time, a South African firm Dada Abdulla and Co. asked for his assistance in a case. Gandhi eagerly agreed and sailed for South Africa in April 1893.

Problems of Indians in South Africa

The small Indian community in South Africa was facing many problems at that time. It consisted mainly of indentured labourers and traders. The indentured labourers were taken there by the European landlords as there was acute labour shortage in South Africa. The condition of these labourers was like slaves. During 1860-1890 around 40,000 labourers were sent from India. Many of them settled there after their agreement periods were completed and started farming or business.

The Europeans did not like it. They did not want free Indians in South Africa. They also found it difficult to face competition from Indian traders. Therefore the White Rulers imposed many restrictions and heavy taxes on the Indians. They were not given citizenship rights, like right to vote. They were treated like dirt and constantly humiliated. All Indians were called 'coolies'. The newspapers carried out the propaganda that the Indians were dirty and uncivilized. The Indians could not travel in the railways and could not enter hotels meant for Europeans. They were hated and radically discriminated in all matters by the dominant White community.

Gandhi Fights Racial Discrimination

Right since his arrival, Gandhi began to feel the pinch of racial iscrimination in South Africa. Indian community was ignorant and divided and therefore unable to fight it. In connection with his case, Gandhi had to travel to Pretoria. He was travelling in the first class, but a White passenger and railway officials asked him to leave the first class compartment. Gandhi refused, whereupon he was thrown out along with his luggage. On the platform of Maritzburg station. It was a severely cold night. Gandhi spent the night shivering and thinking furiously. He ultimately made up his mind to stay in South Africa, fight the racial discrimination and suffer hardships. It was a historic decision. It transformed Gandhi.

He had also to travel some distance by a stage-coach. During this travel also, he was insulted and beaten. On reaching Pretoria, Gandhi called a meeting of the local Indians. There he learnt a lot about the condition of Indians. It was there that he made his first Public Speech and suggested formation of an association. He offered his services for the cause. Gandhi later settled the case, for which he had come, through arbitration. He then decided to return home. But at the farewell party, he came to know about a bill to restrict Indian franchise. Gandhi thought that it had grave implications. The people then pressed him to stay for some time. He agreed.

Gandhi's first major fight had started. He addressed meetings petitioned to the legislative assembly, conducted a signature campaign. He also started regular legal practice there and soon became a successful and leading Lawyer. For sustained agitations, a permanent organisation was needed and the Natal Indian Congress was born. Illiterate indentured labourers also joined the struggle. A proposed tax on them was fought and got abolished after a fierce battle.

In1886, Gandhi visited India for a brief period. In India, he met renowned leaders and gave wide publicity to the South African struggle. Rumours reached South Africa that Gandhi had maligned the Whites there and that he was coming with a large number of Indians to swamp the Natal colony. It was wrong. But it made the Whites furious. Gandhi had to face the fury, when he returned with his wife and children, he had to enter the port town secretly, but he was found out and assaulted. The Whites wanted to hang him but he was saved by the Police Superintendent and his wife. He forgave his assailants.

The Boer War

Gandhi, however, remained a loyal citizen of the British Empire. In that spirit, he decided to help the British during the Boer War. The Boer were the Dutch colonizers who ruled some of the South African colonies. They were simple and sturdy people with strong racial prejudices. The British wanted to rule whole of the South Africa. The British-Boer broke out in 1899. Gandhi's sympathies were with the Boers. But being a British citizen, he considered it his duty to help the British. He also wanted to show that Indians were not cowards and were ready to make sacrifices for the empire while fighting for their rights.

Gandhi raised an ambulance corps of 1100 persons. The work consisted of carrying the wounded on stretchers. At times, it required walking more than 20 miles. The corps had sometimes to cross the firing line. The Indians worked hard, their work was praised and the leaders of the corps were awarded medals. Indian community learnt a lot from this experience. Its stature increased. British won the war, although the Boers fought with determination, which made a deep impression on Gandhi.

The Fight Continues

In 1901, Gandhi returned to India. He travelled widely and worked closely with Gopal Krishna Gokhale, whom he considered his guru. He was about to settle down in Bombay, when he received an urgent telegram from South Africa to rush there. Gandhi again went to South Africa. He found that the condition of Indians had worsened. Gandhi had to devote himself to public work. In 1904, Gandhi started the journal 'Indian Opinion.'

The Phoenix Settlement

In 1904, Gandhi happened to read Ruskin's book 'Unto This Last.' He was deeply impressed by Ruskin's ideas and decided to put them in practice immediately. They were: (I) That the good of the individual is contained in the good of all. (ii) that all work has the same value and (iii) that the life of labour is the life worth-living.

Gandhi purchased some land near Phoenix station and established the Phoenix settlement in mid-1904. The settlers had to erect structures to accommodate themselves and the printing press. 'Indian Opinion' was transferred to Phoenix. The settlers had to go through many trials to print the issue in time. Everyone had to join in the work. The settlers were divided in two classes. The 'Schemers' made their living by manual labour. A few were paid labourers. To make a living by manual labour, land was divided in pieces of three acres each. Stress was on manual labour. Even the printing press was often worked with hand-power. Sanitary arrangements were primitive and everyone had to be his own scavenger. The colony was to be self-supporting and the material needs were to be kept to the minimum. A spirit of self-reliance pervaded the colony. Gandhi, however, could stay there only for brief periods. He had to be in Johannesburg in connection with his work.

The Zulu Rebellion

The Zulu 'rebellion' broke out in April 1906. It was not in fact a rebellion, but a man-hunt. The British wanted to crush the freedom-loving Zulu tribals. The operation to massacre them was, therefore, started under a flimsy pretext. Out of a sense of loyalty to the British empire, Gandhi offered the services of the Indian community, though his heart was with the Zulus. An ambulance corps of 24 persons was formed. Its duty was to carry the wounded Zulus and nurse them. The Zulus were flogged and tortured and left with festering wounds. Whites were not ready to nurse them. Gandhi was happy to nurse them. He had to work hard and walk miles through hills. It was a thought-provoking experience. He saw the cruelty of the British and the horrors of the war. While marching through Zululand, Gandhi thought deeply. Two ideas became fixed in his mind-Brahmacharya and the adoption of voluntary poverty.

Birth of Satyagraha

The White rulers were bent on keeping South Africa under their domination. They wanted as few Indians there as possible and that too as slave-labourers. In Transvaal, Indians were required to register themselves. The procedure was humiliating. The registration was proposed to be made stricter in 1906.

Gandhi realised that it was a matter of life or death for the Indians. A mammoth meeting was held in September 1906 to oppose the bill. People took oath in the name of God not to submit to the bill at any cost. A new principle had come into being - the principle of Satyagraha.The bill about registration was however passed. Picketing against registration was organised. A wave of courage and enthusiasm swept the Indian community. The Indian community rose as one man for the sake of its survival and dignity.

The agitation was first called 'passive Resistance'. Gandhi, however, did not like that term. It did not convey the true nature of the struggle. It implied that it was the weapon of the weak and the disarmed. It did not denote complete faith in nonviolence. Moreover, Gandhi did not like that the Indian struggle should be known by an English name. The term 'Sadagrah' was suggested. Gandhi changed it to 'Satyagrah' to make it represent fully, the whole idea. Satyagraha means asserting truth through non-violence. It aims at converting the opponents through self-suffering.

Gandhi was ordered to leave the colony. He disobeyed and was jailed for two months. Indians filled the jails. Repression failed to yield the results. General Smuts called Gandhi and promised that the law would be withdrawn if the Indians agreed to voluntary registration.

An Attempt of Gandhi's Life

Gandhi agreed. He and his co-workers were set free. Gandhi exhorted Indians to register voluntarily. He was criticized for this by some workers. A Pathan named Mir Alam was unconvinced by Gandhi's arguments and vowed to kill the first man who would register himself. Gandhi came forward to be the first man to register himself. When he was going to the registration office, Mir Alam and his friends assaulted him with lathis.

Gandhi fainted with the words 'He Ram' on his lips. It was 10th February 1908. His colleagues tried to save him otherwise it would have been the last day for him. Mir Alam and his friends were caught and handed over to the police. When Gandhi regained consciousness, he inquired about Mir Alam. When told that he had been arrested, Gandhi told that he should be released. Gandhi was taken by his friend Rev. Doke to his house and was nursed there. Rev. Doke later became his first biographer.

Gandhi Betrayed

Smuts however, betrayed Gandhi. The agitation was again resumed. The voluntary registration certificates were publicly burnt. Meanwhile, Transvaal passed Immigration Restriction Act. This too was opposed by the Indians. They crossed Transvaal border illegally and were jailed. Gandhi, too, was arrested and convicted. The fight continued in spite of the repression.

Tolstoy Farm

Gandhi realised that the fight would be a long one. He, therefore, desired to have a center where the Satyagrahis could lead a simple community life and get training for the struggle. Phoenix was at about 30 hours distance from Johannesburg. Gandhi's German friend Kallenbach therefore bought 1100 acres of land at a distance of about 20 miles from Johannesburg, where Tolstoy Farm was established. The community was named after Tolstoy to pay respect to the great Russian writer whose book 'The Kingdom of God is within You' had greatly influenced Gandhi and made him a firm believer in non-violence.

The inmates numbered about 50-75. It was a heterogeneous group. It was a tribute to Gandhi's leadership that they remained together happily under hard conditions. The inmates erected sheds to accommodate themselves. They did all their work themselves. Drinking, smoking and meat-eating were prohibited. All ate in the community kitchen. Small Cottage Industries were started for self-sufficiency. Gandhi and his colleagues learnt shoe-making. A school was started. Gandhi himself undertook the responsibility of educating the children. The life was simple, hard, but joyful. Experiments at Tolstoy Farm proved to be a source of purification and penance for Gandhi and his co-workers.

The Last Phase of Satyagraha

Satyagraha continued for four years. Gandhi discontinued his legal practice in 1910. After many ups and downs, the last phase of Satyagraha began in September 1913. A Black Law imposing three pounds tax on Indians provided occasion for it. Satyagrahis crossed Transvaal border defying the law. Even the women were invited to join. Indian workers in the Natal coal-mines struck work and joined the struggle. Gandhi led a large contingent of these workers. They were about 2200 in number. It was on epic march.

It aroused sympathy for Satyagraha and indignation for the South African Government throughout England and India. Indian National Congress supported the Satyagraha. Gandhi was arrested. The Satyagrahis marched to Natal without their leader. There, they were arrested and jailed. Thousands of labourers struck work in sympathy. The public outcry in India forced the Indian Government to express sympathy for the Indian cause. The repression having failed, General Smuts had to bow ultimately. Indian demands were accepted. The fight was over. Gandhi now could return to India where a great work awaited him.

It was South Africa which made Gandhi. He had gone there as a young, shy, Briefless Barrister. He returned as an extraordinary leader who had mobilised masses to an unprecedented extent for a novel fight. In South Africa, Gandhi's ideas were shaped. He was influenced by Ruskin, Tolstoy and Thoreau. He made a deep study of religions there and became a staunch believer in nonviolence. The principle of Satyagraha was born in S. Africa.

Gandhi in India: Rise of Leadership

Gandhi returned to India in January 1915. He was welcomed and honoured as a hero. He spent a year touring the country at the instance of Gokhale, his guru. He travelled mostly in third class railway compartments. He saw the conditions in the country first-hand. He founded the Satyagraha Ashram in May 1915 and started getting involved in the social and political life of the country. The Champaran Satyagraha was his first major struggle.

Champaran Satyagraha

Champaran was a district in Northern Bihar. When Gandhi was called there, it was virtually under the rule of European indigo planters. They cruelly exploited and terrorised the tenants. Under the 'tinkathia' system, the tenants had to cultivate indigo in 3/20 th part of the land. The tenants were oppressed and fear-stricken. The British administration supported the planters.

Gandhi was invited to visit Champaran by Rajkumar Shukla, a peasant from the area, in December 1916. Gandhi was first reluctant. But Shukla's persistent requests made him change his mind. He went to Champaran in April 1917 to know the conditions there and the grievances of the peasants. Before visiting the district, Gandhi visited Muzaffarpur and Patna. He discussed the matter with lawyers and social workers. Gandhi declined to seek legal remedies as he felt that law courts were useless when the people were fear-stricken. For him, removal of fear was most important. He made request to the lawyers for clerical assistance. Many of them gladly offered the same.

Gandhi first met the planters and the District Commissioner. They were hostile. Gandhi was ordered to leave the area. He ignored the order. He was then summoned to the court. The news electrified the area. Crowds gathered at the court. Gandhi pleaded guilty, saying that he was obeying a higher law, the voice of conscience. The case against him was later dropped. Gandhi and his co-workers met thousands of the peasants. They recorded about 8000 statements. Efforts were made to ensure that they were true. Recording was done in the presence of police officials. Undue publicity and exaggeration were avoided. Planters' campaign of slander was ignored. The masses in Champaran overcame their fear. Public opinion in the country was aroused. The Government ultimately appointed an enquiry committee in June 1917, with Gandhi as a member. The committee recommended abolition of tinkathia system and partial refund of money taken illegal by the planters. The

Satyagraha was thus successful. Champaran Satyagraha was the first Satyagraha on the Indian soil. It was Gandhi's first major political work in India. It was carried out strictly in accordance with the principles of Satyagraha. Attention was paid to constructive work like sanitation, education and primary health-care.

Ahmedabad Satyagraha

A dispute between the textile mill-owners and the labourers at Ahmedabad arose in 1918, about the grant of bonus and dearness allowance. The labourers wanted 50% increase allowance due to steep rise in prices. The mill-owners were ready to give only 20% increase. Gandhi was approached to find a solution. He persuaded both the parties to agree to arbitration. But after a few days, some misunderstanding led to a strike. The mill-owners seized the opportunity and declared lock-out. Gandhi studied the case. He thought that 35% increase would be reasonable. He advised the labourers to demand the same. Regular strike began on the 26th February 1918. Thousands of labourers struck work. They took a pledge not to resume work till their demand was met or arbitration was agreed upon. They also decided to observe non-violence and maintain peace.

Gandhi had friends in both the camps. The mill-owners being led by Shri Ambalal Sarabhai. His sister Ansuyaben was leading the labourers. During the struggle, Gandhi's co-workers regularly visited the labourers' quarters to solve their problems and to keep high their morale. Daily meetings and prayers were held. Bulletins were issued. Gandhi did not like charity. Efforts were made to find alternative employments for the workers. However, after a fortnight, the workers started getting tired. It was difficult to face starvation. It was unbearable for Gandhi that they should break the vow.

He then decided to undertake an indefinite fast. This strengthened the workers. It brought moral pressure on the mill-owners. They consented to arbitration after three days. Gandhi broke his fast. The Satyagraha was successful. The arbitrator studied the case for three months and recommended 35% increase in dearness allowance. The workers' demand was thus fully met. However, Gandhi's fast did involve in an element of coercion. But it was a spontaneous decision. The situation demanded some drastic action. The Satyagraha was significant in many respects. It was the first Satyagraha by industrial workers. It was wholly peaceful. It showed how workers could fight non-violently. It also gave rise to a strong Gandhian Labour Union.

Kheda Satyagraha

Kheda was a district in Gujarat. In 1917, there was a crop failure due to famine. Peasants were unable to pay the land revenue. The rules permitted suspension of revenue collection when the crops were less than four annas. According to the peasants' estimate, the crops were less than four annas. Gandhi's inquiries, as well as inquiries by independent observers, showed that the peasants were right. The Government, however, thought otherwise. It even turned down a suggestion of an impartial enquiry. It started coercing the peasants to collect revenue. Petitions etc. were of no avail. Satyagraha was therefore started on the 22nd March 1918.

Gandhi advised the peasants to withhold payment to revenue. Satyagrahis took a pledge not to pay the same and resolved to be ready to face the consequences. Volunteers went to villages to keep up the morale of the peasants. As in Champaran, Gandhi's main concern was to remove the fear from the peasants' minds. The officials started attaching the property of the peasants including cattle and even standing crops. Notices were sent for attachment of the land. An occasion for civil disobedience arose when standing onion crop was attached at one place. Gandhi advised one Mohanlal Pandya and a few volunteers to remove the crop. This was done. The volunteers were arrested. Pandya earned the nickname 'Onion Thief.'

The struggle went on for about four months till July 1918. It tested the people's patience. The Government discontinued coercive measures. It advised that if the well-to-do peasants paid up, the poor ones would be granted suspension. In one sense, the Satyagraha was thus successful. The peasants' demand was not, however, fully met. Gandhi was not satisfied. He wanted people to come out stronger after Satyagraha. However, the Satyagraha resulted in awakening the peasants. It educated them politically. It was the first peasant struggle under Gandhi's leadership, the first nonviolent mass civil disobedience campaign organised by Gandhi in India. The peasants became aware of their rights and learnt to suffer for them.

Rowlatt Act

British Government appointed a Committee in 1917 under the chairmanship of Justice Rowlatt, (1) to enquire and report to the Government about the nature and extent of anti-government activities, and (2) to suggest legal remedies to enable the Government to suppress those activities. The Committee submitted its report in April 1918. Its work was carried out in secrecy. The Committee's recommendations were embodied in two bills.

The first bill sought to make a permanent change in the Criminal Law. The second bill intended to deal with the situation arising out of the expiry of Defence of India Rules. The first bill made punishable the possession of an antigovernment document with mere intention to circulate it. The second bill also gave sweeping powers to the officers. There were other harsh provisions also. The bills shocked the entire country. All the leaders considered the bills unjust, unwarranted and destructive of elementary human rights and dignity. The second bill was eventually dropped and the first one passed as a Law in March 1919.

Satyagraha against the Rowlatt Act

India had helped the British in the World War. She expected substantial political rights. Instead, she received the Black Rowlatt bills.

Gandhi had decided to help the British war efforts during the war. He undertook a recruiting campaign and worked hard which ruined his health. While he was recovering, he heard about Rowlatt bills. He was shocked. He took up the matter and started propaganda against the bill. Gandhi carried out propaganda against the bill. A separate body called Satyagraha Sabha was formed. A Satyagraha pledge was drafted and signed by selected leaders. The Government was, however, adamant. It then suddenly it occurred to Gandhi that a call for nation-wide hartal should be given. Everybody in the country should suspend his business and spend the day in fasting and prayers. Public meetings should be held everywhere and resolutions passed for withdrawal of the Act.

The programme was taken up. 30 March was fixed as the day of the hartal, but it was later postponed to 6th April. The notice was very short. Still the masses rose to the occasion. The country rose like one man. Hartal was observed throughout India. Communal prejudices were forgotten. All fear disappeared. In Delhi, Swami Shraddhanand, the Hindu sanyasi was invited to Jama Masjid. It was also decided that civil disobedience should be offered to selected laws which could easily be disobeyed by the people. Gandhi suggested breaking of the Salt law and the sale of the banned literature. The civil disobedience was a great success. Throughout India, meetings were held and processions taken out.

The public awakening was unprecedented. It startled the British. Repression was let loose. Processions were broken up by mounted police and firing was done at several places. Many persons were killed. At some places, people lost balance in the face of repression. In such a situation, Gandhi thought it fit to suspend the Civil Disobedience Campaign. It was done on the 18th April. Satyagraha against the Rowlatt Act was historic. It was the first nation-wide struggle, in which crores of people participated and showed exemplary courage. The Indian freedom movement was transformed into a truly people's movement. The period also witnessed Hindu-Muslim friendship to an extent that was never surpassed thereafter.

Jallianwala Bagh

Satyagraha in Punjab was also quite successful. Its leaders Dr. Satyapal and Dr. Kitchlew were arrested. People observed hartal and took out a procession in Amritsar to demand their release. It was fired upon, and many persons were killed. The crowd therefore became violent and killed 5-6 Englishmen. Some public buildings were burnt. Army troops were rushed in to stop the violence. This was on April 10th 1919. On April 11, a peaceful funeral procession was taken out.

General Dyer then took command of the troops. Meetings and gatherings were prohibited. Still a large meeting was held on April 12th at Jallianwala Bagh. General Dyer took no steps to prevent the meeting. But when the meeting was taking place, he surrounded the place and without any warning, gave orders of firing. The crowd of nearly 10,000 men and women was peaceful and unarmed. They had no idea that they would be fired upon. When the firing started the people became panicky. There was only one exit. Bullets were showered on the trapped people. 1650 rounds were fired. About 400 persons were killed and 1200 injured. General Dyer did this deliberately to teach the Indians a lesson. Jallianwala Bagh massacre shocked the country. It showed how brutal the British power could get. It was followed by many more atrocities. They turned Gandhi fully against the British Empire.

Amritsar Congress

The annual session of the Indian National Congress was held at Amritsar in Punjab in December 1919. Most of the leaders in jails were released before or during the session. The session was attended by 8000 delegates including 1500 peasants. It was the last Congress session attended by Lokmanya Tilak. The Moderates, however, did not attend it. Pandit Motilal Nehru was in the Chair. The Congress was now acquiring a mass character. The proceedings were conducted mainly in Hindustani.

The Congress passed a resolution for removal of General Dyer, the butcher of Jallianwala Bagh. Recall of the Punjab Governor and the Viceroy was also demanded. It was decided to erect a memorial for the Jallianwala Bagh martyrs. Gandhi moved a resolution condemning violence on the part of the people and got it passed. It was a very significant event. The resolution also urged the people to remain peaceful. The

Congress also reiterated the demand for responsible Government. The Montague Reforms were considered inadequate, disappointing and unsatisfactory. But it was decided to work the reforms. Revival of hand-spinning and hand-weaving was recommended. The Congress appointed a subcommittee for reconsideration of the Congress Constitution with Gandhi as the Chairman. It was the first Congress session in which Gandhi took an active part. His leadership was strengthened in Amritsar Congress.

The Khilafat Question

During the First World Way, Turkey sided with Germany against the British. The Sultan of Turkey was the Khalifa, the religious head of the Muslim world. The future of Khalifa, therefore, became a matter of concern for Indian Muslims. The British Government promised them that the Khilafat would not be violated and favourable peace terms would be offered to Turkey. But when Turkey was defeated in the war, the promises were forgotten. Turkish Empire was broken. Indian Muslims felt agitated over this.

Gandhi sympathised with the Khilafat cause. He felt that Hindus should help the Muslim in their need. For him, it was an excellent opportunity to forge communal unity, bring Muslims in the freedom movement and form a common front against the British. The Khilafat Committee was formed. It demanded that terms of treaty with Turkey should be changed to satisfy the Indian Muslims. Gandhi suggested the programme of Non-Cooperation with the British Government. This programme was adopted by the Committee in May 1920.

The Non Co-operation Movement

The redressal of injustice of Punjab and Khilafat and the attainment of Swaraj became the key issue. The masses were getting awakened. Gandhi announced the inauguration of Non-violent Non-Co-operation Movement on the 1st August 1920. A special session of Congress in September accepted the programme. The Nagpur Congress in December 1920 endorsed it enthusiastically.

The programme consisted of the following points -

- Surrender of titles and honours given by the British Government
- Boycott of law-courts
- Boycott of educational institutions
- Boycott of councils and elections
- Boycott of foreign cloth
- Boycott of Government functions
- Picketing of liquor shops
- Refusal to get recruited in the army

The programme was not just negative. It included the building of new institutions. National Education was encouraged. Stress was laid on Khadi. Charkha became the symbol of freedom.

The Congress was completely reorganised and a new constitution drafted by Gandhi was adopted to make it a mass organisation and a useful tool for the struggle. The movement started with hartal, fasting and prayers. It soon spread like wildfire. The freedom movement had become a mass movement. Gandhi declared the Swaraj could be won within one year if the programme was fully implemented. People showed great unity, determination and courage. Hundreds of National schools were established. Tilak Swaraj Fund was over-subscribed. About 20 lakh charkhas began to be plied in the country. The boycott shook the Government.

1921 was the year of the rise of Indian Nationalism Gandhi became a Mahatma, the most loved and revered figure in the country. Masses looked to him as a saint, as an incarnation of God who had come to free them from slavery and poverty. The Government started repression. Arrests were made. Firing took place at some places. The country boycotted the visit of Prince of Wales, the British Prince in November 1921. Disturbances broke out at Bombay and Gandhi had to fast to control the situation. By the end of 1921, the number of prisoners had risen to 30,000. Processions and meetings were being broken up.

The masses were getting impatient. Call was given for Civil Disobedience. Gandhi wanted to start the campaign step-by-step. He chose Bardoli in Gujarat for starting the campaign. Notice was given to Government on the 1st February 1922. However, the movement had to be called off within a few days. On the 5th February, a mob including Congressmen set fire to a police station at Chauri Chaura in U.P., killing about 22 policemen. Gandhi was shocked. He realised that people had not fully accepted non-violence. He persuaded the Congress to suspend the agitation. Gandhi was arrested in March and was sentenced to 6 years' imprisonment. He was kept in the Yeravda jail near Pune.

The Life of Mahatma Gandhi (1922-1948)

Gandhi was freed from jail in 1924 on the ground of health. The country was witnessing a wave of communal riots. Gandhi fasted for 21 days in October 1924. He toured the entire country. He laid stress on the charkha and the removal of untouchability. Political atmosphere in the country began to change slowly. There was a wave of labour strikes in 1928-29. Armed revolutionaries stepped up their activities. There was widespread discontent among the peasants. The historic Satyagraha at Bardoli in Gujarat showed its intensity.

Bardoli Satyagraha

Bardoli was a tehsil in Gujarat. Government increased the land revenue assessment there by 30%. Protests brought it down to 22%. The peasants thought it unjust. Vallabhbhai Patel studied the case. He was convinced that the peasants were right. The peasants decided to withhold the payment until the enhancement was cancelled or an impartial tribunal appointed for setting the case. Gandhi blessed the Satyagraha. It started in February 1928.

Vallabhbhai Patel led the struggle. He organised sixteen camps under the charge of 250 volunteers. His organisation was superb. It earned him the title 'Sardar'. The government tried its best to terrorise the people and extract the payment. It tried flattery, bribery, fines, imprisonment and lathi-charge.

Pathans were brought in to threaten the people. The cattle was taken away and lands auctioned at several places. Patel kept up the people's morale. His volunteers were arrested. People imposed a social boycott on the Government officials and against those who bought auctioned property. Seven members of the Legislative Council resigned in protest against the Government repression. Several village officials, too, resigned their posts.

(1) The Government issued an ultimatum for payment. Patel demanded that

(2) The Satyagrahi prisoners should be released.

(3) The lands sold and forfeited, should be returned.

(4) The cost of seized movables should be refunded.

All the dismissals and punishments should be undone. Gandhi and Patel promised to call off the agitation if these demands were met and an inquiry ordered. The Government ultimately yielded. An Inquiry Committee was appointed. The Committee recommended an increase of 5.7% only. The satyagraha was thus successful. The Bardoli struggle was very well organised one. The peasants remained united against all odds. Women took part in the struggle on a large scale. The struggle became a symbol of hope, strength and victory for the peasants in the country.

Rising Discontent

The discontent against the British Government was increasing. The Government appointed Simon Commission to decide about the grant of political rights of India. Indian leaders had not been consulted. There was no Indian Member in the Commission. The country boycotted Simon Commission.

Gandhi had regarded himself as a 'Prisoner' and refrained from political activities till 1928, when his jail term was to expire. He thereafter took the reins of Congress in his hands. Congress resolved in 1929 to fight for complete independence. Confrontation with the Government became imminent. Gandhi launched Civil Disobedience Campaign - the famous Salt Satyagraha.

The Salt Satyagraha

Gandhi wrote to the Viceroy, listing eleven demands which, according to him, formed the substance of self-government. They were rejected. Gandhi then decided to start Civil Disobedience by breaking the Salt Law, which heavily taxed the salt, an article of daily consumption for the poorest of the poor. He started his epic Dandi March on the 12 March 1930 from Ahmedabad.

A carefully selected band of 78 Satyagrahis accompanied Gandhi in this March to Dandi, a deserted village on the sea-coat, at about 240 miles from Ahmedabad. As the March progressed, the atmosphere in the country was electrified. Several village officials resigned their posts. Gandhi declared that he would not return to Sabarmati Ashram till Independence was won. Congress Committee met on the 21st March to plan the strategy.

Gandhi reached Dandi on the 6th April and broke the Salt law symbolically by picking up a pinch of salt. It was signal for the nation. Civil Disobedience campaign was started throughout the country. Salt Law broken at many places by illegal production of salt and its sale. Gandhi went to the surrounding places and started a campaign to cut toddy trees. Picketing of liquor and foreign cloth shops was started. Women were on the forefront in picketing the liquor shops. The whole country was stirred. Some other laws like Forest Laws were also taken up for disobedience at some places.

Government intensified the repression. Most of the important leaders including Gandhi were arrested. But the agitation grew in strength. People bravely faced police brutalities and even firing at many places. A wave of strikes and hartals swept the country. At Peshawar, soldiers of Garhwali regiment refused to fire on the unarmed people. They were court-martialled. Before his arrest, Gandhi hit upon a novel idea to raid salt depots. The Dharasana raid, in which several non-violent Satyagrahis were mercilessly beaten, sent shock-waves throughout the world. It lowered the British prestige. The movement progressed till January 1931. The boycott of foreign cloth, liquor and British goods was almost complete. Gandhi and other leaders were subsequently released from jail. Government started negotiations. Gandhi-Irvin Pact was signed in March. The Satyagraha was discontinued. This was a major Satyagraha, during which 111 Satyagrahis died in firings and about one lakh persons went to jail.

A Phase of Repression

Gandhi took part in the Round Table Conference in England in 1931 as the representative of the Congress. It was a frustrating experience for him. The British were bent on prolonging their rule by following the policy of Divide and Rule'. Gandhi stayed in London in a poor locality. He even met the unemployed textile mill-workers who had lost the jobs due to Gandhi's movement of Swadeshi and Boycott. He explained to them the rationale behind Khadi. The workers showered love on him.

The Round Table Conference yielded nothing. Gandhi returned in December 1931. He was arrested and the Civil Disobedience Campaign was resumed. The Congress was declared illegal. The Government was determined to crush the movement. The leaders and a large number of workers were arrested. Ordinances w ere issued to arm the Government with wide powers. Gandhi was lodged in the Yervada jail.

Yeravda Pact

While Gandhi was in Yeravda jail the British Prime Minister Ramsay MacDonald announced the provisional scheme of minority representation, known as the Communal Award. The depressed classes (now known as Scheduled Castes) were recognised as a minority community and given separate electorates.

Gandhi was shocked. It was an attempt to divide and destroy the Hindu Society and the Nation and in turn to perpetuate India's slavery. It was not good for the depressed also. Gandhi announced his decision to fast unto death from the 20th September 1932. He was fully for the representation to the depressed classes, but he was against their being considered as a minority community and given separate electorates. Gandhi's decision stirred the country. Indian leaders began hectic efforts to save Gandhi's life. But Dr. Ambedkar described the fast as a political Stunt. Gandhi's decision awakened the Hindu Society. It dealt a blow to the orthodoxy. Hindu leaders resolved to fight untouchability. Several temples were thrown open to the Harijans.

The fast began on 20th September. Attempts to evolve an alternative scheme were continuing. Gandhi's health started deteriorating. He had several rounds of discussions with Dr. Ambedkar. At last, an agreement was reached on the 24th September. The Government was urged to accept the same. The British Government ultimately gave its consent. Gandhi broke his fast on 26th September. The agreement is known as the Yeravda Pact or the Poona Pact. It provided for doubling the number of representatives of depressed classes. Separate electorates were however, done away with. It was decided that for every reserved seat, members of the depressed classes would elect four candidates and the representative would be elected from them by joint electorate. The system of primary election was to be for ten years.

Anti-untouchability Campaign

Yeravda Pact gave a great boost to the anti-untouchability work. Harijan Sevak Sangh was established. 'Harijan' Weekly was started. After his release, Gandhi put aside political activities and devoted himself to Harijan service and other constructive work. All-India Village Industries Association was also formed. Gandhi gave the Sabarmati Ashram to the Harijan Sevak Sangh and later settled at Wardha. He toured the entire country and collected Harijan Fund. The massive anti-untouchability propaganda launched by him had spectacular results. He had, of course, of face opposition. Even a bomb was once thrown at him. The campaign destroyed the legitimacy of untouchability. It cleared the way for legal ban. In 1936, Gandhi settled down at Sevagram, a village near Wardha. In 1937, he presided over the Educational Conference, which gave rise to the scheme of Basic Education.

India and the War

While Gandhi was busy in the constructive work, elections to the provincial assemblies were held in 1937. Congress Ministers were formed in several provinces. the Second World War began in 1939. The British Government dragged India into the War without consulting Indian leaders. Congress Ministries resigned in protest. The Congress expressed expressed sympathy for the Allied powers' fight against Nazism and Fascism and offered co-operation provided responsible Self-Government was granted. Gandhi was however against any co-operation in war efforts on the ground of NonViolence. When the Government turned down the Congress demand, Gandhi was requested to resume the leadership.

Gandhi decided to launch Anti-War individual Satyagraha against curtailment of freedom. It was inaugurated by Vinoba in October 1940. Pandit Nehru was the Second Satyagrahi. The Satyagrahis were arrested. By May 1941, the number of Satyagrahi prisoners had crossed 25000.

Cripps Mission

The War was approaching India's borders with the advance of Japan. England was in difficulties. It could not afford any agitation in India. There were various other pressures on the British Government to make political concessions. As a result, Sir Stafford Cripps was sent to India in March 1942.

Cripps discussed the matter with the Indian leaders. He proposed Dominion Status with power to the States and the provinces to secede and convening of a constitution-making body after the War. But the adherence to the constitution drafted by that body was not to be obligatory. Indian leaders including Gandhi found the Cripps Proposals disappointing. They were aptly termed as post dated cheque on a crashing bank. The Muslim League wanted a definite pronouncement about Pakistan and therefore criticised the Cripps proposals. Congress rejected the Cripps scheme because it did not provide for the participation of the people of the states and the principles of non-accession was against Indian unity. The Cripps Mission failed.

'Quit India' Movement

The country wanted nothing but Complete Independence. The Congress passed the historic 'Quit India' resolution on 8th August 1942. Gandhi and other leaders were arrested. The country now rose in revolt. With most of the leaders in jail, it fought in the way it thought fit. Railway lines and telegraphic communications were interfered with. Government property was burnt or destroyed in several places. The people displayed unprecedented courage and heroism. Unarmed people faced police lathis and bullets. Young boys suffered flogging without flinching. Government machinery was paralysed and parallel Government was set up at some places.

Many workers went underground. About 1000 people died in firings during the movement. About 1600 were injured and 60000 people were arrested. It was noteworthy that violence was done to Government property only. Englishmen were safe throughout the Movement. There was little personal violence. Thus, while the masses rose to great heights of heroism, they also displayed remarkable restraint. It was surely Gandhi's contribution. The rebellion was, however, gradually put down.

Gandhi was in Agakhan Palace jail. He was blamed by the British for the disturbances. He could not tolerate questioning of his faith and honesty and fasted for 21 days. Gandhi lost his wife Kasturba and his Secretary Mahadev Desai in the Agakhan Palace. It was a great blow to him. His health was not in a good condition. He was finally released in May 1944 on health grounds. He then started efforts to break the political stalemate.

Background of the Partition

The Hindu-Muslim unity, forged at the time of the Khilafat agitation, collapsed thereafter. The country witnessed a wave of communal riots. The British encouraged Muslim communalism and used it to obstruct the path of the Freedom Movement. M. A. Jinnah, an erstwhile liberal leader, who had been sidelined when the Congress became a mass organisation, assumed the leadership of Muslim communalism.

The Muslim League under his leadership became more aggressive, unreasonable and violent. The two-nation theory- that Hindus and Muslims were two separate Muslim homeland called 'Pakistan,' consisting of the Muslim-majority provinces. Jinnah's shrewdness, ambition and ruthlessness, communalisation of large sections of society and the British support for Jinnah, brought about such a situation that the Muslim demands became an obstacle in the way of India's Independence. Jinnah kept the demands fluid and utilised every opportunity to frustrate the Nationalist Movement and further his end with the support of the British rulers.

The two-nation theory was an untruth. The Hindus and Muslims had lived together in India for centuries. Gandhi fought this untruth with all his might. He did everything possible, including meeting Jinnah several times. But he failed. Jinnah wanted recognition of the League as the sole representative of the Muslims. It was not acceptable to the Congress.

Cabinet Mission

The War ended in 1945. After an election, Labour Party's Government came to power in England. England had been extremely weakened financially and militarily. The Azad Hind Sena had shown that even the army was not untouched by nationalism. Mutiny of the naval ratings in February 1946 gave the same indication. The people were in an agitated mood. The British rule had lost legitimacy in the eyes of the people. The British, therefore, decided to withdraw from India.

Cabinet Mission was sent to India to help in the formation of Interim Government and to purpose a scheme regarding the transfer of power. The mission proposed that the provinces be divided in three groups, in one of which Hindus were in the majority while in the other two Muslims. Subjects like defence, foreign affairs, communications etc, were to be with the Central Authority and the groups were to be free to frame constitutions about other subjects. Gandhi found the proposals defective. Muslim League declared 'Direct Action' to get Pakistan. 'Direct Action' meant unleashing of violence. The Hindus retaliated.

In Calcutta alone, over 6000 people were killed 4 days. The Hindu communalism too became stronger.

The Noakhali Massacre

In the Noakhali area of East Bengal, where Muslims formed 82% of the population, a reign of terror was let loose in a planned and systematic way in October 1946. The Hindus were killed and beaten, their property was burnt, thousands of Hindus were forcibly converted and thousands of Hindu women were abducted and raped. Temples were defiled and destroyed.

The League Government in Bengal aided the goondas. Even ex-serviceman joined in committing the atrocities. In Noakhali, about three-fourth of the land belonged to the Hindu landlords and the tenants were mostly Muslims. The peasant unrest was naturally there. It was now turned along communal channels. The Noakhali massacre had few parallels in the history. It showed to what level communal politics could stop to. It was meant to terrorise, kill, convert or drive away the Hindus from Muslim-majority areas so that Pakistan could become a reality.

Gandhi's Noakhali March

Gandhi was deeply shocked. He could not bear the defeat of his long-cherished principles. On 6th November 1946, he rushed to Noakhali. It was to be his final and perhaps the most glorious battle.

Gandhi reached Shrirampur and camped there for a few days. He sent his associates including Pyarelal and Sushila Nayyar to different villages which were mostly deserted by the Hindus. He did all his personal work himself. He worked like a possessed man. He walked barefooted, went from house to house, talked to Hindus and Muslims, heard their points of view, and reasoned with them and addressed meetings.

He wanted to instill fearlessness into the Hindus. He exhorted them to die nonviolently, if need be, but not to submit to terror. He did not appease the Muslim. He told the truth bluntly. He wanted to win their confidence and make them see reason and earn the confidence of the Hindus. He did not only preach, he served the village poor. He was testing his NonViolence. It was very difficult to establish mutual trust. The League had made poisonous propaganda against him. But Gandhi's mission began to yield results. It boosted the morale of Hindus. Passions began to subside. Some evacuees started returning home. Some even returned to their original faith. Gandhi gradually succeeded in earning the love and confidence of even the Muslims.

India wins Independence

Noakhali had its reaction in Bihar, where Hindus resorted to violence. The country was seized by communal madness. Gandhi went to Bihar and brought the situation under control.

The situation in the country was explosive. Civil War was imminent. The Congress ultimately consented to the partition of India. Despite Gandhi's bitter opposition, he could not do anything to prevent the partition.

While the country was celebrating the Independence. Day on 15th August 1947, Gandhi was in Bengal to fight communal madness. Partition was followed by riots, a massacre of unparalleled dimensions. It witnessed movement of about one crore persons and killing of at least six lakh persons. Calcutta was once more on the verge of riots. Gandhi under-took a fast which had a magical effect. Lord Mountbatten described him as 'one-man peace army'. Gandhi continued to plead for sanity in those turbulent days.

Gandhi's Death

It was January 1948. Communal feelings were high due to the partition of the country. Hindu communalists thought that Gandhi was pro-Muslim. His fact for communal amity which resulted in the Government of India honouring its obligation of giving Rs. 50 Crores. to Pakistan had further angered them. Gandhi was staying at the Birla house in New Delhi. He used to hold evening prayer meetings regularly. He used to speak on various issues. Once a bomb was thrown during his prayer meeting. Still, Gandhi did not permit security checks.

On 30th of January 1948, about 500 people had gathered for the prayer meeting on the lawns of the Birla House. Gandhi was a bit late as Sardar Patel had come to see him. At 5.10 p.m. he left the room and walked to the prayer ground. He was supporting himself on the shoulders of Abha and Manu, his granddaughter-in-law and granddaughter respectively. People rushed forward to get his darshan and to touch his feet.

Gandhi folded his hands to greet them. When he was a few yards away from the prayer platform, a young man came forward. He saluted Gandhi, suddenly took out a small pistol and fired three shots. The bullets hit Gandhi on and below the chest. He fell to the ground with the words. 'He Ram' on his lips. He died within minutes. The crowd was shocked. The assassin was Nathuram Godse,' a worker of Hindu Mahasabha. He was caught and handed over to the Police.

Gandhi's body was taken to Birla House. People thronged the place and wept bitterly. The whole world was plunged in sorrow. The next morning, Gandhi's body was placed on a gun-carriage and taken to Rajghat. Millions of people joined the procession to have the last darshan (glimpse) of the Mahatma. His son Ramdas lit the funeral pyre. The Mahatma had become a martyr for communal unity.

3

The Story of my Experiments with Truth

BIRTH AND PARENTAGE

The Gandhis belong to the Bania caste and seem to have been originally grocers. But for three generations, from my grandfather, they have been Prime Ministers in several Kathiawad States.2 1 Ramayana, "Balakanda" 2 Vide "Open Letter to Kathiawar Princes", August 8, 1921. Uttamchand Gandhi1, alias Ota Gandhi, my grandfather, must have been a man of principle. State intrigues compelled him to leave Porbandar, where he was Diwan, and to seek refuge in Junagadh.

There he saluted the Nawab with the left hand. Someone, noticing the apparent discourtesy, asked for an explanation, which was given thus : "The right hand is already pledged to Porbandar." Ota Gandhi married a second time, having lost his first wife. He had four sons by his first wife and two by his second wife. I do not think that in my childhood I ever felt or knew that these sons of Ota Gandhi were not all of the same mother.

The fifth of these six brothers was Karamchand Gandhi, alias Kaba Gandhi, and the sixth was Tulsidas Gandhi. Both these brothers were Prime Ministers in Porbandar, one after the other. Kaba Gandhi was my father. He was a member of the Rajasthanik Court. It is now extinct, but in those days it was a very influential body for settling disputes between the chiefs and their fellow-clansmen. He was for some time Prime Minister in Rajkot and then in Vankaner. He was a pensioner of the Rajkot State when he died.

Kaba Gandhi married four times in succession, having lost his wife each time by death. He had two daughters by his first and second marriages. His last wife, Putlibai, bore him a daughter and three sons, I being the youngest.

My father was a lover of his clan, truthful, brave and generous, but short-tempered. To a certain extent he might have been given to carnal pleasures. For he married for the fourth time when he was over forty. But he was incorruptible and had earned a name for strict impartiality in his family as well as outside. His loyalty to the State was well known. An Assistant Political Agent spoke insultingly of the Rajkot Thakore Saheb, his chief, and he stood up to the insult. The Agent was angry and asked Kaba Gandhi to apologize. This he refused to do and was therefore kept under detention for a few hours.

But when the Agent saw that Kaba Gandhi was adamant, he ordered him to be released.2 My father never had any ambition to accumulate riches and left us very little property.

He had no education, save that of experience. At best, he might be said to have read up to the fifth Gujarati standard. Of history and 1 For the genealogical table, vide Appendix to An Autobiography "Geneal ogical Table of Gandhiji".

But his rich experience of practical affairs stood him in good stead in the solution of the most intricate questions and in managing hundreds of men. Of religious training he had very little, but he had had that kind of religious culture which frequent visits to temples and listening to religious discourses make available to many Hindus. In his last days he began reading the Gita at the instance of a learned Brahmin friend of the family, and he used to repeat aloud some verses every day at the time of worship.

The outstanding impression my mother has left on my memory is that of saintliness1. She was deeply religious. She would not think of taking her meals without her daily prayers.

Going to Haveli-the Vaishnava temple-was one of her daily duties. As far as my memory can go back, I do not remember her having ever missed the Chaturmas2. She would take the hardest vows and keep them without flinching. Illness was no excuse for relaxing them. I can recall her once falling ill when she was observing the Chandrayana3 vow, but the illness was not allowed to interrupt the observance. To keep two or three consecutive fasts was nothing to her. Living on one meal a day during Chaturmas was a habit with her. Not content with that, she fasted every alternate day during one Chaturmas. During another Chaturmas she vowed not to have food without seeing the sun.

We children on those days would stand, staring at the sky, waiting to announce the appearance of the sun to our mother. Everyone knows that at the height of the rainy season the sun often does not condescend to show his face. And I remember days when, at his 1 Mahadev Desai has reported the following conversation with Gandhiji in Yeravda Prison in 1932; "In the morning while examining the proofs of the abridged edition of An Autobiography, I asked Bapu; "You have spoken of your mother"s austere vows such as ekadashi, chaturmas kandrayana, etc., but you have used the word saintliness. Do you not wish to say penance instead of saintliness here ? Cannot the word austerity be put in ?" Bapu : No. I have used the word saintliness deliberately. In penance there may be external renunciation, endurance and even hypocrisy. But saintliness is an inner quality. My mother"s inner life would reflect itself in her austerity. If you notice any purity in me, that is not my father"s but my mother"s. My mother died at the age of forty, so I have seen her in the prime of life, but I have never seen in her any frivolity, recourse to beauty aids or interest in the pleasures of life or hypocrisy. The one lasting impression that she left on my mind is that of saintliness." [From Gujarati] Mahadevbhaini Diary I, p. 67.

My mother had strong common sense. She was well informed about all matters of State, and ladies of the court thought highly of her intelligence. Often I would accompany her, exercising the priv ilege of childhood, and I still remember many lively discussions she had with the widowed mother of the Thakore Saheb. Of these parents I was born at Porbandar, otherwise known as Sudamapuri, on the 2nd October,1869. I passed my childhood in Porbandar. I recollect having been put to school. It was with some difficulty that I got through the multiplication tables. The fact that I recollect nothing more of those days than having learnt, in company with other boys, to call our teacher all kinds of names, would strongly suggest that my intellect must have been sluggish, and my memory raw.

CHILDHOOD

I must have been about seven when my father left Porbandar for Rajkot to become a member of the Rajasthanik Court. There I was put into a primary school, and I can well recollect those days, including the names and other particulars of the teachers who taught me. As at Porbandar, so here, there is hardly anything to note about my studies.

I could only have been a mediocre student. From this school I went to the suburban school and thence to the high school, having already reached my twelfth year. I do not remember having ever told a lie during this short period, either to teachers or to my school-mates. I used to be very shy and avoided all company. My books and my lessons were my sole companions. To be at school at the stroke of the hour and to run back home as soon as the school closed-that was my daily habit. I literally ran back, because I could not bear to talk to anybody. I was even afraid lest anyone should poke fun at me.

There is an incident which occurred at the examination during my first year at the high school and which is worth recording. Mr. Giles, the Educational Inspector, had come on a visit of inspection. He had set us five words to write as a spelling exercise. One of the words was "kettle". I had mis-spelt it. The teacher tried to prompt me with the point of his boot, but I would not be prompted. It was beyond me to see that he wanted me to copy the spelling from my neighbour"s slate, for I had thought that the teacher was there to supervise us against copying. The result was that all the boys, except myself, were found to have spelt every word correctly. Only I had been stupid. The teacher tried later to bring this stupidity home to me, but without effect. I never could learn the art of "copying".

Yet the incident did not in the least diminish my respect for my teacher. I was by nature, blind to the faults of elders. Later I came to know of many other failings of this teacher, but my regard for him remained the same. For I had learnt to carry out the orders of elders, not to scan their actions.

Two other incidents belonging to the same period have always clung to my memory. As a rule I had a distaste for any reading beyond my school books. The daily lessons had to be done, because I disliked being taken to task by my teacher as much as I disliked deceiving him. Therefore I would do the lessons, but often without my mind in them. Thus when even the lessons could not be done properly, there was of course no question of any extra reading. But somehow my eyes fell on a book purchased by my father. It was Shravana Pitribhakti Nataka (a play about Shravana"s devotion to his parents). I read it with intense interest. There came to our place about the same time itinerant showmen. One of the pictures I was shown was of Shravana carrying, by means of slings fitted for his shoulders, his blind parents on a pilgrimage. The book and the picture left an indelible impression on my mind. Here is an example for you to copy," I said to myself. The agonized lament of the parents over Shravan"s death is still fresh in my memory. The melting tune moved me deeply, and I played it on a concertina which my father had purchased for me.

There was a similar incident connected with another play. Just about this time, I had secured my father"s permission to see a play performed by a certain dramatic company. This play-Harishchan dra1 -captured my heart. I could never be tired of seeing it. But how often should I be permitted to go ? It haunted me and I must have acted Harishchandra to myself times without number. "Why should not all be truthful like Harishchandra?" was the question I asked myself day and night. To follow truth and to go through all the ordeals Harishchandra went through was the one ideal it inspired in me. I literally believed in the story of Harishchandra. The thought of it all often made me weep. My common sense tells me today that Harishchandra could not have been a historical character. Still both Harishchandra and Shravana are living realities for me, and I am sure I should be moved as before if I were to read those plays again today.

CHILD MARRIAGE

Much as I wish that I had not to write this chapter, I know that I shall have to swallow many such bitter draughts in the course of this narrative. And I cannot do otherwise, if I claim to be a worshipper of Truth. It is my painful duty to have to record here my marriage at the age of thirteen. As I see the youngsters of the same age about me who are under my care, and think of my own marriage, I am inclined to pity myself and to congratulate them on having escaped my lot. I can see no moral argument in support of such a preposterously early marriage.

Let the reader make no mistake. I was married, not betrothed.

For in Kathiwad there are two distinct rites-betrothal and marriage.

Betrothal is a preliminary promise on the part of the parents of the boy and the girl to join them in marriage, and it is not inviolable. The death of the boy entails no widowhood on the girl. It is an agreement purely between the parents, and the children have no concern with it.

Often they are not even informed of it. It appears that I was betrothed thrice, though without my knowledge. I was told that two girls chosen for me had died in turn, and therefore I infer that I was betrothed three times. I have a faint recollection, however, that the third betro that took place in my seventh year. But I do not recollect having been informed about it. In the present chapter I am talking about my marriage, of which I have the clearest recollection.

It will be remembered that we were three brothers. The first was already married. The elders decided to marry my second brother, who was two or three years my senior, a cousin, possibly a year older, and me, all at the same time. In doing so there was no thought of our welfare, much less our wishes. It was purely a question of their own convenience and economy.

Marriage among Hindus is no simple matter. The parents of the bride and the bridegroom often bring themselves to ruin over it. They waste their substance, they waste their time. Months are taken up over the preparations-in making clothes and ornaments and in preparing budgets for dinners. Each tries to outdo the other in the number and variety of courses to be prepared. Women, whether they have a voice or no, sing themselves hoarse, even get ill, and disturb the peace of their neighbours. These in their turn quietly put up with all the turmoil and bustle, all the dirt and filth, representing the remains of the feasts, because they know that a time will come when they also will be behaving in the same manner.

It would be better, thought my elders, to have all this bother over at one and the same time. Less expense and greater eclat. For money could be freely spent if it had only to be spent once instead of thrice.

My father and my uncle were both old, and we were the last children they had to marry. It is likely that they wanted to have the last best time of their lives. In view of all these considerations, a triple wedding was decided upon, and as I have said before, months were taken up in preparation for it.

It was only through these preparations that we got warning of the coming event. I do not think it meant to me anything more than the prospect of good clothes to wear, drum beating, marriage processions, rich dinners and a strange girl to play with. The carnal desire came later. I propose to draw the curtain over my shame, except for a few details worth recording. To these I shall come later.

But even they have little to do with the central idea I have kept before me in writing this story. So my brother and I were both taken to Porbandar from Rajkot. There are some amusing details of the preliminaries to the final drama-e.g., smearing our bodies all over with turmeric paste-but I must omit them.

My father was a Diwan, but nevertheless a servant, and all the more so because he was in favour with the Thakore Saheb. The latter would not let him go until the last moment. And when he did so, he ordered for my father special stage-coaches, reducing the journey by two days. But the fates had willed otherwise. Porbandar is 120 miles from Rajkot-a cart journey of five days. My father did the distance in three, but the coach toppled over in the third stage, and he sustained severe injuries. He arrived bandaged all over. Both his and our interest in the coming event was half destroyed, but the ceremony had to be gone through. For how could the marriage dates be changed ? However, I forgot my grief over my father"s injuries in the childish amusement of the wedding.

I was devoted to my parents. But no less was I devoted to the passions that flesh is heir to. I had yet to learn that all happiness and pleasure should be sacrificed in devoted service to my parents. And yet, as though by way of punishment for my desire for pleasures, an incident happened, which has ever since rankled in my mind and which I will relate later. Nishkulanand1 sings :"Renunciation of objects, without the renunciation of desires, is short-lived, however hard you may try." Whenever I sing this song or hear it sung, this bitter untoward incident rushes to my memory and fills me with shame.

A Gujarati poet of the Swaminarayan cult My father put on a brave face in spite of his injuries, and took full part in the wedding. As I think of it, I can even today call before my mind"s eye the places where he sat as he went through the different details of the ceremony. Little did I dream then that one day I should severely criticize my father for having married me as a child.

Everything on that day seemed to me right and proper and pleasing.

There was also my own eagerness to get married. And as everything that my father did then struck me as beyond reproach, the recollection of those things is fresh in my memory. I can picture to myself, even today, how we sat on our wedding dais, how we performed the Sapta padi1, how we, the newly wedded husband and wife, put the sweet kansar2 into each other"s mouth, and how we began to live together, and oh! that first night. Two innocent children all unwittingly hurled themselves into the ocean of life. My brother"s wife had thoroughly coached me about my behaviour on the first night. I do not know who had coached my wife. I have never asked her about it, nor am I inclined to do so now.

The reader may be sure that we were too nervous to face each other. We were certainly too shy. How was I to talk to her, and what was I to say ? The coaching could not carry me far. But no coaching is really necessary in such matters. The impressions of the former birth are potent enough to make all coaching superfluous. We gradually began to know each other, and to speak freely together. We were the same age. But I took no time in assuming the authority of a husband.

PLAYING THE HUSBAND

About the time of my marriage, little pamphlets costing a pice, or a pie (I now forget how much), used to be issued, in which conjugal love, thrift, child marriages, and other such subjects were discussed.

Whenever I came across any of these, I used to go through them cover to cover, and it was a habit with me to forget what I did not like, and to carry out in practice whatever I liked. Lifelong faithfulness to the wife, inculcated in these booklets as the duty of the husband, remained permanently imprinted on my heart. Furthermore, the passion for truth was innate in me, and to be false to her was therefore out of the question. And then there was very little chance of my being faithless at that tender age.

But the lesson of faithfulness had also an untoward effect. "If I 1 A ceremony consisting of seven steps in which a Hindu bride and bridegroom walk together, making at the same time promises of mutual fidelity and devotion, after which the marriage becomes irrevocable. For details, vide "With Bare Religious Rites", March 7, 1926.

I do not know whether Kasturbai had any such ambition. She was illiterate. By nature she was simple, independent, persevering and, with me at least, reticent. She was not impatient of her ignorance and I do not recollect my studies having ever spurred her to go in for a sim ilar adventure. I fancy, therefore, that my ambition was all one-sided.

My passion was entirely centred on one woman, and I wanted it to be reciprocated. But even if there were no reciprocity, it could not be all unrelieved misery because there was active love on one side at least.

I must say I was passionately fond of her. Even at school I used to think of her, and the thought of nightfall and our subsequent meeting was ever haunting me. Separation was unbearable. I used to keep her awake till late in the night with my idle talk. If with this devouring passion there had not been in me a burning attachment to duty, I should either have fallen a prey to disease and premature death, or have sunk into a burdensome existence. But the appointed tasks had to be gone through every morning, and lying to anyone was out of the question. It was this last thing that saved me from many a pitfall. I have already said that Kasturbai was illiterate. I was very anxious to teach her, but lustful love left me no time. For one thing the teaching had to be done against her will, and that too at night. I dared not meet her in the presence of the elders, much less talk to her.

Kathiawad had then, and to a certain extent has even today, its own peculiar, useless and barbarous purdah. Circumstances were thus unfavourable. I must therefore confess that most of my efforts to instruct Kasturbai in our youth were unsuccessful. And when I awoke from the sleep of lust, I had already launched forth into public life, which did not leave me much spare time. I failed likewise to instruct her through private tutors. As a result, Kasthurbai can now with difficulty write simple letters and understand simple Gujarati. I am sure that, had my love for her been absolutely untainted with lust, she would be a learned lady today; for I could then have conquered her dislike for studies. I know that nothing is impossible for pure love.

I have mentioned one circumstance that more or less saved me from the disasters of lustful love. There is another worth noting.

Numerous examples have convinced me that God ultimately saves him whose motive is pure. Along with the cruel custom of child marriages, Hindu society has another custom which to a certain extent diminishes the evils of the former. Parents do not allow young couples to stay together long. The child-wife spends more than half her time at her father"s place. Such was the case with us. That is to say, during the first five years of our married life (from the age of 13 to 18), we could not have lived together longer than an aggregate period of three years. We would hardly have spent six months together, when there would be a call to my wife from her parents. Such calls were very unwelcome in those days, but they saved us both. At the age of eighteen I went to England, and this meant a long and healthy spell of separation. Even after my return from England we hardly stayed together longer than six months. For I had to run up and down between Rajkot and Bombay. Then came the call from South Africa, and that found me already fairly free from the carnal appetite.

AT THE HIGH SCHOOL

I have already said that I was learning at the high school when I was married. We three brothers were learning at the same school. The eldest brother was in a much higher class, and the brother who was married at the same time as I was, only one class ahead of me. Mar riage resulted in both of us wasting a year. Indeed the result was even worse for my brother, for he gave up studies altogether. Heaven knows how many youths are in the same plight as he. Only in our present Hindu society do studies and marriage go thus hand in hand.

My studies were continued. I was not regarded as a dunce at the high school. I always enjoyed the affection of my teachers. Certifi cates of progress and character used to be sent to the parents every year. I never had a bad certificate. In fact I even won prizes after I passed out of the second standard. In the fifth and sixth I obtained scholarships of rupees four and ten respectively, an achievement for which I have to thank good luck more than my merit. For the scholarships were not open to all, but reserved for the best boys amongst those coming from the Sorath Division of Kathiawad. And in those days there could not have been many boys from Sorath in a class of forty to fifty.

My own recollection is that I had not any high regard for my ability. I used to be astonished whenever I won prizes and scholar ships. But I very jealously guarded my character. The least little ble mish drew tears from my eyes. When I merited, or seemed to the teacher to merit, a rebuke, it was unbearable for me. I remember hav ing once received corporal punishment. I did not so much mind the punishment, as the fact that it was considered my desert. I wept piteously. That was when I was in the first or second standard. There was another such incident during the time when I was in the seventh standard. Dorabji Edulji Gimi was the head master then. He was pop ular among boys, as he was a disciplinarian, a man of method and a good teacher. He had made gymnastics and cricket compulsory for boys of the upper standards. I disliked both. I never took party in any exercise, cricket or football, before they were made compulsory. My shyness was one of the reasons for this aloofness, which I now see was wrong. I then had the false notion that gymnastics had nothing to do with education. Today I know that physical training should have as much place in the curriculum as mental training.

I may mention, however, that I was none the worse for abstaining from exercise. That was because I had read in books about the benefits of long walks in the open air, and having liked the advice, I had formed a habit of taking walks, which has still remained with me. These walks gave me a fairly hardy constitution.

The reason of my dislike for gymnastics was my keen desire to serve as nurse to my father. As soon as the school closed, I would hurry home and begin serving him. Compulsory exercise came directly in the way of this service. I requested Mr. Gimi to exempt me from gymnastics so that I might be free to serve my father. But he would not listen to me. Now it so happened that one Saturday, when we had school in the morning, I had to go from home to the school for gymnastics at 4 o"clock in the afternoon. I had no watch, and the clouds deceived me. Before I reached the school the boys had all left. The next day Mr. Gimi, examining the roll, found me marked absent.

Being asked the reason for absence, I told him what had happened. He refused to believe me and ordered me to pay a fine of one or two annas (I cannot now recall how much).

I was convicted of lying ! That deeply pained me. How was I to prove my innocence ? There was no way. I cried in deep anguish. I saw that a man of truth must also be a man of care. This was the first and last instance of my carelessness in school. I have a faint recollec tion that I finally succeeded in getting the fine remitted. The exemp tion from exercise was of course obtained, as my father wrote himself to the head master saying that he wanted me at home after school.

But though I was none the worse for having neglected exercise, I am still paying the penalty of another neglect. I do not know whence I got the notion that good handwriting was not a necessary part of education, but I retained it until I went to England. When later, especially in South Africa, I saw the beautiful handwriting of lawyers and young men born and educated in South Africa, I was ashamed of myself and repented of my neglect. I saw that bad handwriting should be regarded as a sign of an imperfect education. I tried later to improve mine, but it was too late. I could never repair the neglect of my youth. Let every young man and woman be warned by my example, and understand that good handwriting is a necessary part of education. I am now of opinion that children should first be taught the art of drawing before learning how to write. Let the child learn his letters by observation as he does different objects, such as flowers, birds, etc., and let him learn handwriting only after he has learnt to draw objects. He will then write a beautifully formed hand.

Two more reminiscences of my school days are worth recording. I had lost one year because of my marriage, and the teacher wanted me to make good the loss by skipping a class-a privilege usually allowed to industrious boys. I therefore had only six months in the third standard and was promoted to the fourth after the examinations which are followed by the summer vacation. English became the medium of instruction in most subjects from the fourth standard. I found myself completely at sea. Geometry was a new subject in which I was not particularly strong, and the English medium made it still more difficult for me. The teacher taught the subject very well, but I could not follow him. Often I would lose heart and think of going back to the third standard, feeling that the packing of two years" studies into a single year was too ambitious. But this would discredit not only me, but also the teacher; because, counting on my industry, he had recommended my promotion. So the fear of the double discredit kept me at my post. When, however, with much effort I reached the thirteenth proposition of Euclid, the utter simplicity of the subject was suddenly revealed to me. A subject which only required a pure and simple use of one"s reasoning powers could not be difficult. Ever since that time geometry has been both easy and interesting for me.

Samskrit, however, proved a harder task. In geometry there was nothing to memorize, whereas in Samskrit, I thought, everything had to be learnt by heart. This subject also was commenced from the fourth standard. As soon as I entered the sixth I became disheartened.

The teacher was a hard taskmaster, anxious, as I thought, to force the boys. There was a sort of rivalry going on between the Samskrit and the Persian teachers. The Persian teacher was lenient. The boys used to talk among themselves that Persian was very easy and the Persian teacher very good and considerate to the students. The "easiness" tempted me and one day I sat in the Persian class. The Samskrit teacher was grieved. He called me to his side and said: "How can you forget that you are the son of a Vaishnava1 father ? Won"t you learn the language of your own religion ? If you have any difficulty, why not come to me ? I want to teach you students Samskrit to the best of my ability. As you proceed further, you will find in it things of absorbing interest. You should not lose heart. Come and sit again in the Samskrit class." This kindness put me to shame. I could not disregard my teacher"s affection. Today I cannot but think with gratitude of Krishnashankar Pandya. For if I had not acquired the little Samskrit that I learnt then, I should have found it difficult to take any interest in our sacred books. In fact I deeply regret that I was not able to acquire a more thorough knowledge of the language, because I have since realized that every Hindu boy and girl should possess sound Samskrit learning.

It is now my opinion that in all Indian curricula of higher education there should be a place for Hindi, Samskrit, Persian, Arabic and English, besides of course the vernacular. This big list need not frighten anyone. If our education were more systematic, and the boys free from the burden of having to learn their subjects through a foreign medium, I am sure learning all these languages would not be an irksome task, but a perfect pleasure. A scientific knowledge of one language makes a knowledge of other languages comparatively easy.

In reality, Hindi, Gujarati and Samskrit may be regarded as one language, and Persian and Arabic also as one. Though Persian 1 Member of the Vaishnava sect; a worshipper of Vishnu belongs to the Aryan, and Arabic to the Semitic family of languages, there is a close relationship between Persian and Arabic, because both claim their full growth through the rise of Islam. Urdu I have not regarded as a distinct language, because it has adopted the Hindi grammar and its vocabulary is mainly Persian and Arabic, and he who would learn good Urdu must learn Persian and Arabic, as one who would learn good Gujarati, Hindi, Bengali or Marathi must learn Samskrit.

A TRAGEDY

Amongst my few friends at the high school I had, at different times, two who might be called intimate. One of these friendships did not last long, though I never forsook my friend. He forsook me, because I made friends with the other1. This latter friendship I regard as a tragedy in my life. It lasted long. I formed it in the spirit of a reformer.

This companion was originally my elder brother"s friend. They were classmates. I knew his weaknesses, but I regarded him as a faithful friend. My mother, my eldest brother, and my wife warned me that I was in bad company. I was too proud to heed my wife"s warning. But I dared not go against the opinion of my mother and my eldest brother. Nevertheless I pleaded with them saying, "I know he has the weaknesses you attribute to him, but you do not know his virtues. He cannot lead me astray, as my association with him is meant to reform him. For I am sure that if he reforms his ways, he will be a splendid man. I beg you not to be anxious on my account." I do not think this satisfied them, but they accepted my explana tion and let me go my way.

I have seen since that I had calculated wrongly. A reformer can-not afford to have close intimacy with him whom he seeks to reform. True friendship is an identity of souls rarely to be found in this world. Only between like natures can friendship be altogether worthy and endu-ring. Friends react on one another. Hence in friendship there is very little scope for reform. I am of opinion that all exclusive intimacies are to be avoided; for man takes in vice far more readily than virtue. And he who would be friends with God must remain alone, or make the whole world his friend. I may be wrong, but my effort to cultivate in intimate friendship proved a failure.

A wave of "reform" was sweeping over Rajkot at the time when I first came across this friend. He informed me that many of our teachers were secretly taking meat and wine. He also named many 1 Sheikh Mehtab; vide "London Diary", November 12, 1888.

You know how hardy I am, and how great a runner too. It is because I am a meat-eater. Meat-eaters do not have boils or tumours, and even if they sometimes happen to have any, these heal quickly. Our teachers and other distinguished people who eat meat are no fools. They know its virtues. You should do likewise. There is nothing like trying. Try, and see what strength it gives." All these pleas on behalf of meat-eating were not advanced at a single sitting. They represent the substance of a long and elaborate argument which my friend was trying to impress upon me from time to time. My elder brother had already fallen. He therefore supported my friend"s argument. I certainly looked feeble-bodied by the side of my brother and this friend. They were both hardier, physically stronger, and more daring. This friend"s exploits cast a spell over me.

He could run long distances and extraordinarily fast. He was an adept in high and long jumping. He could put up with any amount of corporal punishment. He would often display his exploits to me and, as one is always dazzled when he sees in others the qualities that he lacks himself, I was dazzled by this friend"s exploits. This was followed by a strong desire to be like him. I could hardly jump or run. Why should not I also be as strong as he ? Moreover, I was a coward. I used to be haunted by the fear of thieves, ghosts and serpents. I did not dare to stir out of doors at night.

Darkness was a terror to me. It was almost impossible for me to sleep in the dark, as I would imagine ghosts coming from one direction, thieves from another and serpents from a third. I could not therefore bear to sleep without a light in the room. How could I disclose my fears to my wife, no child, but already at the threshold of youth, sleeping by my side ? I knew that she had more courage than I, and I felt ashamed of myself. She knew no fear of serpents and ghosts. She could go out anywhere in the dark. My friend knew all these weak nesses of mine. He would tell me that he could hold in his hand live serpents, could defy thieves and did not believe in ghosts. And all this was, of course, the result of eating meat.

A doggerel of the Gujarati poet Narmad was in vogue amongst us schoolboys, as follows : Behold the mighty Englishman He rules the Indian small, Because being a meat-eater He is five cubits tall.

All this had its due effect on me. I was beaten. It began to grow on me that meat-eating was good, that it would make me strong and daring, and that, if the whole country took to meat-eating, the English could be overcome.

A day was thereupon fixed for beginning the experiment. It had to be conducted in secret. The Gandhis were Vaishnavas.

My parents were particularly staunch Vaishnavas. They would regularly visit the Haveli. The family had even its own temples. Jainism was strong in Gujarat, and its influence was felt everywhere and on all occasions.

The opposition to and abhorrence of meat-eating that existed in Gujarat among the Jains and Vaishnavas were to be seen nowhere else in India or outside in such strength. These were the traditions in which I was born and bred. And I was extremely devoted to my parents. I knew that the moment they came to know of my having eaten meat, they would be shocked to death. Moreover, my love of truth made me extra cautious. I cannot say that I did not know then that I should have to deceive my parents if I began eating meat.

But my mind was bent on the "reform". It was not a question of pleasing the palate. I did not know that it had a particularly good relish. I wished to be strong and daring and wanted my countrymen also to be such, so that we might defeat the English and make India free. The word "swaraj" I had not yet heard. But I knew what freedom meant. The frenzy of the "reform" blinded me. And having ensured secrecy, I persuaded myself that mere hiding the deed from parents was no departure from truth.

A TRAGEDY

So the day came. It is difficult fully to describe my condition.

There were, on the one hand, the zeal for "reform" and the novelty of making a momentous departure in life. There was, on the other, the shame of hiding like a thief to do this very thing. I cannot say which of the two swayed me more. We went in search of a lonely spot by the river, and there I saw, for the first time in my life-meat. There was baker"s bread also. I relished neither. The goat"s meat was as tough as leather. I simply could not eat it. I was sick and had to leave off eating.I had a very bad night afterwards. A horrible nightmare haunted me. Every time I dropped off to sleep it would seem as though a live goat were bleating inside me, and I would jump up full of remorse.

But then I would remind myself that meat-eating was a duty and so become more cheerful.

My friend was not a man to give in easily. He now began to cook various delicacies with meat, and dress them neatly. And for dining, no longer was the secluded spot on the river chosen, but a State house, with its dining-hall, and tables and chairs, about which my friend had made arrangements in collusion with the chief cook there.

This bait had its effect. I got over my dislike for bread, forswore my compassion for the goats, and became a relisher of meat-dishes, if not of meat itself. This went on for about a year. But not more than half a dozen meat-feasts were enjoyed in all; because the State house was not available every day, and there was the obvious difficulty about frequently preparing expensive savoury meat-dishes. I had no money to pay for this "reform". My friend had therefore always to find the wherewithal. I had no knowledge where he found it. But find it he did, because he was bent on turning me into a meat-eater. But even his means must have been limited, and hence these feasts had necessarily to be few and far between.

Whenever I had occasion to indulge in these surreptiitous feasts, dinner at home was out of the question. My mother would naturally ask me to come and take my food and want to know the reason why I did not wish to eat. I would say to her, "I have no appetite today; there is something wrong with my digestion." It was not without compunction that I devised these pretexts. I knew I was lying, and lying to my mother. I also knew that, if my mother and father came to know of my having become a meat-eater, they would be deeply shocked. This knowledge was gnawing at my heart.

Therefore I said to myself : "Though it is essential to eat meat, and also essential to take up food reform in the country yet deceiving and lying to one"s father and mother is worse than not eating meat. In their lifetime, therefore, meat-eating must be out of the question.

When they are no more and I have found freedom, I will eat meat openly, but until that moment arrives I will abstain from it." This decision I communicated to my friend, and I have never since gone back to meat. My parents never knew that two of their sons had become meat-eaters.

I abjured meat out of the purity of my desire not to lie to my parents, but I did not abjure the company of my friend. My zeal for reforming him had proved disastrous for me, and all the time I was completely unconscious of the fact.

The same company would have led me into faithlessness to my wife. But I was saved by the skin of my teeth. My friend once took me to a brothel. He sent me in with the necessary instructions. It was all pre-arranged. The bill had already been paid. I went into the jaws of sin, but God in His infinite mercy protected me against myself. I was almost struck blind and dumb in this den of vice. I sat near the woman on her bed, but I was tongue-tied. She naturally lost patience with me, and showed me the door, with abuses and insults. I then felt as though my manhood had been injured, and wished to sink into the ground for shame. But I have ever since given thanks to God for having saved me. I can recall four more similar incidents in my life, and in most of them my good fortune, rather than any effort on my part, saved me. From a strictly ethical point of view, all these occasions must be regarded as moral lapses; for the carnal desire was there, and it was as good as the act. But from the ordinary point of view, a man who is saved from physically committing sin is regarded as saved. And I was saved only in that sense. There are some actions from which an escape is a godsend both for the man who escapes and for those about him. Man, as soon as he gets back his consciousness of right, is thankful to the Divine mercy for the escape. As we know that a man often succumbs to temptation, however much he may resist it, we also know that Providence often intercedes and saves him in spite of himself. How all this happens-how far a man is free and how far a creature of circumstances-how far free will comes into play and where fate enters on the scene-all this is a mystery and will remain a mystery.

But to go on with the story. Even this was far from opening my eyes to the viciousness of my friend"s company. I therefore had many more bitter draughts in store for me, until my eyes were actually ope ned by an ocular demonstration of some of his lapses quite unexpec ted by me. But of them later, as we are proceeding chronologically.

One thing, however, I must mention now, as it pertains to the same period. One of the reasons of my differences with my wife was undoubtedly the company of this friend. I was both a devoted and a jealous husband, and this friend fanned the flame of my suspicions about my wife. I never could doubt his veracity. And I never have forgiven myself the violence of which I have been guilty in often having pained my wife by acting on his information.

Perhaps only a Hindu wife would tolerate these hardships, and that is why I have regarded woman as an incarnation of tolerance. A servant wrongly suspected may throw up his job, a son in the same case may leave his father"s roof, and a friend may put an end to the friendship. The wife, if she suspects her husband, will keep quiet3, but if the husband suspects her, she is ruined. Where is she to go ? A Hindu wife4 may not seek divorce in a law-court. Law has no remedy for her. And I can Vide "Power of "Ramanama"", May 17, 1925.

never forget or forgive myself for having driven my wife to that desperation.

The canker of suspicion was rooted out only when I understood ahimsa in all its bearings. I saw then the glory of brahmacharya1 and realized that the wife is not the husband"s bondslave, but his companion and his helpmate, and an equal partner in all his joys and sorrows-as free as the husband to choose her own path6. Whenever I think of those dark days of doubts and suspicions, I am filled with loathing of my folly and my lustful cruelty, and I deplore7 my blind devotion to my friend.

STEALING AND ATONEMENT

I have still to relate some of my failings during this meat-eating period and also previous to it, which date from before my marriage or soon after.

A relative and I became fond of smoking. Not that we saw any good in smoking, or were enamoured of the smell of a cigarette. We simply imagined a sort of pleasure in emitting clouds of smoke from our mouths. My uncle had the habit, and when we saw him smoking, we thought we should copy his example. But we had no money. So we began pilfering stumps of cigarettes thrown away by my uncle.

The stumps, however, were not always available, and could not emit much smoke either. So we began to steal coppers from the servant"s pocket-money in order to purchase Indian cigarettes. But the question was where to keep them. We could not of course smoke in the presence of elders. We managed somehow for a few weeks on these stolen coppers. In the mean time we heard that the stalks of a certain plant were porous and could be smoked like cigarettes. We got them and began this kind of smoking.

But we were far from being satisfied with such things as these.

Our want of independence began to smart. It was unbearable that we should be unable to do anything without the elder"s permission. At last, in sheer disgust, we decided to commit suicide ! But how were we to do it? From where were we to get the poison? We heard that dhatura seeds were an effective poison. Off we went to the jungle in search of these seeds, and got them. Evening was thought to be the auspicious hour. We went to Kedarji Mandir, put ghee in the temple-lamp, had the darshan and then looked for a lonely corner. But our courage failed us. Supposing we were not Literally, "conduct that leads one to God"; hence self-restraint, parti cularly in sex Belladonna instantly killed ? And what was the good of killing ourselves ? Why not rather put up with the lack of independence? But we swallowed two or three seeds nevertheless. We dared not take more. Both of us fought shy of death, and decided to go to Ramji-Mandir to compose ourselves, and to dismiss the thought of suicide.

I realized that it was not as easy to commit suicide as to contemplate it. And since then, whenever I have heard of someone threatening to commit suicide, it has had little or no effect on me.

The thought of suicide ultimately resulted in both of us bidding good-bye to the habit of smoking stumps of cigarettes and of stealing the servant"s coppers for the purpose of smoking.

Ever since I have been grown up, I have never desired to smoke and have always regarded the habit of smoking as barbarous, dirty and harmful. I have never understood why there is such a rage for smoking throughout the world. I cannot bear to travel in a compart ment full of people smoking. I become choked.

But much more serious than this theft was the one I was guilty of a little later. I pilfered the coppers when I was twelve or thirteen, possibly less. The other theft was committed when I was fifteen. In this case I stole a bit of gold out of my meat-eating brother"s armlet. This brother had run into a debt of about twenty-five rupees. He had on his arm an armlet of solid gold. It was not difficult to clip a bit out of it.

Well, it was done, and the debt cleared. But this became more than I could bear. I resolved never to steal again. I also made up my mind to confess it to my father. But I did not dare to speak. Not that I was afraid of my father beating me. No. I do not recall his ever having beaten any of us. I was afraid of the pain that I should cause him.

But I felt the risk should be taken; that there could not be a cleansing without a clean confession.

I decided at last to write out the confession, to submit it to my father, and ask his forgiveness. I wrote it on a slip of paper and handed it to him myself. In this note not only did I confess my guilt, but I asked adequate punishment for it, and closed with a request to him not to punish himself for my offence. I also pledged myself never to steal in future.

I was trembling as I handed the confession to my father. He was then suffering from a fistula and was confined to bed. His bed was a plain wooden plank. I handed him the note and sat opposite the plank.

He read it through, and pearl-drops trickled down his cheeks, wetting the paper. For a moment he closed his eyes in thought and then tore up the note. He had sat up to read it. He again lay down. I also cried. I could see my father"s agony. If I were a painter I could draw a picture of the whole scene today. It is still so vivid in my mind.

Those pearl-drops of love cleansed my heart, and washed my sin away. Only he who has experienced such love can know what it is. As the hymn says : "Only he Who is smitten the arrows of love, Knows its power." This was, for me, an object-lesson in ahimsa. Then I could read in it nothing more than a father"s love, but today I know that it was pure ahimsa. When such ahimsa becomes all-embracing, it transforms every-thing it touches. There is no limit to its power.

This sort of sublime forgiveness was not natural to my father. I had thought that he would be angry, say hard things, and strike his forehead. But he was so wonderfully peaceful, and I believe this was due to my clean confession. A clean confession, combined with a promise never to commit the sin again, when offered before one who has the right to receive it, is the purest type of repentance. I know that my confession made my father feel absolutely safe about me, and increased his affection for me beyond measure.

MY FATHER"S DEATH AND MY DOUBLE SHAME

The time of which I am now speaking is my sixteenth year. My father, as we have seen, was bed-ridden, suffering from a fistula. My mother, an old servant of the house, and I were his principal attendants. I had the duties of a nurse, which mainly consisted in dressing the wound giving my father his medicine, and compounding drugs whenever they had to be made up at home. Every night I massaged his legs and retired only when he asked me to do so or after he had fallen asleep. I loved to do this service. I do not remember ever having neglected it. All the time at my disposal, after the performance of the daily duties, was divided between school and attending on my father. I would only go out for an evening walk either when he permitted me or when he was feeling well.

This was also the time when my wife was expecting a baby,-a circumstance which, as I can see today, meant a double shame for me.

For one thing I did not restrain myself, as I should have done whilst I Vide "Letter to Manilal Gandhi", March 25, 1925 : "My keenest enjoyment was to nurse my father." was yet a student. And secondly, this carnal lust got the better of what I regarded as my duty to study, and of what was even a greater duty, my devotion to my parents, Shravana having been my ideal since childhood. Every night whilst my hands were busy massaging my father"s legs, my mind was hovering about the bed-room-and that too at a time when religion, medical science and common sense alike forbade sexual intercourse. I was always glad to be relieved from my duty, and went straight to the bed-room after doing obeisance to my father.At the same time my father was getting worse every day. Ayur vedic physicians had tried all their ointments, hakims their plasters, and local quacks their nostrums. An English surgeon had also used his skill. As the last and only resort he had recommended a surgical operation. But the family physician came in the way. He disapproved of an operation being performed at such an advanced age. The physician was competent and well known, and his advice prevailed.

The operation was abandoned, and various medicines purchased for the purpose were of no account. I have an impression that, if the phys ician had allowed the operation, the wound would have been easily healed. The operation also was to have been performed by a surgeon who was then well known in Bombay. But God had willed otherwise.

When death is imminent, who can think of the right remedy? My father returned from Bombay with all the paraphernalia of the ope ration, which were now useless. He despaired of living any longer. He was getting weaker and weaker, until at last he had to be asked to per form the necessary functions in bed. But up to the last he refused to do anything of the kind, always insisting on going through the strain of leaving his bed. The Vaishnavite rules about external cleanliness are so inexorable.

Such cleanliness is quite essential no doubt, but Western medical science has taught us that all the functions, including a bath, can be done in bed with the strictest regard to cleanliness, and without the slightest discomfort to the patient, the bed always remaining spotlessly clean. I should regard such cleanliness as quite consistent with Vais hnavism. But my father"s insistence on leaving the bed only struck me with wonder then, and I had nothing but admiration for it.

The dreadful night came. My uncle was then in Rajkot. I have a faint recollection that he came to Rajkot having had news that my father was getting worse. The brothers were deeply attached to each other. My uncle would sit near my father"s bed the whole day, and would insist on sleeping by his bedside after sending us all to sleep.

No one had dreamt that this was to be the fateful night. The danger of course was there.

It was 10.30 or 11 p.m. I was giving the massage. My uncle offered to relieve me. I was glad and went straight to the bed-room.

My wife, poor thing, was fast asleep. But how could she sleep when I was there? I woke her up. In five or six minutes, however, the servant knocked at the door. I started with alarm. "Get up," he said, "Father is very ill." I knew of course that he was very ill, and so I guessed what "very ill" meant at that moment. I sprang out of bed.

"What is the matter ? Do tell me !" "Father is no more." So all was over ! I had but to wring my hands. I felt deeply ashamed and miserable. I ran to my father"s room. I saw that, if animal passion had not blinded me, I should have been spared the torture of separation from my father during his last moments. I should have been massaging him, and he would have died in my arms. But now it was my uncle who had had this privilege. He was so deeply devoted to his elder brother that he had earned the honour of doing him the last services ! My father had forebodings of the coming event. He had made a sign for pen and paper, and written : "Prepare for the last rites." He had then snapped the amulet of his arm and also his gold necklace of tulasi1 beads and flung them aside. A moment after this he was no more.

The shame, to which I have referred in a foregoing chapter, was this shame of my carnal desire even at the critical hour of my father"s death, which demanded wakeful service. It is a a blot I have never been able to efface or forget, and I have always thought that, although my devotion to my parents knew no bounds and I would have given up anything for it, yet it was weighed and found unpardonably wanting becuase my mind was at the same moment in the grip of lust.

I have therefore always regarded myself as a lustful, though a faithful, husband. It took me long to get free from the shackles of lust, and I had to pass through many ordeals before I could overcome it.

Before I close this chapter of my double shame, I may mention that the poor mite that was born to my wife scarcely breathed for more than three or four days. Nothing else could be expected. Let all those who are married0 be warned by my example.

GLIMPSES OF RELIGION

From my sixth or seventh year up to my sixteenth I was at school, being taught all sorts of things except religion. I may say that I failed to get from the teachers what they could have given me 1 An aromatic plant the leaves of which are offered in worship. Prayer beads are made out of its stalk. without any effort on their part. And yet I kept on picking up things here and there from my surroundings. The term "realigion" I am using in its broadest sense, meaning thereby self-relization or knowledge of self.

Being born in the Vaishnava faith, I had often to go to the Haveli. But it never appealed to me. I did not like its glitter and pomp.

Also I heard rumours of immorality being practised there, and lost all interest in it. Hence I could gain nothing from the Haveli.

But what I failed to get there I obtained from my nurse, an old servant of the family, whose affection for me I still recall. I have said before that there was in me a fear of ghosts and spirits. Rambha, for that was her name, suggested, as a remedy for this fear, the repetition of Ramanama. I had more faith in her than in her remedy, and so at a tender age I began repeating Ramanama to cure my fear of ghosts and spirits. This was of course short-lived, but the good seed sown in childhood was not sown in vain. I think it is due to the seed sown by that good woman Rambha that today Ramanama is an infallible remedy for me. Just about this time, a cousin of mine who was a devotee of the Ramayana arranged for my second brother and me to learn Rama Raksha.

We got it by heart, and made it a rule to recite it every mor ning after the bath. The practice was kept up as long as we were in Porbandar. As soon as we reached Rajkot, it was forgotten. For I had not much belief in it. I recited it partly because of my pride in being able to recite Rama Raksha with correct pronunciation.

What, however, left a deep impression on me was the reading of the Ramayana before my father. During part of his illness my father was in Porbandar. There every evening he used to listen to the Ramayana. The reader was a great devotee of RamaLadha Mah araj of Bileshwar. It was said of him that he cured himself of his leprosy not by any medicine, but by applying to the affected parts bilva leaves which had been cast away after being offered to the image of Mahadeva in Bileshwar temple, and by the regular repetition of Ramanama. His faith, it was said, had made him whole. This may or may not be true. We at any rate believed the story. And it is a fact that when Ladha Maharaj began his reading of the Ramayana his body Name of Rama, name of God Vide "Speech at Suppressed Classes Conference, Ahmedabad", April 13.

A hymn invoking Rama"s protection Lord Siva, God of destruction in the Hindu Trinity St. Matthew, ix. 22 and St. Mark and St. Luke was entirely free from leprosy. He had a melodious voice. He would sing the dohas (couplets) and chopais (quatrains), and explain them, losing himself in the discourse and carrying his listeners along with him. I must have been thirteen at that time, but I quite remember being enraptured by his reading. That laid the foundation of my deep devotion to the Ramayana. Today I regard the Ramayana of Tul asidas as the greatest book in all devotional literature.

A few months after this we came to Rajkot. There was no Ramayana reading there. The Bhagavata, however, used to be read on every Ekadashi1 day. Sometimes I attended the reading, but the reciter was uninspiring. Today I see that the Bhagavata is a book which can evoke religious fervour. I have read it in Gujarati with intense interest. But when I heard portions of the original read by Pandit Madan Mohan Malaviya during my twenty-one days" fast, I wished I had heard it in my childhood from such a devotee as he is, so that I could have formed a liking for it at an early age. Impressions formed at that age strike roots deep down into one"s nature, and it is my perpetual regret that I was not fortunate enough to hear more good books of this kind read during that period.

In Rajkot, however, I got an early grounding in toleration for all branches of Hinduism and sister religions. For my father and mother would visit the Haveli as also Shiva"s and Rama"s temples, and would take or send us youngsters there. Jain monks also would pay frequent visits to my father, and would even go out of their way to accept food from us-non-Jains.0 They would have talks with my father on subjects religious and mundane.

He had, besides, Mussalman and Parsi friends, who would talk to him about their own faiths, and he would listen to them always with respect, and often with interest. Being his nurse, I often had a chance to be present at these talks. These many things combined to inculcate in me a toleration for all faiths.

Only Christianity was at the time an exception. I developed a sort of dislike for it. And for a reason. In those days Christian missionaries used to stand in a corner near the high school and hold forth, pouring abuse on Hindus and their gods. I could not endure this. I must have stood there to hear them3 once only, but that was enough to dissuade me from repeating the experiment. About the same time, I heard of a well-known Hindu having been converted to 1 Eleventh day of the bright and the dark half of a lunar month.

But the fact that I had learnt to be tolerant to other religions did not mean that I had any living faith in God. I happened, about this time, to come across Manusmriti which was amongst my father"s collection. The story of the creation and similar things in it did not impress me very much, but on the contrary made me incline somewhat towards atheism.

There was a cousin of mine, still alive, for whose intellect I had great regard. To him I turned with my doubts. But he could not resolve them. He sent me away with this answer : "When you grow up, you will be able to solve these doubts yourself. These questions ought not to be raised at your age." I was silenced, but was not comforted.

Chapters about diet and the like in Manusmriti seemed to me to run contrary to daily practice. To my doubts as to this also, I got the same answer. "With intellect more developed and with more reading I shall understand it better," I said to myself.

Manusmriti at any rate did not then teach me ahimsa. I have told the story of my meat-eating. Manusmriti seemed to support it. I also felt that it was quite moral to kill serpents, bugs and the like. I remember to have killed at that age bugs and such other insects, regarding it as a duty.

But one thing took keep root in me-the conviction that morality is the basis of things, and that truth is the substance of all morality. Truth became my sole objective. It began to grow in magnitude every day, and my definition of it also has been ever widening.

A Gujarati didactic stanza likewise gripped my mind and heart.

Its precept-return good for evil-became my guiding principle. It became such a passion with me that I began numerous experiments in it. Here are those (for me)4 wonderful lines : For a bowl of water give a goodly meal; For a kindly greeting bow thou down with zeal; 1 Laws of Manu, Hindu law-giver. They have the sanction of religion.

For a simple penny pay thou back with gold; If thy life be rescued, life do not withhold.

Thus the words and actions of the wise regard; Every little service tenfold they reward.

But the truly noble know all men as one, And return with gladness good for evil done.

PREPARATION FOR ENGLAND

I passed the matriculation examination in 1887. It then used to be held at two centres, Ahmedabad and Bombay. The general poverty of the country naturally led Kathiawad students to prefer the nearer and the cheaper centre. The poverty of my family likewise dictated to me the same choice. This was my first journey from Rajkot to Ahmedabad and that too without a companion.

My elders wanted me to pursue my studies at college after the matriculation. There was a college in Bhavnagar as well as in Bombay, and as the former was cheaper, I decided to go there and join the Samaldas College. I went, but found myself entirely at sea. Every thing was difficult. I could not follow, let alone taking interest in, the professors" lectures. It was no fault of theirs. The professors in that College were regarded as first-rate. But I was so raw. At the end of the first term, I returned home.

We had in Mavji Dave2, who was a shrewd and learned Brah min, an old friend and adviser of the family. He had kept up his connection with the family even after my father"s death. He happened to visit us during my vacation. In conversation with my mother and elder brother, he inquired about my studies.

Learning that I was at Samaldas College, he said: "The times are changed. And none of you can expect to succeed to your father"s gadi without having had a proper education. Now as this boy is still pursuing his studies, you should all look to him to keep the gadi. It will take him four or five years to get his B.A. degree, which will at best qualify him for a sixty rupees" post, not for a Diwanship. If like my son he went in for law, it would take him still longer, by which time there would be a host of lawyers, aspiring for a Diwan"s post. I would far rather that you sent him to England. My son Kevalram says By Shamal Bhatt 2 Alias Mavji Joshi, a leading lawyer of Kathiawar; for another account of the decision on going to England and of the voyage to England, vide "London Diary", November 12, 1888.

Think of that barrister who has just come back from England. How stylishly he lives! He could get the Diwanship for the asking. I would strongly advise you to send Mohandas to England this very year.

Kevalram has numerous friends in England. He will give notes of introduction to them, and Mohandas will have an easy time of it there."Joshiji-that is how we used to call old Mavji Dave-turned to me with complete assurance, and asked: "Would you not rather go to England than study here?" Nothing could have been more welcome to me. I was fighting shy of my difficult studies. So I jumped at the proposal and said that the sooner I was sent the better. It was no easy business to pass examinations quickly. Could I not be sent to qualify for the medical profession? My brother interrupted me: "Father never liked it. He had you in mind when he said that we Vaishnavas should have nothing to do with dissection of dead bodies. Father intended you for the bar." Joshiji chimed in: "I am not opposed to the medical profession as was Gandhiji. Our Shastras are not against it.

But a medical degree will not make a Diwan of you, and I want you to be Diwan, or if possible something better. Only in that way could you take under your protecting care your large family. The times are fast changing and getting harder every day. It is the wisest thing therefore to become a barrister." Turning to my mother he said: "Now, I must leave. Pray ponder over what I have said. When I come here next I shall expect to hear of preparations for England. Be sure to let me know if I can assist in any way." Joshiji went away, and I began building castles in the air.

My elder brother was greatly exercised in his mind. How was he to find the wherewithal to send me? And was it proper to trust a young man like me to go abroad alone? My mother was sorely perplexed. She did not like the idea of parting with me. This is how she tried to put me off: "Uncle," she said, is now the eldest member of the family. He should first be consulted.

If he consents we will consider the matter." My brother had another idea. He said to me: "We have a certain claim on the Porbandar State. Mr. Lely is the Administrator. He thinks highly of our family and uncle is in his good books. It is just possible that he might recommend you for some State help for your education in England." I liked all this and got ready to start off for Porbandar. There was no railway in those days. It was a five days" bullock-cart journey.

I have already said that I was a coward. But at that moment my cowar dice vanished before the desire to go to England, which com-pletely possessed me. I hired a bullock-cart as far as Dhoraji, and from Dhoraji I took a camel in order to get to Porbandar a day quicker.

This was my first camel-ride.

I arrived at last, did obeisance to my uncle, and told him ever ything. He thought it over and said: "I am not sure whether it is possible for one to stay in England without prejudice to one"s own religion. From all I have heard, I have my doubts. When I meet these big barristers, I see no difference between their life and that of Euro peans. They know no scruples regarding food. Cigars are never out of their mouths. They dress as shamelessly as Englishmen. All that would not be in keeping with our family tradition. I am shortly going on a pilgrimage and have not many years to live. At the threshold of death, how dare I give you permission to go to England, to cross the seas? But I will not stand in your way. It is your mother"s permission which really matters. If she permits you, then godspeed! Tell her I will not interfere. You will go with my blessings." "I could expect nothing more from you," said I. "I shall now try to win mother over. But would you not recommend me to Mr. Lely?" "How can I do that ?" said he. "But he is a good man. You ask for an appointment telling him how you are connected. He will certainly give you one and may even help you." I cannot say why my uncle did not give me a note of recom mendation. I have a faint idea that he hesitated to co-operate directly in my going to England, which was in his opinion an irreligious act.

I wrote to Mr. Lely, who asked me to see him at his residence.

He saw me as he was ascending the staircase; and saying curtly, "Pass your B.A. first and then see me. No help can be given you now", he hurried upstairs. I had made elaborate preparations to meet him. I had carefully learnt up a few sentences and had bowed low and saluted him with both hands. But all to no purpose! I thought of my wife"s ornaments. I thought of my elder brother, in whom I had the utmost faith. He was generous to a fault, and he loved me as his son.

I returned to Rajkot from Porbandar and reported all that had happened. I consulted Joshiji, who of course advised even incurring a debt if necessary. I suggested the disposal of my wife"s ornaments, which could fetch about two to three thousand rupees. My brother promised to find the money somehow.

My mother, however, was still unwilling. She had begun making minute inquiries. Someone had told her that young men got lost in England. Someone else had said that they took to meat; and yet another that they could not live there without liquor. "How about all this?" she asked me. I said: "Will you not trust me? I shall not lie to you. I swear that I shall not touch any of those things. If there were any such danger, would Joshiji let me go?" "I can trust you," she said. "But how can I trust you in a distant land? I am dazed and know not what to do. I will ask Becharji Swami." Becharji Swami was originally a Modh Bania, but had now become a Jain monk. He too was a family adviser like Joshiji. He came to my help, and said: "I shall get the boy solemnly to take the three vows, and then he can be allowed to go." He administered the oath and I vowed not to touch wine, woman and meat. This done, my mother gave her permission.

The high school had a send-off in my honour. It was an uncommon thing for a young man of Rajkot to go to England. I had written out a few words of thanks. But I could scarcely stammer them out. I remember how my head reeled and how my whole frame shook as I stood up to read them.1 With the blessings of my elders, I started for Bombay. This was my first journey from Rajkot to Bombay. My brother accompanied me. But there is many a slip," twixt the cup and the lip. There were difficulties to be faced in Bombay.

OUTCASTE

With my mother"s permission and blessings, I set off exultantly for Bombay, leaving my wife with a baby of a few months. But on arrival there friends told my brother that the Indian Ocean was rough in June and July, and as this was my first voyage, I should not be allowed to sail until November. Someone also reported that a steamer had just been sunk in a gale. This made my brother uneasy, and he refused to take the risk of allowing me to sail immediately. Leaving me with a friend in Bombay, he returned to Rajkot to resume his duty.

He put the money for my travelling expenses in the keeping of a brother-in-law, and left word with some friends to give me whatever help I might need.

Time hung heavily on my hands in Bombay. I dreamt conti nually of going to England.

Meanwhile my caste people were agitated over my going

1 Vide "Speech at Alfred High School", July 4, 1888.

abroad. No Modh Bania had been to England up to now, and if I dared to do so, I ought to be brought to book! A general meeting of the caste was called and I was summoned to appear before it. I went.

How I suddenly managed to muster up courage I do not know. Not hing daunted, and without the slightest hesitation, I came before the meeting. The Sheth-the headman of the community-who was distantly related to me and had been on very good terms with my father, thus accosted me: "In the opinion of the caste, your proposal to go to England is not proper. Our religion forbids voyage abroad. We have also heard that it is not possible to live there without compromising our religion.

One is obliged to eat and drink with Europeans!" To which I replied: "I do not think it is at all against our religion to go to England. I intend going there for further studies. And I have already solemnly promised to my mother to abstain from three things you fear most. I am sure the vow will keep me safe." "But we tell you," rejoined the Sheth, "that it is not possible to keep our religion there. You know my relations with your father and you ought to listen to my advice." "I know those relations," said I. "And you are as an elder to me.

But I am helpless in this matter. I cannot alter my resolve to go to England. My father"s friend and adviser, who is a learned Brahmin, sees no objection to my going to England, and my mother and brother have also given me their permission." "But will you disregard the orders of the caste?" "I am really helpless. I think the caste should not interfere in the matter." This incensed the Sheth. He swore at me. I sat unmoved. So the Sheth pronounced his order: "This boy shall be treated as an outcaste from today. Whoever helps him or goes to see him off at the dock shall be punishable with a fine of one rupee four annas." The order had no effect on me, and I took my leave of the Sheth. But I wondered how my brother would take it. Fortunately he remained firm and wrote to assure me that I had his permission to go, the Sheth"s order notwithstanding.

The incident, however, made me more anxious than ever to sail.

What would happen if they succeeded in bringing pressure to bear on my brother? Supposing something unforeseen happened? As I was thus worrying over my predicament, I heard that a Junagadh vakil was going to England, for being called to the bar, by a boat sailing on the 4th of September. I met the friends to whose care my brother had commended me. They also agreed that I should not let go the opp ortunity of going in such company. There was no time to be lost. I wired to my brother for permission, which he granted. I asked my brother-in-law to give me the money. But he referred to the order of the Sheth and said that he could not afford to lose caste. I then sought a friend of the family and requested him to accommodate me to the extent of my passage and sundries, and to recover the loan from my brother. The friend was not only good enough to accede to my request, but he cheered me up as well. I was so thankful. With part of the money I at once purchased the passage. Then I had to equip myself for the voyage.

There was another friend who had experience in the matter. He got clothes and other things ready. Some of the clothes I liked and some I did not like at all. The necktie, which I delighted in wearing later, I then abhorred. The short jacket I looked upon as immodest. But this dislike was nothing before the desire to go to England, which was uppermost in me. Of provisions also I had enough and to spare for the voyage. A berth was reserved for me by my friends in the same cabin as that of Sjt. Tryambakrai Mazmudar, the Junagadh vakil. They also commended me to him. He was an experienced man of mature age and knew the world. I was yet a stripling of eighteen without any experience of the world.

Mazmudar told my friends not to worry about me.

I sailed at last from Bombay on the 4th of September.

IN LONDON AT LAST

I did not feel at all sea-sick. But as the days passed, I became fidgety. I felt shy even in speaking to the steward. I was quite unaccustomed to talking English, and except for Sjt. Mazmudar all the other passengers in the second saloon were English. I could not speak to them. For I could rarely follow their remarks when they came up to speak to me, and even when I understood I could not reply. I had to frame every sentence in my mind, before I could bring it out. I was innocent of the use of knives and forks and had not the boldness to inquire what dishes on the menu were free of meat. I therefore never took meals at table but always had them in my cabin, and they consisted principally of sweets and fruits which I had brought with me. Sjt. Mazmudar had no difficulty, and he mixed with everybody. He would move about freely on deck, while I hid myself in the cabin the whole day, only venturing up on deck when there were but few people. Sjt. Mazmudar kept pleading with me to associate with the passengers and to talk with them freely. He told me that lawyers should have a long tongue, and related to me his legal 1 In 1888 experiences. He advised me to take every possible opportunity of talking English, and not to mind making mistakes which were obviously unavoidable with a foreign tongue. But nothing could make me conquer my shyness.

An English passenger, taking kindly to me, drew me into conversation. He was older than I. He asked me what I ate, what I was, where I was going, why I was shy, and so on. He also advised me to come to table. He laughed at my insistence on abjuring meat, and said in a friendly way when we were in the Red Sea: "It is all very well so far but you will have to revise your decision in the Bay of Biscay.

And it is so cold in England that one cannot possibly live there without meat." "But I have heard that people can live there without eating meat," I said.

"Rest assured it is a fib," said he. "No one, to my knowledge, lives there without being a meat-eater. Don"t you see that I am not asking you to take liquor, though I do so? But I do think you should eat meat, for you cannot live without it." "I thank you for your kind advice, but I have solemnly promised to my mother not to touch meat, and therefore I cannot think of taking it. If it be found impossible to get on without it, I will far rather go back to India than eat meat in order to remain there."

We entered the Bay of Biscay, but I did not begin to feel the need either of meat or liquor. I had been advised to collect certificates of my having abstained from meat, and I asked the English friend to give me one. He gladly gave it and I treasured it for some time. But when I saw later that one could get such a certificate in spite of being a meat-eater, it lost all its charm for me. If my word was not to be trusted, where was the use of possessing a certificate in the matter ? However, we reached Southampton, as far as I remember, on a Saturday. On the boat I had worn a black suit, the white flannel one, which my friends had got me, having been kept especially for wearing when I landed. I had thought that white clothes would suit me better when I stepped ashore, and therefore I did so in white flannels. Those were the last days of September, and I found I was the only person wearing such clothes. I left in charge of an agent of Grindlay and Co. all my kit, including the keys, seeing that many others had done the same and I must follow suit.

I had four notes of introduction : to Dr. P. J. Mehta, to Sjt.

Dalpatram Shukla, to Prince Ranjitsinhji and to Dadabhai Naoroji.

Someone on board had advised us to put up at the Victoria Hotel in London. Sjt. Mazmudar and I accordingly went there. The shame of being the only person in white clothes was already too much for me.

And when at the Hotel I was told that I should not get my things from Grindlay"s the next day, it being a Sunday, I was exasperated.

Dr. Mehta, to whom I had wired from Southampton, called at about eight o"clock the same evening. He gave me a hearty greeting.

He smiled at my being in flannels. As we were talking, I casually picked up his top-hat, and trying to see how smooth it was, passed my hand over it the wrong way and disturbed the fur. Dr. Mehta looked somewhat angrily at what I was doing and stopped me. But the mischief had been done. The incident was a warning for the future. This was my first lesson in European etiquette, into the details of which Dr. Mehta humorously initiated me. "Do not touch other people"s things," he said. "Do not ask questions as we usually do in India on first acquaintance; do not talk loudly; never address people as "sir" whilst speaking to them as we do in India, only servants and subordinates address their masters that way." And so on and so forth.

He also told me that it was very expensive to live in a hotel and recommended that I should live with a private family. We deferred consideration of the matter until Monday.

Sjt. Mazmudar and I found the hotel to be a trying affair. It was also very expensive. There was, however, a Sindhi fellowpassenger from Malta who had become friends with Sjt. Mazmudar, and as he was not a stranger to London, he offered to find rooms for us. We agreed, and on Monday, as soon as we got our baggage, we paid up our bills and went to the rooms rented for us by the Sindhi friend. I remember my hotel bill came to £3, an amount which shocked me.

And I had practically starved in spite of this heavy bill ! For I could relish nothing. When I did not like one thing, I asked for another, but had to pay for both just the same. The fact is that all this while I had depended on the provisions which I had brought with me from Bombay.

I was very uneasy even in the new rooms. I would continually think of my home and country. My mother"s love always haunted me. At night the tears would stream down my cheeks and home mem ories of all sorts made sleep out of the question. It was impossible to share my misery with anyone. And even if I could have done so, where was the use ? I knew of nothing that would soothe me.

Everything was strange-the people, their ways, and even their dwel lings. I was a complete novice in the matters of English etiquette and continually had to be on my guard. There was the additional inc onvenience of the vegetarian vow. Even the dishes that I could eat were tasteless and insipid. I thus found myself between Scylla and Charybdis. England I could not bear, but to return to India was not to be thought of. Now that I had come, I must finish the three years, said the inner voice.

MY CHOICE

Dr. Mehta went on Monday to the Victoria Hotel expecting to find me there. He discovered that we had left, got our new address, and met me at our rooms. Through sheer folly I had managed to get ringworm on the boat. For washing and bathing we used to have sea water, in which soap is not soluble. I, however, used soap, taking its use to be a sign of civilization, with the result that instead of cleaning the skin it made it greasy. This gave me ringworm. I showed it to Dr. Mehta, who told me to apply acetic acid. I remember how the burning acid made me cry. Dr. Mehta inspected my room and its appoint ments and shook his head in disapproval. "This place won"t do," he said. "We come to England not so much for the purpose of studies as for gaining experience of English life and customs. And for this you need to live with a family. But before you do so, I think you had better serve a period of apprenticeship with- . I will take you there." I gratefully accepted the suggestion and removed to the friend"s rooms. He was all kindness and attention. He treated me as his own brother, initiated me into English ways and manners, and accustomed me to talking the language.

My food, however, became a serious question. I could not relish boiled vegetables cooked without salt or condiments. The landlady was at a loss to know what to prepare for me. We had oatmeal porridge for breakfast, which was fairly filling, but I always starved at lunch and dinner. The friend continually reasoned with me to eat meat, but I always pleaded my vow and then remained silent. Both for luncheon and dinner we had spinach and bread and jam too. I was a good eater and had a capacious stomach; but I was ashamed to ask for more than two or three slices of bread, as it did not seem correct to do so. Added to this, there was no milk either for lunch or dinner. The friend once got disgusted with this state of things, and said: "Had you been my own brother, I would have sent you packing. What is the value of a vow made before an illiterate mother, and in ignorance of conditions here ? It is no vow at all. It would not be regarded as a vow in law. It is pure superstition to stick to such a promise. And I tell you this persistence will not help you to gain anything here. You confess to having eaten and relished meat.

You took it where it was absolutely unnecessary, and will not where it is quite essential. What a pity!" But I was adamant.

Day in and day out the friend would argue, but I had an eternal negative to face him with. The more he argued, the more uncompro mising I became. Daily I would pray for God"s protection and get it.

Not that I had any idea of God. It was faith that was at work-faith of which the seed had been sown by the good nurse Rambha.

One day the friend began to read to me Bentham"s Theory of Utility. I was at my wit"s end. The language was too difficult for me to understand. He began to expound it. I said: "Pray excuse me. These abstruse things are beyond me. I admit it is necessary to eat meat. But I cannot break my vow. I cannot argue about it. I am sure I cannot meet you in argument. But please give me up as foolish or obstinate. I appreciate your love for me and I know you to be my well-wisher. I also know that you are telling me again and again about this because you feel for me. But I am helpless. A vow is a vow. It cannot be broken." The friend looked at me in surprise. He closed the book and said: "All right. I will not argue any more." I was glad. He never discussed the subject again. But he did not cease to worry about me.

He smoked and drank, but he never asked me to do so. In fact he asked me to remain away from both. His one anxiety was lest I should become very weak without meat, and thus be unable to feel at home in England.

That is how I served my apprenticeship for a month. The friend"s house was in Richmond, and it was not possible to go to London more than once or twice a week. Dr. Mehta and Sjt. Dal patram Shukla therefore decided that I should be put with some family. Sjt. Shukla hit upon an Anglo-Indian"s house in West Kensin gton and placed me there. The landlady was a widow. I told her about my vow. The old lady promised to look after me properly, and I took up my residence in her house. Here too I practically had to starve. I had sent for sweets and other eatables from home, but nothing had yet come. Everything was insipid. Every day the old lady asked me whether I liked the food, but what could she do? I was still as shy as ever and dared not ask for more than was put before me. She had two daughters. They insisted on serving me with an extra slice or two of bread. But little did they know that nothing less than a loaf would have filled me.

But I had found my feet now. I had not yet started upon my regular studies. I had just begun reading newspapers, thanks to Sjt. Shukla. In India I had never read a newspaper. But here I succeeded in cultivating a liking for them by regular reading. I always glanced over The Daily News, The Daily Telegraph, and The Pall Mall Gazette.

This took me hardly an hour. I therefore began to wander about. I launched out in search of a vegetarian restaurant. The landlady had told me that there were such places in the city. I would trot ten or twelve miles each day, go into a cheap restaurant and eat my fill of bread, but would never be satisfied. During these wanderings I once hit on a vegetarian restaurant in Farringdon Street. The sight of it filled me with the same joy that a child feels on getting a thing after its own heart. Before I entered I noticed books for sale exhibited under a glass window near the door. I saw among them Salt"s Plea for Vegetarianism. This I purchased for a shilling and went straight to the dining-room. This was my first hearty meal since my arrival in England. God had come to my aid.

I read Salt"s book from cover to cover and was very much impressed by it. From the date of reading this book, I may claim to have become a vegetarian by choice. I blessed the day on which I had taken the vow before my mother. I had all along abstained from meat in the interests of truth and of the vow I had taken, but had wished at the same time that every Indian should be a meat-eater, and had looked forward to being one myself freely and openly some day, and to enlisting others in the cause. The choice was now made in favour of vegetarianism, the spread of which henceforward became by mission.

PLAYING THE ENGLISH GENTLEMAN

My faith in vegetarianism grew on me from day to day. Salt"s book whetted my appetite for dietetic studies. I went in for all books available on vegetarianism and read them. One of these, Howard Williams"s The Ethics of Diet, was a "biographical history of the liter ature of humane dietetics from the earliest period to the present day".

It tried to make out, that all philosophers and prophets from Pythagoras and Jesus down to those of the present age were vegetarians. Dr. Anna Kingsford"s The Perfect Way in Diet was also an attractive book. Dr. Allinson"s writings on health and hygiene were likewise very helpful. He advocated a curative system based on regulation of the dietary of patients. Himself a vegetarian, he prescribed for his patients also a strictly vegetarian diet. The result of reading all this literature was that dietetic experiments came to take an important place in my life. Health was the principal consideration of these experiments to begin with. But later on religion became the supreme motive.

Meanwhile my friend had not ceased to worry about me. His love for me led him to think that, if I persisted in my objections to meat-eating, I should not only develop a weak constitution, but should remain a duffer, because I should never feel at home in English society. When he came to know that I had begun to interest myself in books on vegetarianism, he was afraid lest these studies should muddle my head; that I should fritter my life away in experiments, forgetting my own work, and become a crank. He therefore made one last effort to reform me. He one day invited me to go to the theatre. Before the play we were to dine together at the Holborn Restaurant, to me a palatial place and the first big restaurant I had been to since leaving the Victoria Hotel. The stay at that hotel had scarcely been a helpful experience, for I had not lived there with my wits about me. The friend had planned to take me to this restaurant evidently imagining that modesty would forbid any questions. And it was a very big company of diners in the midst of which my friend and I sat sharing a table between us. The first course was soup. I wondered what it might be made of, but durst not ask the friend about it. I therefore sum moned the waiter. My friend saw the movement and sternly asked across the table what was the matter. With considerable hesitation I told him that I wanted to inquire if the soup was a vegetable soup.

"You are too clumsy for decent society," he passionately exclaimed.

"If you cannot behave yourself, you had better go. Feed in some other restaurant and await me outside." This delighted me. Out I went. There was a vegetarian restaurant close by, but it was closed. So I went without food that night. I accompanied my friend to the theatre, but he never said a word about the scene I had created. On my part of course there was nothing to say.

That was the last friendly tussle we had. It did not affect our relations in the least. I could see and appreciate the love by which all my friend"s efforts were actuated, and my respect for him was all the greater on account of our differences in thought and action.

But I decided that I should put him at ease, that I should assure him that I would be clumsy no more, but try to become polished and make up for my vegetarianism by cultivating other accomplishments which fitted one for polite society. And for this purpose I undertook the all too impossible task of becoming an English gentleman.

The clothes after the Bombay cut that I was wearing were, I thought, unsuitable for English society, and I got new ones at the Army and Navy Stores. I also went in for a chimney-pot hat costing nineteen shillings-an excessive price in those days. Not content with this, I wasted ten pounds on an evening suit made in Bond Street, the centre of fashionable life in London; and got my good and noble hearted brother to send me a double watch-chain of gold. It was not correct to wear a ready-made tie and I learnt the art of tying one for myself. While in India, the mirror had been a luxury permitted on the days when the family barber gave me a shave. Here I wasted ten minutes every day before a huge mirror, watching myself arranging my tie and parting my hair in the correct fashion. My hair was by no means soft, and every day it meant a regular struggle with the brush to keep it in position. Each time the hat was put on and off, the hand would automatically move towards the head to adjust the hair, not to mention the other civilized habit of the hand every now and then operating for the same purpose when sitting in polished society.

As if all this were not enough to make me look the thing, I directed my attention to other details that were supposed to go towards the making of an English gentleman. I was told it was necessary for me to take lessons in dancing, French and elocution.1 French was not only the language of neighbouring France, but it was the lingua franca of the Continent over which I had a desire to travel. I decided to take dancing lessons at a class and paid down £3 as fees for a term.

I must have taken about six lessons in three weeks. But it was beyond me to achieve anything like rhythmic motion. I could not follow the piano and hence found it impossible to keep time.3 What then was I do? The recluse in the fable kept a cat to keep off the rats, and then a cow to feed the cat with milk, and a man to keep the cow and so on.

My ambitions also grew like the family of the recluse. I thought I should learn to play the violin in order to cultivate an ear for Western music. So I invested £3 in a violin14 and something more in fees. I sought a third teacher to give me lessons in elocution and paid him a preliminary fee of a guinea. He recommended Bell"s Standard Elocutionist as the text-book, which I purchased. And I began with a speech of Pitt"s.

But Mr. Bell rang the bell of alarm in my ear and I awoke.

I had not to spend a lifetime in England, I said to myself. What then was the use of learning elocution? And how could dancing make a gentleman of me? The violin I could learn even in India. I was a student and ought to go on with my studies. I should qualify myself to join the Inns of Court. If my character made a gentleman of me, so much the better. Otherwise I should forgo the ambition.

These and similar thoughts possessed me, and I expressed them in a letter which I addressed to the elocution teacher, requesting him to excuse me from further lessons. I had taken only two or three. I wrote a similar letter to the dancing teacher, and went personally to the violin teacher with a request to dispose of the violin for any price it might fetch. She was rather friendly to me, so I told her how I had discovered that I was pursuing a false idea. She encouraged me in the determination to make a complete change.

This infatuation must have lasted about three months. The punctiliousness in dress persisted for years. But henceforward I became a student.

CHANGES

Let no one imagine that my experiments in dancing and the like marked a stage of indulgence in my life. The reader will have noticed that even then I had my wits about me. That period of infatuation was not unrelieved by a certain amount of self-intro-spection on my part.

I kept account of every farthing I spent, and my expenses were carefully calculated. Every little item, such as omnibus fares or postage or a couple of coppers spent on newspapers, would be entered, and the balance struck every evening before going to bed.

That habit has stayed with me ever since, and I know that as a result, though I have had to handle public funds amounting to lakhs, I have succeeded in exercising strict economy in their disbursement and, instead of outstanding debts, have had invariably a surplus balance in respect of all the movements I have led. Let every youth take a leaf out of my book and make it a point to account for everything that comes into and goes out of his pocket, and like me he is sure to be a gainer in the end. As I kept strict watch over my way of living, I could see that it was necessary to economize. I therefore decided to reduce my expenses by half. My accounts showed numerous items spent on fares. Again my living with a family meant the payment of a regular weekly bill. It also included the courtesy of occasionally taking members of the family out to dinner, and likewise attending parties with them. All this involved heavy items for conveyances, especially as, if the friend was a lady, custom required that the man should pay all the expenses. Also dining out meant extra cost, as no deduction could be made from the regular weekly bill for meals not taken. It seemed to me that all these items could be saved, as likewise the drain on my purse caused through a false sense of propriety.

So I decided to take rooms on my own account, instead of living any longer in a family, and also to remove from place to placet6 according to the work I had to do, thus gaining experience at the same time. The rooms were so selected as to enable me to reach the place of business on foot in half an hour, and so save fares. Before this I had always some kind of conveyance whenever I went anywhere and had to find extra time for walks. The new arrangement combined walks and economy, as it meant a saving of fares and gave me walks of eight or ten miles a day. It was mainly this habit of long walks that kept me practically free from illness throughout my stay in England and gave 1 Vide "Satyagraha in South Africa

Deputation to England".

me a fairly strong body.

Thus I rented a suite of rooms; one for a sitting-room and another for a bedroom. This was the second stage. The third was yet to come.

These changes saved me half the expense. But how was I to utilize the time? I knew that Bar examinations did not require much study, and I therefore did not feel pressed for time. My weak English was a perpetual worry to me. Mr. (afterwards Sir Frederic) Lely"s words, "Graduate first and then come to me," still rang in my ears. I should, I thought, not only be called to the Bar, but have some literary degree as well. I inquired about the Oxford and Cambridge University courses, consulted a few friends, and found that, if I elected to go to either of these places, that would mean greater expense and a much longer stay in England than I was prepared for. A friend suggested that, if I really wanted to have the satisfaction of taking a difficult examination, I should pass the London Matriculation. It meant a good deal of labour and much addition to my stock of general knowledge, without any extra expense worth the name. I welcomed the sugges tion. But the syllabus frightened me. Latin and a modern language were compulsory ! How was I to manage Latin ? But the friend entered a strong plea for it: "Latin is very valuable to lawyers. Know ledge of Latin is very useful in understanding law-books. And one paper in Roman Law is entirely in Latin. Besides, a knowledge of Latin means greater command over the English language." It went home and I decided to learn Latin, no matter how difficult it might be.

French I had already begun, so I thought that should be the modern language. I joined a private Matriculation class. Examinations were held every six months and I had only five months at my disopsal. It was an almost impossible task for me. But the aspirant after being an English gentleman chose to convert himself into a serious student. I framed my own time-table to the minute; but neither my intelligence nor memory promised to enable me to tackle Latin and French besides other subjects within the given period. The result was that I was ploughed in Latin. I was sorry0 but did not lose heart. I had acquired a taste for Latin, also I thought my French would be all the better for another trial and I would select a new subject in the science group. Chemistry which was my subject in science had no attraction for want of experiments, whereas1 it ought to have been a deeply interesting study. It was one of the compulsory subjects in India and so I had selected it for the London Matriculation. This time, however, I chose Heat and Light instead of Chemistry. It was said to be easy and I found it to be so.

With my preparation for another trial, I made an effort to simplify my life still further. I felt that my way of living did not yet befit the modest means of my family. The thought of my struggling brother, who nobly responded to my regular calls for monetary help, deeply pained me. I saw that most of those who were spending from eight to fifteen pounds monthly had the advantage of scholarships. I had before me examples of much simpler living. I came across a fair number of poor students living more humbly than I. One of them was staying in the slums in a room at two shillings a week and living on twopence worth of cocoa and bread per meal from Lockhart"s cheap Cocoa Rooms. It was far from2 me to think of emulating him, but I felt I could surely have one room instead of two and cook some of my meals at home. That would be a saving of4 four to five pounds each5 month. I also came across books on simple living. I gave up the suite of rooms and rented one instead, invested in a stove, and began cooking my breakfast at home. The process scarcely took me more than twenty minutes, for there was only oatmeal porridge to cook and water to boil for cocoa. I had lunch out and for dinner bread and cocoa at home. Thus I managed to live on a shilling and three pence a day. This was also a period of intensive study. Plain living saved me plenty of time and I passed my examination.

Let not the reader think that this living made my life by any means a dreary affair. On the contrary the change harmonized my inward and outward life. It was also more in keeping with the means of my family. My life was certainly more truthful6 and my soul knew no bounds of joy.

EXPERIMENTS IN DIETETICS

As I searched myself deeper, the necessity for changes both internal and external began to grow on me. As soon as, or even before, I made alterations in my expenses and my way of living, I began to make changes in my diet. I saw that the writers on vegetaria nism had examined the question very minutely, attacking it in its religious, scientific, practical and medical aspects. Ethically they had arrived at the conclusion that man"s supremacy over the lower animals meant not that the former should prey upon the latter, but that the higher should protect the lower, and that there should be mutual aid between the two as between man and man. They had also brought out the truth that man eats not for enjoyment but to live. And some of them accordingly suggested and effected in their lives abstention not only from fleshmeat but from eggs and milk.

Scientifically some had concluded that man"s physical structure showed that he was not meant to be a cooking but a frugivorous animal, that he could take only his mother"s milk and, as soon as he had teeth, should begin to take solid foods.

Medically they had suggested the rejection of all spices and condiments. According to the practical and economic argument they had demonstrated that a vegetarian diet was the least expensive. All these considerations had their effect on me, and I came across vegetarians of all these types in vegetarian restaurants. There was a Vegetarian Society in England with a weekly journal1 of its own. I subscribed to the weekly, joined the Society and very shortly found myself on the Executive Committee. Here I came in contact with those who were regarded as pillars of vegetarianism, and began my own experiments in dietetics.

I stopped taking the sweets and condiments I had got from home. The mind having taken a different turn, the fondness for condiments wore away, and I now relished the boiled spinach, which in Richmond tasted insipid, cooked without condiments. Many such experiments taught me that the real seat of taste was not the tongue but the mind.

The economic consideration was of course constantly before me. There was in those days a body of opinion which regarded tea and coffee as harmful and favoured cocoa. And as I was convinced that one should eat only articles that sustained the body, I gave up tea and coffee as a rule, and substituted cocoa.

There were two divisions in the restaurants I used to visit. One division, which was patronized by fairly well-to-do people, provided any number of courses from which one chose and paid for a la carte, each dinner thus costing from one to two shillings. The other division provided six-penny dinners of three courses with a slice of bread. In my days of strict frugality I usually dined in the second division.

There were many minor experiments going on along with the main one; as for example, giving up starchy foods at one time; living on bread and fruit alone at another, and once living on cheese, milk and eggs. This last experiment is worth noting. It lasted not even a fortnight.2 The reformer who advocated starchless food had spoken highly of eggs and held that eggs were not meat. It was apparent that there was no injury done to living creatures in taking eggs. I was taken in by this plea and took eggs in spite of my vow. But the lapse was momentary. I had no business to put a new interpretation on the vow. The interpretation of my mother who administered the vow was 1 The Vegetarian; commenced publication in 1888 as an independent journal and became the London Vegetarian Society"s official organ 2 However, in a paper read in London on 2-5-1891, Gandhiji stated : "I am sorry to say that I have been taking eggs for about a month and half". Vide "The Foods of India", June 1, 189 therefor me. I knew that her definition of meat included eggs. And as soon as I saw the true import of the vow I gave up eggs and the experiment alike.

There is a nice point underlying the argument, and worth noting. I came across three definitions of meat in England. Accor ding to the first, meat denoted only the flesh of birds and beasts.

Vegetarians who accepted that definition abjured the flesh of birds and beasts, but ate fish, not to mention eggs. According to the second definition, meat meant flesh of all living creatures. So fish was here out of the question, but eggs were allowed. The third definition included under meat the flesh of all living beings, as well as all their products, thus covering eggs and milk alike. If I accepted the first definition, I could take not only eggs, but fish also. But I was conv inced that my mother"s definition was the definition binding on me.

If, therefore, I would observe the vow I had taken, I must abjure eggs.

I therefore did so. This was a hardship inasmuch as inquiry showed that even in vegetarian restaurants many courses used to contain eggs.

This meant that unless I knew what was what, I had to go through the awkward process of ascertaining whether a particular course contained eggs or no, for many puddings and cakes were not free from them.

But though the revelation of my duty caused this difficulty, it simplified my food. The simplification in its turn brought me annoyance in that I had to give up several dishes I had come to relish.

These difficulties were only passing, for the strict observance of the vow produced an inward relish disinctly more healthy, delticate and permanent.

The real ordeal, however, was still to come, and that was in respect of the other vow. But who dare harm whom God protects ? A few observations about the interpretation of vows or pledges may not be out of place here. Interpretation of pledges has been a fruitful source of strife all the world over. No matter how explicit the pledge, people will turn and twist the text to suit their own purposes. They are to be met with among all classes of society, from the rich down to the poor, from the prince down to the peasant.

Selfishness turns them blind, and by a use of the ambiguous middle they deceive themselves and seek to deceive the world and God. One golden rule is to accept the interpretation honestly put on the pledge by the party administering it.1 Another is to accept the interpretation of the weaker party, where there are two interpretations possible.

Rejection of these two rules gives rise to strife and iniquity, which are rooted in untruthfulness. He who seeks truth alone easily follows the golden rule. He need not seek learned advice for interpretation. My mother"s interpretation of meat was, according to the golden rule, the only true one for me, and not the one my wider experience or my pride of better knowledge might have taught me.

My experiments in England were conducted from the point of view of economy and hygiene. The religious aspect of the question was not considered until I went to South Africa where I undertook strenuous experiments which will be narrated later. The seed, however, for all of them was sown in England.

A convert"s enthusiasm for his new religion is greater than that of a person who is born in it. Vegetarianism was then a new cult in England, and likewise for me, because, as we have seen, I had gone there a convinced meat-eater, and was intellectually converted to vegetarianism later. Full of the neophyte"s zeal for vegetarianism. I decided to start a vegetarian club in my locality, Bayswater. I invited Sir Edwin Arnold, who lived there, to be Vice-President. Dr. Oldfield who was Editor of The Vegetarian became President. I myself became the Secretary. The club went well for a while, but came to an end in the course of a few months. For I left the locality, according to my custom of moving from place to place periodically. But this brief and modest experience gave me some little training in organizing and conducting institutions.

SHYNESS MY SHIELD

I was elected to the Executive Committee of the Vegetarian Society, and made it a point to attend every one of its meetings, but I always felt tongue-tied. Dr. Oldfield once said to me, "You talk to me quite all right, but why is it that you never open your lips at a committee meeting ? You are a drone." I appreciated the banter. The bees are ever busy, the drone is a thorough idler. And it was not a little curious that whilst others expressed their opinions at these meetings, I sat quite silent. Not that I never felt tempted to speak. But I was at a loss to know how to express myself. All the rest of the members appeared to me to be better informed than I. Then it often happened that just when I had mustered up courage to speak, a fresh subject would be started. This went on for a long time.

Meantime a serious question came up for discussion. I thought it wrong to be absent, and felt it cowardice to register a silent vote.

The discussion arose somewhat in this wise. The President of the Society was Mr. Hills, proprietor of the Thames Iron Works. He was a puritan. It may be said that the existence of the Society depended practically on his financial assistance. Many members of the Committee were more or less his proteges. Dr. Allinson of vegetarian fame was also a member of the Committee. He was an advocate of the then new birthcontrol movement, and preached its methods among the working classes. Mr. Hills regarded these methods as cutting at the root of morals. He thought that the Vegetarian Society had for its object not only dietetic but also moral reform, and that a man of Dr. Allinson"s anti-puritanic views should not be allowed to remain in the Society. A motion was therefore brought for his removal. The question deeply interested me. I considered Dr. Allinson"s views regarding artificial methods of birth control as dangerous, and I believed that Mr. Hills was entitled, as a puritan, to oppose him. I had also a high regard for Mr. Hills and his generosity. But I thought it was quite improper to exclude a man from a vegetarian society simply because he refused to regard puritan morals as one of the objects of the Society. Mr. Hills view regarding the exclusion of anti puritans from the Society was personal to himself, and it had nothing to do with the declared object of the Society, which was simply the promotion of vegetarianism and not of any system of morality. I therefore held that any vegetarian could be a member of the Society irrespective of his views on other morals.

There were in the Committee others also who shared my view, but I felt myself personally called upon to express my own. How to do it was the question. I had not the courage to speak and I therefore decided to set down0 my thoughts in writing1 . I went to the meeting with the document in my pocket. So far as I recollect, I did not find myself equal even to reading it, and the President had it read by someone else. Dr. Allinson lost the day. Thus in the very first battle of the kind I found myself siding with the losing party. But I had comfort in the thought that the cause was right. I have a faint recollection that, after this incident, I resigned from the Committee This shyness I retained throughout my stay in England. Even when I paid a social call the presence of half a dozen or more people would strike me dumb.

I once went to Ventnor with Sjt. Mazmudar. We stayed there with a vegetarian family. Mr. Howard, the author of The Ethics of Diet, was also staying at the same watering-place. We met him, and he invited us to speak at a meeting for the promotion of vegetarianism. I had ascertained that it was not considered incorrect to read one"s speech. I knew that many did so to express themselves coherently and briefly. To speak extempore would have been out of the question for me. I had therefore written down my speech. I stood up to read it, but could not. My vision became blurred and I trembled, though the speech hardly covered a sheet of foolscap. Sjt. Mazmudar had to read it for me. His own speech was of course excellent and was received with applause. I was ashamed of myself and sad at heart for my incapacity.

My last effort to make a public speech in England was on the eve of my departure for home. But this time too I only succeeded in making myself ridiculous. I invited my vegetarian friends to dinner in the Holborn Restaurant referred to in these chapters. "A vegetarian dinner could be had," I said to myself, "in vegetarian restaurants as a matter of course. But why should it not be possible in a non-veg etarian restaurant too?" And I arranged with the manager of the Holborn Restaurant to provide a strictly vegetarian meal. The vegetarians hailed the new experiment with delight. All dinners are meant for enjoyment, but the West has developed the thing into an art.

They are celebrated with great eclat, music and speeches. And the little dinner party that I gave was also not unaccompanied by some such display. Speeches, therefore, there had to be. When my turn for speaking came, I stood up to make a speech. I had with great care thought out one which would consist of a very few sentences.

But I could not proceed beyond the first sentence. I had read of Addison that he began his maiden speech in the House of Commons, repeating "I conceive" three times, and when he could proceed no further, a wag stood up and said, "The gentleman conceived thrice but brought forth nothing." I had thought of making a humorous speech taking this anecdote as the text. I therefore began with it and stuck there. My memory entirely failed me and in attempting a humorous4 speech I made myself ridiculous. "I thank you, gentlemen, for having kindly responded to my invitation," I said abruptly, and sat down.

It was only in South Africa that I got over this shyness, though I never completely overcame it. It was impossible for me to speak impromptu. I hesitated whenever I had to face strange audiences and avoided making a speech whenever I could. Even today I do not think I could or would even be inclined to keep a meeting of friends engaged in idle talk.

I must say that, beyond occasionally exposing me to laughter, my constitutional shyness has been no disadvantage whatever. In fact I can see that, on the contrary, it has been all to my advantage. My hesitancy in speech, which was once an annoyance, is now a pleasure.

Its greatest benefit has been that it has taught me the economy of words. I have naturally formed the habit of restraining my thoughts.

For a report of this "nervous" speech, vide Speech at Farewell Dinner", June 11, 1891. And I can now give myself the certificate that a thoughtless word hardly ever escapes my tongue or pen. I do not recollect ever having had to regret anything in my speech or writing. I have thus been spared many a mishap and waste of time. Experience has taught me that silence is part of the spiritual discipline of a votary of truth.

Proneness to exaggerate, to suppress or modify the truth, wittingly or unwittingly, is a natural weakness of man, and silence is necessary in order to surmount it. A man of few words will rarely be thoughtless in his speech; he will measure every word. We find so many people impatient to talk.

There is no chairman of a meeting who is not pestered with notes for permission to speak. And whenever the permission is given the speaker generally exceeds the time-limit, asks for more time, and keeps on talking without permission. All this talking can hardly be said to be of any benefit to the world. It is so much waste of time. My shyness has been in reality my shield and buckler. It has allowed me to grow. It has helped me in my discernment of truth.

THE CANKER OF UNTRUTH

There were comparatively few Indian students in England forty years ago. It was a practice with them to affect the bachelor even though they might be married. School or college students in England are all bachelors, studies being regarded as incompatible with married life. We had that tradition in the good old days, a student then being invariably known as a brahmchari1. But in these days we have child marriages, a thing practically unknown in England. Indian youths in England, therefore, felt ashamed to confess that they were married.

There was also another reason for dissembling, namely that in the event of the fact being known it would be impossible for the young man to go about or flirt with the young girls of the family in which they lived. The flirting was more or less innocent. Parents even encouraged it; and that sort of association between young men and young women may even be a necessity there, in view of the fact that every young man has to choose his mate. If, however, Indian youths on arrival in England indulge in these relations, quite natural to English youths, the result is likely to be disastrous, as has often been found. I saw that our youths had succumbed to the temptation and chosen a life of untruth for the sake of companionships which, however innocent in the case of English youths, were for them undesirable. I too caught the contagion. I did not hesitate to pass myself of as a bachelor though I was married and the father of a One who observes brahmacharya, i.e., complete self-restraint son. But I was none the happier for being a dissembler. Only my reserve and my reticence saved me from going into deeper waters. If I did not talk, no girl would think it worth her while to enter into conversation with me or to go out with me.

My cowardice was on a par with my reserve. It was customary in families like the one in which I was staying at Ventnor for the dau ghter of the landlady to take out guests for a walk. My landlady"s daughter took me one day to the lovely hills round Ventnor. I was no slow walker, but my companion walked even faster, dragging me after her and chattering away all the while. I responded to her chatter sometimes with a whispered "yes" or "no", or at the most "yes, how beautiful !" She was flying like a bird whilst I was wondering when I should get back home. We thus reached the top of a hill. How to get down again was the question. In spite of her high-heeled boots this sprightly young lady of twenty-five darted down the hill like an arrow. I was shamefacedly struggling to get down0. She stood at the foot smiling and cheering me and offering to come and drag me. How could I be so chicken-hearted ? With the greatest difficulty, and crawling at intervals, I somehow managed to scramble to the bottom.

She loudly laughed "bravo" and shamed me all the more, as well she might.

But I could not escape scatheless everywhere. For God wanted to rid me of the canker of untruth. I once went to Brighton, another watering-place like Ventnor. This was before the Ventnor visit. I met there at a hotel an old widow of moderate means. This was my first year in England. The courses on the menu were all described in French, which I did not understand. I sat at the same table as the old lady. She saw that I was a stranger and puzzled, and immediately came to my aid. "You seem to be a stranger," she said, "and look perplexed.

Why have you not ordered anything ?" I was spelling through the menu and preparing to ascertain the ingredients of the courses from the waiter, when the good lady thus intervened. I thanked her, and explaining my difficulty told her that I was at a loss to know which of the courses were vegetarian as I did not understand French.

"Let me help you," she said, "I shall explain the card to you and show you what you may eat." I gratefully availed of her help.

This was the beginning of an acquaintance that ripened into frien dship and was kept up all through my stay in England and long after.

She gave me her London address and invited me to dine at her house every Sunday. On special occasions also she would invite me, help me to conquer my bashfulness and introduce me to young ladies and draw me into conversation with them. Particularly marked out for these conversations was a young lady who stayed with her, and often we would be left entirely alone together. I found all this very trying at first. I could not start a conversation nor could I indulge in any jokes. But she put me in the way. I began to learn; and in course of time looked forward to every Sunday and came to like the conversations with the young friend.

The old lady went on spreading her net wider every day. She felt interested in our meetings. Possibly she has her own plans about us.1 I was in a quandary. "How I wished I had told the good lady that I was married !" I said to myself. "She would then have not thou ght of an engagement between us. It is, however, never too late to mend. If I declare the truth, I might yet be saved more misery." With these thoughts in my mind, I wrote a letter to her somewhat to this effect :"Ever since we met at Brighton you have been kind to me. You have taken care of me even as a mother of her son. You also think that I should get married and with that view you have been introducing me to young ladies.

Rather than allow matters to go further, I must confess to you that I have been unworthy of your affection. I should have told you when I begen by visits to you that I was married. I knew that Indian students in England dissembled the fact of their marriage and I followed suit. I now see that I should not have done so. I must also add that I was married while yet a boy, and am the father of a son. I am pained that I should have kept this knowledge from you so long.

But I am glad God has now given me the courage to speak out the truth. Will you forgive me ? I assure you I have taken no improper liberties with the young lady you were good enough to introduce to me. I knew my limits. You, not knowing that I was married, naturally desired that we should be engaged. In order that things should not go beyond the present stage, I must tell you the truth.2 "If on receipt of this, you feel that I have been unworthy of your hospitality, I assure you I shall not take it amiss. You have laid me under an everlasting debt of gratitude by your kindness and solicitude. If, after this, you do not reject me but continue to regard me as worthy of your hospitality, which I will spare no pains to deserve, I shall naturally be happy and count it a further token of your kindness." Let the reader know that I could not have written such a letter in a moment. I must have drafted and redrafted it many times over. But it lifted a burden that was weighing me down. Almost by return post came her reply somewhat as follows : "I have your frank letter. We were both very glad and had a hearty laugh over it. The untruth you say you have been guilty of is pardonable. But it is well that you have acquainted us with the real state of things. My inviation still stands and we shall certainly expect you next Sunday and look forward to hearing all about your child marriage and to the pleasure of laughing at your expense. Need I assure you that our friendship is not in the least affected by this incident ?" I thus purged myself of the canker of untruth, and I never thenceforward hesitated to talk of my married state wherever necessary.

ACQUAINTANCE WITH RELIGIONS

Towards the end of my second year in England I came across two Theosophists, brothers, and both unmarried. They talked to me about the Gita. They were reading Sir Edwin Arnold"s translation The Song Celestial-and they invited me to read the original with them. I felt ashamed, as I had read the divine poem neither in Samskrit nor in Gujarati. I was constrained to tell them that I had not read the Gita, but that I would gladly read it with them, and that though my knowledge of Samskrit was meagre, still I hoped to be able to understand the original to the extent of telling where the translation failed to bring out the meaning. I began reading the Gita with them.

The verses in the second chapter If one Ponders on objects of the sense, there springs Attraction; from attraction grows desire, Desire flames to fierce passion, passion breeds Recklessness; then the memory-all betrayed Lets noble purpose go, and saps the mind, Till purpose, mind, and man are all undone.

The book struck me as one of priceless worth. The impression has ever since been growing on me with the result that I regard it today as the book par excellence for the knowledge of Truth. It has afforded me invaluable help in my moments of gloom. I have read almost all the English translations of it, and I regard Sir Edwin Arnold"s as the best. He has been faithful to the text, and yet it does not read like a translation. Though I read the Gita with these friends, I cannot [illegible] studied it then. It was only after some years that it became a book of daily reading.

The brothers also recommended The Light of Asia by Sir Edwin Arnold, whom I knew till then as the author only of The Song Celestial, and I read it with even greater interest than I did the Bhagavad Gita. Once I had begun it I could not leave off. They also took me on one occasion to the Blavatsky Lodge and introduced me toMadame Blavatsky and Mrs. Besant. The latter had just then joined the Theosophical Society, and I was following with great interest the controversy about her conversion. The friends advised me to join the Society, but I politely declined saying, With, my meagre knowledge of my own religion I do 63 not want to belong to any religious body." I recall having read, at the brothers" instance, Mad-ame Blavatsky"s Key to Theosophy. This book stimulated in me the desire to read books on Hinduism, and disabused me of the notion fostered by the missionaries that Hinduism was rife with superstition.

About the same time I met a good Christian from Manchester in a vegetarian boarding house. He talked to me about Christianity. I narrated to him my Rajkot recollections. He was pained to hear them.

He said, "I am a vegetarian. I do not drink. Many Charistians are meat-eaters and drink, no doubt; but neither meat-eating nor drinking is enjoined by Scripture. Do please read the Bible." I accepted his advice, and he got me a copy. I have a faint recollection that he himself used to sell copies of the Bible, and I purchased from him an edition containing maps, concordance, and other aids. I began reading it, but I could not possibly read through the Old Testament. I read the book of Genesis, and the chapters that followed invariably sent me to sleep. But just for the sake of being able to say that I had read it, I plodded through the other books with much difficulty and without the least interest or understanding. I disliked reading the book of Numbers.

But the New Testament produced a different impression, especially the Sermon on the Mount which went straight to my heart. I compared it with the Gita. The verses, "But I say unto you, that ye resist not evil : but whosoever shall smite thee on thy right cheek, turn to him the other also. And if any man take away thy coat let him have thy cloak too," delighted me beyond measure and put me in mind of Shamal Bhatt"s "For a bowl of water, give a goodly meal" etc. My young mind tried to unify the teaching of the Gita, The Light of Asia and the Sermon on the Mount. That renunciation was the highest form of religion appealed to me greatly.

This reading whetted my appetite for studying the lives of other religious teachers. A friend recommended Carlyle"s Heroes and Hero-warship. I read the chapter on the Hero as a prophet and learnt of the Prophet"s greatness and bravery and austere living. Beyond this acquaintance with religion I could not go at the moment, as reading for the examination left me scarcely any time for outside subjects. But I took mental note of the fact that I should read more religious books and acquaint myself with all the principal religions.

And how could I help knowing something of atheism too ? Every Indian knew Bradlaugh"s name and his so-called atheism. I read some book about it, the name of which I forget. It had no effect on me, for I had already crossed the Sahara of atheism. Mrs. Besant who was then very much in the limelight, had turned to theism from atheism, and that fact also strengthened my aversion to atheism. I had read her book0 How I Became a Theosophist.

It was about this time that Bradlaugh died. He was buried in the Woking Cemetery. I attended the funeral, as I believe every Indian residing in London did. A few clergymen also were present to do him the last honours. On our way back from the funeral we had to wait at the station for our train. A champion atheist from the crowd heckled one of these clergymen."Well, Sir, you believe in the existence of God?" "I do," said the good man in a low tone.

"You also agree that the circumference of the Earth is 28,000 miles, don"t you ?" said the atheist with a smile of self-assurance.

"Indeed." "Pray tell me then the size of your God and where he may be ?" "Well, if we but knew, He resides in the hearts of us both." "Now, now, don"t take me to be a child," said the champion with a triumphant look at us.

The clergyman assumed a humble silence.

This talk still further increased my prejudice against atheism.

Though I had acquired a nodding acquaintance with Hinduism and other religions of the world, I should have known that it would not be enough to save me in my trials. Of the thing that sustains him through trials man has no inkling, much less knowledge, at the time. If an unbeliever, he will attribute his safety to chance. If a believer, he will say God saved him. He will conclude as well he may, that his religious study or spiritual discipline was at the back of the state of grace within him. But in the hour of his deliverance he does not know whether his spiritual discipline or something else saves him.

"Nirbalke Bal Ram"-refrain of Surdas"s famous hymn, "Rama the help of the helpless, the strength of the weak" Who that has prided himself on his spiritual strength has not seen it humbled to the dust? A knowledge of religion, as distinguished from experience, seems but chaff in such moments of trial.

It was in England that I first discovered the futility of mere religious knowledge. How I was saved on previous occasions is more than I can say, for I was very young then1 ; but not I was twenty and had gained some experience as husband and father.

During the last year, as far as I can remember, of my stay in England, that is in 1890,2 there was a Vegetarian Conference at Port smouth to which an Indian friend and I were invited. Portsmouth is a sea-port with a large naval population. It has many houses with women of ill fame, women not actually prostitutes, but at the same time, not very scrupulous about their morals. We were put up in one of these houses. Needless to say, the Reception Committee did not know anything about it. It would have been difficult in a town like Portsmouth to find out which were good lodgings and which were bad for occasional travellers like us.

We returned from the Conference in the evening. After dinner we sat down to play a rubber of bridge, in which our landlady joined, as is customary in England even in respectable households. Every player indulges in innocent jokes as a matter of course, but here my companion and our hostess began to make indecent ones as well. I did not know that my friend was an adept in the art. It captured me and I also joined in. Just when I was about to go beyond the limit, leaving the cards and the game to themselves, God through the good comp anion uttered the blessed warning : "Whence this devil in you, my boy ? Be off, quick !" I was ashamed. I took the warning and expressed within myself gratefulness to my friend. Remembering the vow I had taken before my mother, I fled from the scene. To my room I went quaking, trembling, and with beating heart, like a quarry escaped from its pursuer.

I recall this as the first occasion on which a woman, other than my wife, moved me to lust. I passed that night sleeplessly, all kinds of thoughts assailing me. Should I leave this house ? Should I run away from the place ? Where was I ? What would happen to me if I had not my wits about me ? I decided to act thenceforth with great caution; not to leave the house, but somehow leave Portsmouth. The Conference was not to go on for more than two days, and I remember I left Portsmouth the next evening, my companion staying there some 1 Vide also "Power of "Ramanama"", May 17, 1925.

I did not then know the essence of religion or of God, and how He works in us. Only vaguely I understood that God had saved me on that occasion. On all occasions of trial He has saved me. I know that the phrase "God saved me" has a deeper meaning for me today, and still I feel that I have not yet grasped its entire meaning. Only richer experience can help me to a fuller understanding. But in all my tria ls-of a spiritual nature, as a lawyer, in conducting institutions, and in politics-I can say that God saved me. When every hope is gone, "when helpers fail and comforts flee," I find that help arrives some how, from I know not where. Supplication, worship, prayer are no superstition; they are acts more real than the acts of eating, drinking, sitting or walking. It is no exaggeration to say that they along are real, all else is unreal.

Such worship or prayer is no flight of eloquence; it is no lip homage. It springs from the heart. If, therefore, we achieve that purity of the heart when it is "emptied of all but love", if we keep all the chords in proper tune, they "trembling pass in music out of sight".

Prayer needs no speech. It is in itself independent of any sensuous effort. I have not the slightest doubt that prayer is an unfailing means of cleansing the heart of passions. But it must be combined with the utmost humility.

NARAYAN HEMCHANDRA

Just about this time Narayan Hemchandra came to England. I had heard of him as a writer.1 We met at the house of Miss Manning of the National Indian Association. Miss Manning knew that I could not make myself sociable. When I went to her place I used to sit tongue-tied, never speaking except when spoken to. She introduced me to Narayan Hemchandra. He did not know English. His dress was queer-a clumsy pair of trousers, a wrinkled, dirty, brown coat after the Parsi fashion, no necktie or collar, and a tasselled woollen cap. He grew a long beard.

He was lightly built and short of stature. His round face was scarred with small-pox, and had a nose which was neither pointed nor blunt. With his hand he was constantly turning over his beard.

Such a queer-looking and queerly dressed person was bound to be singled out in fashionable society.

Gandhiji mentions him as the author of a biography of the Prophet Mohammed; vide "letter to Jamnadas Gandhi", August 28, 1911.

Died in 1905; for an obituary by Gandhiji, vide "The Late Miss Manning", September 16, 1905. "I have heard a good deal about you," I said to him. "I have also read some of your writings. I should be very pleased if you were kind enough to come to my place." Narayan Hemchandra had a rather hoarse voice. With a smile on his face he replied : "Yes, where do you stay ?" "In Store Street." Then we are neighbours. I want to learn English. Will you teach me ?""I shall be happy to teach you anything I can, and will try my best. If you like, I will go to your place." "Oh, no. I shall come to you. I shall also bring with me a Translation Exercise Book." So we made an appointment. Soon we were close friends.

Narayan Hemchandra was innocent of grammar. "Horse" was a verb with him and "run" a noun. I remember many such funny instances. But he was not to be baffled by his ignorance. My little knowledge of grammar could make no impression on him. Certainly he never regarded his ignorance of grammar as a matter for shame.

With perfect nonchalance he said : "I have never been to school like you. I have never felt the need of grammar in expressing my thoughts. Well, do you know Bengali ? I know it. I have travelled in Bengal. It is I who have given Maharshi Devendranath Tagore"s works to the Gujarati-speaking world. And I wish to translate into Gujarati the treasures of man other languages. And you know I am never literal in my translations. I always content myself with bringing out the spirit. Others, with their better knowledge, may be able to do more in future. But I am quite satisfied with what I have achieved without the help of grammar. I know Marathi, Hindi, Bengali, and now I have begun to know English. What I want is a copious vocabulary. And do you think my ambition ends here ? No fear. I want to go to France and learn French. I am told that language has an extensive literature. I shall go to Germany also, if possible, and there learn German." And thus he would talk on unceasingly. He had a boundless ambition for learning languages and for foreign travel.

"Then you will go to America also ?" "Certainly. How can I return to India without having seen the New World ?" "But where will you find the money ?" "What do I need money for ? I am not a fashionable fellow like you. The minimum amount of food and the minimum amount of clothing suffice for me. And for this what little I get out of my books and from my friends is enough. I always travel third class. While going to America also I shall travel on deck." Narayan Hemchandra"s simplicity was all his own, and his frankness was on a par with it. Of pride he had not the slightest trace, excepting, of course, a rather undue regard for his own capacity as a writer.We met daily. There was a considerable amount of similarity between our thoughts and actions. Both of us were vegetarians. We would often have our lunch together. This was the time when I lived on 17s. a week and cooked for myself. Sometimes I would go to his room, and sometimes he would come to mine. I cooked in the English style. Nothing but Indian style would satisfy him. He could not do without dal. I would make soup of carrots, etc., and he would pity me for my taste. Once he somehow hunted out mung1, cooked it and brought it to my place. I ate it with delight. This led on to a regular system of exchange between us. I would take my delicacies to him and he would bring his to me.

Cardinal Manning"s name was then on every lip. The dock labourers" strike had come to an early termination owing to the efforts of John Burns and Cardinal Manning. I told Narayan Hemchandra of Disraeli"s tribute to the Cardinal"s simplicity. "Then I must see the sage," said he.

"He is a big man. How do you expect to meet him ?" "Why ? I know how. I must get you to write to him in my name.

Tell him I am an author and that I want to congratulate him personally on his humanitarian work, and also say that I shall have to take you as interpreter as I do not know English." I wrote a letter to that effect. In two or three days came Cardinal Manning"s card in reply giving us an appointment. So we both called on the Cardinal. I put on the usual visiting suit. Narayan Hemchandra was the same as ever, in the same coat and the same trousers. I tried to make fun of this, but he laughed me out and said : "You civilized fellows are all cowards. Great men never look at a person"s exterior. They think of his heart." We entered the Cardinal"s mansion. As soon as we were seated, a thin, tall, old gentleman made his appearance, and shook hands with us. Narayan Hemchandra thus gave his greetings : "I do not want to take up your time. I had heard a lot about you and I felt I should come and thank you for the good work you have 1 An Indian pulse done for the strikers. It has been my custom to visit the sages of the world and that is why I have put you to this trouble." This was of course my translation of what he spoke in Gujarati.

"I am glad you have come. I hope your stay in London will agree with you and that you will get in touch with people here. God bless you." With these words the Cardinal stood up and said good-bye.

Once Narayan Hemchandra came to my place in a shirt and dhoti. The good landlady opened the door, came running to me in a fright-this was a new landlady who did not know Narayan Hem chandra-and said : "A sort of a madcap wants to see you." I went to the door and to my surprise found Narayan Hemchandra. I was shocked. His face, however, showed nothing but his usual smile.

"But did not the children in the street rag you ?" "Well, they ran after me, but I did not mind them and they were quiet."Narayan Hemchandra went to Paris after a few months" stay in London. He began studying French and also translating French books. I knew enough French to revise his translation, so he gave it to me to read. It was not a translation, it was the substance.

Finally he carried out his determination to visit America. It was with great difficulty that he succeeded in securing a deck ticket. While in the United States he was prosecuted0 for "being indecently dressed", as he once went out in a shirt and dhoti. I have a recollection that he was discharged.

THE GREAT EXHIBITION

There was a great Exhibition at Paris in 1890. I had read about its elaborate preparations, and I also had a keen desire to see Paris. So I thought I had better combine two things in one and go there at this juncture. A particular attraction of the

Exhi bition was the Eiffel Tower, constructed entirely of iron, and nearly 1,000 feet high. There were of course many other things of interest, but the Tower was the chief one, inasmuch as it had been supposed till then that a structure of that height could not safely stand.

I had heard of a vegetarian restaurant in Paris. I engaged a room there and stayed seven days. I managed everything very econ omically, both the journey to Paris and the sightseeing there. This I did mostly on foot and with the help of a map of Paris, as also a map of and guide to the Exhibition. These were enough to direct one to the main streets and chief places off interest.

I remember nothing of the Exhibition excepting its magnitude and variety. I have fair recollection of the Eiffel Tower as I ascended it twice or thrice. there was a restaurant on the first platform, and just for the satisfaction of being able to say that I had had my lunch at a great height, I threw away seven shillings on it.

The ancient churches of Paris are still in my memory. Their grandeur and their peacefulness are unforgettable. The wonderful constru-ction of Notre Dame and the elaborate decoration of the interior with its beautiful sculptures cannot be forgotten. I felt then that those who expended millions on such divine cathedrals could not but have the love of God in their hearts.

I had read a lot about the fashions and frivolity of Paris. These were in evidence in every street, but the churches stood noticeably apart from these scenes. A man would forget the outside noise and bustle as soon as he entered one of these churches. His manner would change, he would behave with dignity and reverence as he passed someone kneeling before the image of the Virgin. The feeling I had then has since been growing on me, that all this kneeling and prayer could not be mere superstition; the devout souls kneeling before the Virgin could not be worshipping mere marble. They were fired with genuine devotion and they worshipped not stone, but the divinity of which it was symbolic. I have an impression that I felt then that by this worship they were not detracting from, but increasing, the glory of God.

I must say a word about the Eiffel Tower. I do not know what purpose it serves today. But I then heard it greatly disparaged as well as praised. I remember that Tolstoy was the chief among those who disparaged it. He said that the Eiffel Tower was a monument of man"s folly, not of his wisdom. Tobacco, he argued, was the worst of all into xicants, inasmuch as a man addicted to it was tempted to commit crimes which a drunkard never dared to do; liquor made a man mad, but tobacco clouded his intellect and made him build castles in the air. The Eiffel Tower was one of the creations of a man under such influence.

There is no art about the Eiffel Tower. In no way can it be said to have contributed to the real beauty of the Exhibition. Men flocked to see it and ascended it as it was a novelty and of unique dimensions.

It was the toy of the Exhibition. So long as we are children we are attracted by toys, and the Tower was a good demonstration of the fact that we are all children attracted by trinkets. That may be claimed to be the purpose served by the Eiffel Tower.

"CALLED"-BUT THEN

I have deferred saying anything up to now about the purpose for which I went to England, viz., being called to the bar. It is time to advert to it briefly.

There were two conditions which had to be fulfilled before a student was formally called to the bar : "keeping terms", twelve terms equivalent to about three years; and passing examinations. "Keeping terms" meant eating one"s terms, i.e., attending at least six out of about twenty-four dinners in a term. Eating did not mean actually partaking of the dinner, it meant reporting oneself at the fixed hours and remaining present throughout the dinner. Usually of course everyone ate and drank the good commons and choice wines pro vided. A dinner cost from two and six to three and six, that is from two to three rupees. This was considered moderate, inasmuch as one had to pay that same amount for wines alone if one dined at a hotel.

To us in India it is a matter for surprise, if we are not "civilized", that the cost of drink should exceed the cost of food. The first revelation gave me a great shock, and I wondered how people had the heart to throw away so much money on drink. Later Icame to understand. I often nothing at these dinners, for the things that I might eat were only bread, boiled potato and cabbage. In the beginning I did not eat these, as I did not like them; and later, when I began to relish them, I also gained the courage to ask for other dishes.

The dinner provided for the benchers used to be better than that for the students. A Parsi student, who was also a vegetarian, and I applied, in the interests of vegetarianism, for the vegetarian courses which were served to the benchers. The application was granted, and we began to get fruits and other vegetables from the benchers" table.

Two bottles of wine were allowed to each group of four, and as I did not touch them, I was ever in demand to form a quartet, so that three might empty two bottles. And there was a "grand night" in each term when extra wines, like champagne, in addition to port and sheery, were served. I was therefore specially requested to attend and was in great demand on that "grand night".

I could not see then, nor have I seen since, how these dinners qualified the students better for the bar. There was once a time when only a few students used to attend these dinners and thus there were opportunities for talks between them and the benchers, and speeches were also made. These occasions helped to give them knowledge of the world with a sort of polish and refinement, and also improved their power of speaking. No such thing was possible in my time, as the benchers had a table all to themselves. The institution had gradually lost all its meaning, but conservative England retained it nevertheless.

The curriculum of study was easy, barristers being humorously known as "dinner barristers". Everyone knew that the examinations had practically no value. In my time there were two, one in Roman Law and the other in Common Law. There were regular text-books prescribed for these examinations which could be taken in compartments, but scarcely anyone read them. I have known many to pass the Roman Law examination by scrambling through notes on Roman Law in a couple of weeks, and the Common Law examination by reading notes on the subject in two or three months. Question papers were easy and examiners were generous. The percentage of passes in the Roman Law examination used to be 95 to 99 and of those in the final examination 75 or even more. There was thus little fear of being plucked, and examinations were held not once but four times in the year. They could not be felt as a difficulty.

But I succeeded in turning them into one. I felt that I should read all the text-books. It was a fraud, I thought, not to read these books. I invested much money in them. I decided to read Roman Law in Latin. The Latin which I had acquired in the London Matriculation stood me in good stead. And all this reading was not without its value later on in South Africa, where Roman Dutch is the common law. The reading of Justinian, therefore, helped me a great deal in understan ding the South African law.

It took me nine months of fairly hard labour to read through the Common Law of England. For Broom"s Common Law, a big but interesting volume, took up a good deal of time. Snell"s Equity was full of interest, but a bit hard to understand. White and Tudor"s Leading Cases, from which certain cases were prescribed, was full of interest and instruction. I read also with interest Williams" and Edwards" Real Property, and Goodeve"s Personal Property. Williams" book read like a novel. The one book I remember to have read on my return to India, with the same unflagging interest, was Mayne"s Hindu Law. But it is out of place to talk here of Indian law-books.

I passed my examinations, was called to the bar on the 10th of June 1891, and enrolled in the High Court on the 11th. On the 12th I sailed for home.

But notwithstanding my study there was no end to my helpless ness and fear. I did not feel myself qualified to practise law.

But a separate chapter is needed to describe this helplessness0 of mine.

MY HELPLESSNESS

It was easy to be called, but it was difficult to practise at the bar.

I had read the laws, but not learnt how to practise law. I had read with interest "Legal Maxims", but did not know how to apply them in my profession. "Sic utere tuo ut alienum non laedas" (Use your property in such a way as not to damage that of others) was one of them, but I was at a loss to know how one could employ this maxim for the bene fit of one"s client. I had read all the leading cases on this maxim, but they gave me no confidence in the application of it in the practice of law. Besides, I had learnt nothing at all of Indian law. I had not the slightest idea of Hindu and Mahomedan Law. I had not even learnt how to draft a plaint, and felt completely at sea. I had heard of Sir Pherozeshah Mehta as one who roared like a lion in law-courts. How, I wondered, could he have learnt the art in England ? It was out of the question for me ever to acquire his legal acumen, but I had serious misgivings as to whether I should be able even to earn a living by the profession.

I was torn with these doubts and anxieties whilst I was studying law. I confided my difficulties to some of my friends. One of them suggested that I should seek Dadabhai Naoroji"s advice. I have already said that, when I went to England, I possessed a note of introduction to Dadabhai. I availed myself of it very late. I thought I had no right to trouble such a great man for an interview. Whenever an address by him was announced, I would attend it, listen to him from a corner of the hall and go away after having feasted my eyes and ears. In order to come in close touch with the students he had founded an association. I used to attend its meetings, and rejoiced at Dadabhai"s solicitude for the students, and the latter"s respect for him. In course of time I mustered up courage to present to him the note of introduction. He said : "You can come and have my advice whenever you like." But I never availed myself of his offer. I thought it wrong to trouble him without the most pressing necessity.

Therefore I dared not venture to accept my friend"s advice to submit my difficulties to Dadabhai at that time. I forget now whether it was the same friend or someone else who recommended me to meet Mr.

Frederick Pincott. He was a Conservative, but his affection for Indian students was pure and unselfish. Many students sought his advice and I also applied to him for an appointment, which he granted. I can 1 Gandhiji often cites this maxim; vide, e.g., "Speech on Swadeshi at Missionary Conference, Madras", February 14, 1916.

never forget that interview. He greeted me as a friend. He laughed away my pessimism. "Do you think," he said, "that everyone must be a Pherozeshah Mehta ? Pherozeshahs and Badruddins are rare. Rest assured it takes no unusual skill to be an ordinary lawyer. Common honesty and industry are enough to enable him to make a living. All cases are not complicated. Well, let me know the extent of your general reading." When I acquainted him with my little stock of reading, he was, as I could see, rather disappointed. But it was only for a moment.

Soon his face beamed with a pleasing smile and he said, "I understand your trouble. Your general reading is meagre. You have no knowledge of the world, a sine qua non for a vakil. You have not even read the history of India. A vakil should know human nature. He should be able to read a man"s character from his face. And every Indian ought to know Indian history. This has no connection with the practice of law, but you ought to have that knowledge I see that you have not even read Kaye and Malleson"s history of the Mutiny of 1857. Get hold of that at once and also read two more books to understand human nature." These were Lavator"s and Shemmelpennick"s books on physiognomy.

I was extremely grateful to this venerable friend. In his presence I found all my fear gone, but as soon as I left him I began to worry again. "To know a man from his face" was the question that haunted me, as I thought of the two books on my way home. The next day I purchased Lavator"s book. Shemmelpennick"s was not available at the shop. I read Lavator"s book and found it more difficult than Snell"s Equity, and scarcely interesting. I studied Shakespeare"s physi ognomy, but did not acquire the knack of finding out the Shak espeares walking up and down the streets of London.

Lavator"s book did not add to my knowledge. Mr. Pincott"s advice did me very little direct service, but his kindness stood me in good stead. His smiling open face stayed in my memory, and I trusted his advice that Pherozeshah Mehta"s acumen, memory and ability were not essential to the making of a successful lawyer; honesty and industry were enough. And as I had a fair share of these last I felt somewhat reassured.

I could not read Kaye and Malleson"s volumes in England, but I did so in South Africa as I had made a point of reading them at the first opportunity.

Thus with just a little leaven of hope mixed with my despair, I landed at Bombay from s.s. Assam. The sea was rough in the harbour, and I had to reach the quay in a launch.

THE STORY OF MY EXPERIMENTS WITH TRUTH/PART II/RAYCHANDBHAI

I said in the last chapter that the sea was rough in Bombay harbour, not an unusual thing in the Arabian Sea in June and July. It had been choppy all the way from Aden. Almost every passenger was sick; I alone was in perfect form, staying on deck to see the stormy surge, and enjoying the splash of the waves. At breakfast there would be just one or two people besides myself, eating their oatmeal porridge from plates carefully held in their laps, lest the porridge itself find its place there.

The outer storm was to me a symbol of the inner. But even as the former left me unperturbed, I think I can say the same thing about the latter. There was the trouble with the caste that was to confront me. I have already adverted to my helplessness in starting on my profession. And then, as I was a reformer. I was taxing myself as to how best to begin certain reforms. But there was even more in store for me than I knew.

My elder brother had come to meet me at the dock. He had already made the acquaintance of Dr. Mehta and his elder brother and as Dr. Mehta insisted on putting me up at his house, we went there. Thus the acquaintance begun in England continued in India and ripened into a permanent friendship between the two families.

I was pining to see my mother. I did not know that she was no more in the flesh to receive me back into her bosom. The sad news was now given me, and I underwent the usual ablution. My brother had kept me ignorant of her death, which took place whilst I was still in England. He wanted to spare me the blow in a foreign land. The news, however, was none the less a severe shock to me. But I must not dwell upon it. My grief was even greater than over my father's death. Most of my cherished hopes were shattered. But I remember that I did not give myself up to any wild expression of grief. I could even check the tears, and took to life just as though nothing had happened.

Dr. Mehta introduced me to several friends, one of them being his brother Shri Revashankar Jagjivan, with whom there grew up a lifelong friendship. But the introduction that I need particularly take note of was the one to the poet Raychand or Rajchandra, the son-in-law of an elder brother of Dr. Mehta, and partner of the firm of jewellers conducted in the name of Revashankar Jagjivan.

He was not above twenty-five then, but my first meeting with him convinced me that he was a man of great character and learning. He was also known as Shatavadhani (one having the faculty of remembering or attending to a hundred things simultaneously), and Dr. Mehta recommended me to see some of his memory feats. I exhausted my vocabulary of all the European tongues I knew, and asked the poet to repeat the words, He did so in the precise order in which I had given them. I envied his gift without, however, coming under its spell. The thing that did cast its spell over me I came to know afterwards. This was his wide knowledge of the scriptures, his spotless character, and his burning passion for self-realization. I saw later that this last was the only thing for which he lived. The following lines of Muktanand were always on his lips and engraved on the tablets of his heart:

'I shall think myself blessed only when I see Him in every one of my daily acts;

Verily He is the thread, Which supports Muktanand's life.'

Raychandbhai's commercial transactions covered hundreds of thousands. He was a connoisseur of pearls and diamonds. No knotty business problem was too difficult for him. But all these things were not the centre round which his life revolved. That centre was the passion to see God face to face. Amongst the things on his business table there were invariably to be found some religious book and his diary. The moment he finished his business he opened the religious book or the diary. Much of his published writings is a reproduction from this diary. The man who, immediately on finishing his talk about weighty business transaction, began to write about the hidden things of the spirit could evidently not be a businessman at all, but a real seeker after Truth. And I saw him thus absorbed in godly pursuits in the midst of business, not once or twice, but very often. I never saw him lose his state of equipoise.

There was no business or other selfish tie that bound him to me, and yet I enjoyed the closest association with him. I was but a briefless barrister then, and yet whenever I saw him he would engage me in conversation of a seriously religious nature. Though I was then groping and could not be said to have any serious interest in religious discussion, Still I found his talk of absorbing interest. I have since met many a religious leader or teacher. I have tried to meet the heads of various faiths, and I must say that no one else has ever made on me the impression that Raychandbhai did. His words went straight home to me. His intellect compelled as great a regard from me as his moral earnestness, and deep down in me was the conviction that he would never willingly lead me astray and would always confide to me his innermost thoughts. In my moments of spiritual crisis, therefore, he was my refuge.

And yet in spite of this regard for him I could not enthrone him in my heart as my Guru. The throne has remained vacant and my search still continues.

I believe in the Hindu theory of Guru and his importance in spiritual realization. I think there is a great deal of truth in the doctrine that true knowledge is impossible without a Guru. An imperfect teacher may be tolerable in mundane matters, but not in spiritual matters. Only a perfect gnanil deserves to be enthroned as Guru. There must, therefore, be ceaseless striving after perfection. For one gets the Guru that one deserves. Infinite striving after perfection is one's right. It is its own reward. The rest is in the hands of God.

Thus, though I could not place Raychandbhai on the throne of my heart as Guru, we shall see how he was, on many occasions, my guide and helper. Three moderns have left a deep impress on my life, and captivated me: Raychandbhai by his living contact; Tolstoy by his book, The Kingdom of God is Within You; and Ruskin by his Unto this Last. But of these more in their proper place.

HOW I BEGAN LIFE

My elder brother had built high hopes on me. The desire for wealth and name and fame was great in him. He had a big heart, generous to a fault. This, combined with his simple nature, had attracted to him many friends, and through them he expected to get me briefs. He had also assumed that I should have a swinging practice and had, in that expectation, allowed the household expenses to become top-heavy. He had also left no stone unturned in preparing the field for my practice. The storm in my caste over my foreign voyage was still brewing. It had divided the caste into two camps, one of which immediately readmitted me, while the other was bent on keeping me out. To please the former my brother took me to Nasik before going to Rajkot, gave me a bath in the sacred river and, on reaching Rajkot. gave a caste dinner. I did not like all this. But my brother's love for me was boundless, and my devotion to him was in proportion to it, and so I mechanically acted as he wished, taking his will to be law.

The trouble about readmission to the caste was thus practically over. I never tried to seek admission to the section that had refused it. Nor did I feel even mental resentment against any of the headmen of that section. Some of these regarded me with dislike, but I scrupulously avoided hurting their feelings. I fully respected the caste regulations about excommunication. According to these, none of my relations, including my father-in-law and mother-in-law, and even my sister and brother-in-law, could entertain me; and I would not so much as drink water at their houses. They were prepared secretly to evade the prohibition, but it went against the grain with me to do a thing in secret that I would not do in public. The result of my scrupulous conduct was that I never had occasion to be troubled by the caste; nay, I have experienced nothing but affection and generosity from the general body of the section that still regards me as excommunicated.

They have even helped me in my work, without ever expecting me to do anything for the caste. It is my conviction that all these good things are due to my non-resistance. Had I agitated for being admitted to the caste, had I attempted to divide it into more camps, had I provoked the castemen, they would surely have retaliated, and instead of steering clear of the storm, I should on arrival from England, have found myself in a whirlpool of agitation, and perhaps a party to dissimulation. My relations with my wife were still not as I desired. Even my stay in England had not cured me of jealousy. I continued my squeamishness and suspiciousness in respect of every little thing, and hence all my cherished desires remained unfulfilled. I had decided that my wife should learn reading and writing and that I should help her in her studies, but my lust came in the way and she had to suffer for my own shortcoming.

Once I went the length of sending her away to her father's house, and consented to receive her back only after I had made her thoroughly miserable. I saw later that all this was pure folly on my part. I had planned reform in the education of children, My brother had children, and my own child which I had left at home when I went to England was now a boy of nearly four. It was my desire to teach these little ones physical exercise and make them hardy, and also to give them the benefit of my personal guidance. In this I had my brother's support and I succeeded in my efforts more or less. I very much liked the company of children, and the habit of playing and joking with them has stayed with me till today. I have ever since thought that I should make a good teacher of children. The necessity for food 'reform' was obvious. Tea and coffee had already found their place in the house. My brother had thought it fit to keep some sort of English atmosphere ready for me on my return, and to that end, crockery and such other things, which used to be kept in the house only for special occasions, were now in general use. My 'reforms' put the finishing touch. I introduced oatmeal porridge, and cocoa was to replace tea and coffee. But in truth it became an addition to tea and coffee.

Boots and shoes were already there. I completed the Europeanization by adding the European dress. Expenses thus went up. New things were added every day. We had succeeded in tying a white elephant at our door. But how was the wherewithal to be found? To start practice in Rajkot would have meant sure ridicule. I had hardly the knowledge of a qualified vakil and yet I expected to be paid ten times his fee! No client would be fool enough to engage me. And even if such a one was to be found, should I add arrogance and fraud to my ignorance, and increase the burden of debt I owed to the world? Friends advised me to go to Bombay for some time in order to gain experience of the High Court, to study Indian law and to try get what briefs I could. I took up the suggestion and went. In Bombay I started a household with a cook as incompetent as myself. He was a Brahman.

I did not treat him as a servant but as a member of the household. He would pour water over himself but never wash. His dhoti was dirty, as also his sacred thread, and he was completely innocent of the scriptures. But how was I to get a better cook? 'Well, Ravishankar,' (for that was his name), I would ask him, 'you may not know cooking, but surely you must know your sandhya (daily worship), etc. '#Sandhya#, sir! the plough is our sandhya and the spade our daily ritual. That is the type of Brahman I am. I must live on your mercy. Otherwise agriculture is of course there for me.' So I had to be Ravishankar's teacher. Time I had enough. I began to do half the cooking myself and introduced the English experiments in vegetarian cookery. I invested in a stove, and with Ravishankar began to run the kitchen. I had no scruples about interdining, Ravishankar too came to have none, and so we went on merrily together. There was only one obstacle. Ravishankar had sworn to remain dirty and to keep the food unclean! But it was impossible for me to get along in Bombay for more than four or five months, there being no income to square with the ever-increasing expenditure. This was how I began life. I found the barrister's profession a bad job - much show and little knowledge. I felt a crushing sense of my responsibility.

THE FIRST CASE

While in Bombay, I began, on the one hand, my study of Indian law and, on the other, my experiments in dietetics in which Virchand Gandhi, a friend, joined me. My brother, for his part, was trying his best to get me briefs. The study of Indian law was a tedious business. The Civil Procedure Code I could in no way get on with. Not so however, with the Evidence Act. Virchand Gandhi was reading for the Solicitor's Examination and would tell me all sorts of stories about barristers and vakils. 'Sir Pherozeshah's ability,' he would say, 'lies in his profound knowledge of law. He has the Evidence Act by heart and knows all the cases on the thirty-second section. Badruddin Tyabji's wonderful power of argument inspires the judges with awe.' The stories of stalwarts such as these would unnerve me. 'It is not unusual,' he would add, 'for a barrister to vegetate for five or seven years. That's why I have signed the articles for solicitorship. You should count yourself luckly if you can paddle your own canoe in three years' time.' Expenses were mounting up every month.

To have a barrister's board outside the house, whilst still preparing for the barrister's profession inside, was a thing to which I could not reconcile myself. Hence I could not give undivided attention to my studies. I developed some liking for the Evidence Act and read Mayne's Hindu Law with deep interest, but I had not the courage to conduct a case. I was helpless beyond words, even as the bride come fresh to her father-in- law's house! About this time, I took up the case of one Mamibai. It was a 'small cause.' 'You will have to pay some commission to the tout,' I was told. I emphatically declined. 'But even that great criminal lawyer Mr. So-and-So, who makes three to four thousand a month, pays commission!' 'I do not need to emulate him,' I rejoined. 'I should be content with Rs. 300 a month. Father did not get more.' 'But those days are gone. Expenses in Bombay have gone up frightfully. You must be businesslike.' I was adamant. I gave no commission, but got Mamibai's case all the same.

It was an easy case. I charged Rs. 30 for my fees. The case was no likely to last longer than a day. This was my debut in the Small Causes Court. I appeared for the defendant and had thus to cross-examine the plaintiff's witnesses. I stood up, but my heart sank into my boots. My head was reeling and I felt as though the whole court was doing likewise. I could think of no question to ask. The judge must have laughed, and the vakils no doubt enjoyed the spectacle. But I was past seeing anything. I sat down and told the agent that I could not conduct the case, that he had better engage Patel and have the fee back from me. Mr. Patel was duly engaged for Rs. 51. To him, of course, the case was child's play. I hastened from the Court, not knowing whether my client won or lost her case, but I was ashamed of myself, and decided not to take up any more cases until I had courage enough to conduct them. Indeed I did not go to Court again until I went to South Africa. There was no virtue in my decision. I had simply made a virtue of necessity. There would be no one so foolish as to entrust his case to me, only to lose it! But there was another case in store for me at Bombay. It was a memorial to be drafted. A poor Mussalman's land was confiscated in Porbandar.

He approched me as the worthy son of a worthy father. His case appeared to be weak, but I consented to draft a memorial for him, the cost of printing to be borne by him. I drafted it and read it out to friends. They approved of it, and that to some extent made me feel confident that I was qualified enough to draft a memorial, as indeed I really was. My business could flourish if I drafted memorials without any fees. But that would bring no grist to the mill. So I thought I might take up a teacher's job. My knowledge of English was good enough, and I should have loved to teach English to Matriculation boys in some school. In this way I could have met part at least of the expenses. I came across an advertisement in the papers: 'Wanted, an English teacher to teach one hour daily. Salary Rs 75.' The advertisment was from a famous high school. I applied for the post and was called for an interview. I went there in high spirits, but when the principal found that I was not a graduate, he regretfully refused me. 'But I have passed the London Matriculation with Latin as my second language.' 'True but we want a graduate.' There was no help for it.

I wrung my hands in despair. My brother also felt much worried. We both came to the conclusion that it was no use spending more time in Bombay. I should settle in Rajkot where my brother, himself a petty pleader, could give me some work in the shape of drafting applications and memorials. And then as there was already a household at Rajkot, the breaking up of the one at Bombay meant a considerable saving. I liked the suggestion. My little establishment was thus closed after a stay of six months in Bombay. I used to attend High Court daily whilst in Bombay, but I cannot say that I learnt anything there. I had not sufficient knowledge to learn much. Often I could not follow the case and dozed off. There were others also who kept me company in this, and thus lightened my load of shame. After a time, I even lost the sense of shame, as I learnt to think that it was fashionable to doze in the High Court.

If the present generation has also its briefless barristers like me in Bombay, I would commend them a little practical precept about living. Although I lived in Girgaum I hardly ever took a carriage or a tramcar. I had made it a rule to walk to the High Court. It took me quite forty- five minutes, and of course I invariably returned home on foot. I had inured myself to the heat of the sun. This walk to and from the Court saved a fair amount of money, and when many of my friends in Bombay used to fall ill, I do not remember having once had an illness. Even when I began to earn money, I kept up the practice of walking to and from the office, and I am still reaping the benefits of that practice.

THE FIRST SHOCK

Disappointed, I left Bombay and went to Rajkot where I set up my own office. Here I got along moderately well. Drafting applications and memorials brought me in, on an average, Rs 300 a month. For this work I had to thank influence rather than my own ability, for my brother's partner had a settled practice. All applications etc. which were, really or to his mind of an important character, he sent to big barristers. To my lot fell the applications to be drafted on behalf of his poor clients. I must confess that here I had to compromise the principle of giving no commission, which in Bombay I had so scrupulously observed. I was told that conditions in the two cases were different; that whilst in Bombay commissions had to be paid to touts, here they had to be paid to vakils who briefed you; and that here as in Bombay all barristers, without exception, paid a percentage of their fees as commission. The argument of my brother was, for me, unanswerable. 'You see,' said he, 'that I am in partnership with another vakil. I shall always be inclined to make over to you all our cases with which you can possibly deal, and if you refuse to pay a commission to my partner, you are sure to embarrass me.

As you and I have a joint establishment, your fee comes to our common purse, and I automatically get a share. But what about my partner? Supposing he gave the same case to some other barrister he would certainly get his commission from him.' I was taken in by this plea, and felt that, if I was to practise as a barrister, I could not press my principle regarding commissions in such cases. That is how I argued with myself, or to put it bluntly, how I deceived myself. Let me add, however, that I do not remember ever to have given a commission in respect of any other case. Though I thus began to make both ends meet, I got the first shock of my life about this time. I had heard what a British officer was like, but up to now had never been face to face with one. My brother had been secretary and adviser to the late Ranasaheb of Porbandar before he was installed on his gadi and hanging over his head at this time was the charge of having given wrong advice when in that office. The matter had gone to the Political Agent who was prejudiced against my brother.

Now I had known this officer when in England, and he may be said to have been fairly friendly to me. My brother thought that I should avail myself of the friendship and, putting in a good word on his behalf, try to disabuse the Political Agent of his prejudice. I did not at all like this idea. I should not, I thought, try to take advantage of a trifling acquaintance in England. If my brother was really at fault, what use was my recommendation? If he was innocent, he should submit a petition in the proper course and, confident of his innocence, face the result. My brother did not relish this advice. 'You do not know Kathiawad, he said, and you have yet to know the world. Only influence counts here. It is not proper for you, a brother, to shirk your duty, when you can clearly put in a good word about me to an officer you know.' I could not refuse him, so I went to the officer much against my will. I knew I had no right to approach him and was fully conscious that I was compromising my self-respect. But I sought an appointment and got it. I reminded him of the old acquaintance, but I immediately saw that Kathiawad was different from England; that an officer on leave was not the same as an officer on duty. The political Agent owned the acquaintance, but the reminder seemed to stiffen him. 'Surely you have not come here to abuse that acquaintance, have you?' appeared to be the meaning of that stiffness, and seemed to be written on his brow. Nevertheless I opened my case. The sahib was impatient. 'Your brother is an intriguer. I want to hear nothing more from you.

I have no time. If your brother has anything to say, let him apply through the proper channel. The answer was enough, was perhaps deserved. But selfishness is blind. I went on with my story. The sahib got up and said· 'You must go now.' 'But please hear me out,' said I. That made him more angry. He called his peon and ordered him to show me the door. I was still hesitating when the peon came in, placed his hands on my shoulders and put me out of the room. The sahib went away as also the peon, and I departed, fretting and fuming. I at once wrote out and sent over a note to this effect: 'You have insulted me. You have assaulted me through your peon. If you make no amends, I shall have to proceed against you.' Quick came the answer through his sowar: 'You were rude to me. I asked you to go and you would not. I had no option but to order my peon to show you the door. Even after he asked you to leave the office, you did not do so. He therefore had to use just enough force to send you out. You are at liberty to proceed as you wish.'

With this answer in my pocket, I came home crest fallen, and told my brother all that had happened. He was grieved, but was at a loss as to how to console me. He spoke to his vakil friends. For I did not know how to proceed against the sahib. Sir Pherozeshah Mehta happened to be in Rajkot at this time, having come down from Bombay for some case. But how could a junior barrister like me dare to see him? So I sent him the papers of my case, through the vakil who had engaged him, and begged for his advice. 'Tell Gandhi,' he said, 'such things are the common experience of many vakils and barristers. He is still fresh from England, and hot-blooded. He does not know British officers. If he would earn something and have an easy time here, let him tear up the note and pocket the insult. He will gain nothing by proceeding against the sahib, and on the contrary will very likely ruin himself. Tell him he has yet to know life.' The advice was as bitter as poison to me, but I had to swallow it. I pocketed the insult, but also profited by it, 'Never again shall I place myself in such a false position, never again shall I try to exploit friendship in this way,' said I to myself, and since then I have never been guilty of a breach of that determination. This shock changed the course of my life.

PREPARING FOR SOUTH AFRICA

I was no doubt at fault in having gone to that officer. But his impatience and overbearing anger were out of all proportion to my mistake. It did not warrant expulsion. I can scarcely have taken up more than five minutes of his time. But he simply could not endure my talking. He could have politely asked me to go, but power had intoxicated him to an inordinate extent. Later I came to know that patience was not one of the virtues of this officer.

It was usual for him to insult his visitors. The slightest unpleasantness was sure to put the sahib out. Now most of my work would naturally be in his court. It was beyond me to conciliate him. I had no desire to curry favour with him, Indeed, having once threatened to proceed against him, I did not like to remain silent. Meanwhile I began to learn something of the petty politics of the country. Kathiawad, being a conglomeration of small states, naturally had its rich crop of politicals. Petty intrigues between states, and intrigues of officers for power were the order of the day.

Princes were always at the mercy of others and ready to lend their ears to sycophants. Even the sahib's peon had to be cajoled, and the sahib's shirastedar was more than his master, as he was his eyes, his ears and his interpreter. The shirastedar's will was law, and his income was always reputed to be more than the sahib's. This may have been an exaggeration, but he certainly lived beyond his salary. This atmosphere appeared to me to be poisonous, and how to remain unscathed was a perpetual problem for me. I was thoroughly depressed and my brother clearly saw it. We both felt that, if I could secure some job, I should be free from this atmosphere of intrigue. But without intrigue a ministership or judgeship was out of the question. And the quarrel with the sahib stood in the way of my practice. Probandar was then under administration, and I had some work there in the shape of securing more powers for the prince. Also I had to see the Administrator in respect of the heavy vighoti (land rent) exacted from the Mers. This officer, though an Indian, was, I found, one better than the sahib in arrogance. He was able, but the ryots appeared to me to be none the better off for his ability. I succeeded in securing a few more powers for the Rana, but hardly any relief for the Mers.

It struck me that their cause was not even carefully gone into. So even in this mission I was comparatively disappointed. I thought justice was not done to my clients, but I had not the means to secure it. At the most I could have appealed to the Political Agent or to the Governor who would have dismissed the appeal saying, 'We decline to interfere.' If there had been any rule or regulation governing such decisions, it would have been something, but here the sahib's will was law. I was exasperated.

In the meantime a Meman firm from Porbandar wrote to my brother making the following offer: 'We have business in South Africa. Ours is a big firm, and we have a big case there in the Court, our claim being £ 40,000. It has been going on for a long time. We have engaged the services of the best vakils and barristers. If you sent your brother there, he would be useful to us and also to himself. He would be able to instruct our counsel better than ourselves. And he would have the advantage of seeing a new part of the world, and of making new acquaintances.' My brother discussed the proposition with me.

I could not clearly make out whether I had simply to instruct the counsel or to appear in court. But I was tempted. My brother introduced me to the late Sheth Abdul Karim Jhaveri a partner of Dada Abdulla & Co; the firm in question. 'It won't be a difficult job' the Sheth assured me. 'We have big Europeans as our friends, whose acquaintance you will make. You can be useful to us our shop. Much of our correspondence is in English and you can help us with that too. You will, of course, be our guest and hence will have no expense whatever.' 'How long do you require my services?' I asked. 'And what will be the payment?' 'Not more than a year. We will pay you a first class return fare and a sum of £ 105, all found.' This was hardly going there as a barrister. It was going as a servant of the firm. But I wanted somehow to leave India. There was also the tempting opportunity of seeing a new country, and of having new experience. Also I could send £105 to my brother and help in the expenses of the household. I closed with the offer without any haggling, and got ready to go to South Africa.

ARRIVAL IN NATAL

When starting for South Africa I did not feel the wrench of separation which I had experienced when leaving for England. My mother was now no more. I had gained some knowledge of the world and of travel abroad, and going from Rajkot to Bombay was no unusual affair. This time I only felt the pang of parting with my wife. Another baby had been born to us since my return from England. Our love could not yet be called free from lust, but it was getting gradually purer. Since my return from Eurpoe, we had lived very little together; and as I had now become her teacher, however indifferent, and helped her to make certain reforms, we both felt the necessity of being more together, if only to continue the reforms. But the attraction of South Africa rendered the separation bearable. 'We are bound to meet again in a year ,' I said to her, by way of consolation, and left Rajkot for Bombay. Here I was to get my passage through the agent of Dada Abdulla and Company.

But no berth was available on the boat, and if I did not sail then, I should be stranded in Bombay. 'We have tried our best,' said the agent, 'to secure a first class passage, but in vain unless you are prepared to go on deck. Your meals can be arranged for in the saloon.' Those were the days of my first class traveling, and how could a barrister travel as a deck passenger? So I refused the offer. I suspected the agent's veracity, for I could not believe that a first class passage was not available. With the agent's consent I set about securing it myself. I went on board the boat and met the chief officer. He said to me quite frankly, 'We do not usually have such a rush. But as the Governor-General of Mozambique is going by this boat, all the berths are engaged.' 'Could you not possibly squeeze me in?' I asked. He surveyed me from top to toe and smiled. There is just one way,' he said. 'There is an extra berth in my cabin, which is usually not available for passengers. But I am prepared to give it to you.' I thanked him and got the agent to purchase the passage. In April 1893 I set forth full of zest to try my luck in South Africa. The first port of call was Lamu which we reached in about thirteen days. The Captain and I had become great friends by this time.

He was fond of playing chess, but as he was quite a novice, he wanted one still more of a beginner for his partner, and so he invited me. I had heard a lot about the game but had never tried my hand at it. Players used to say that this was a game in which there was plenty of scope for the exercise of one's intelligence.

The Captain offered to give me lessons, and he found me a good pupil as I had unlimited patience. Every time I was the loser, and that made him all the more eager to teach me. I liked the game, but never carried my liking beyond the boat or my knowledge beyond the moves of the pieces. At Lamu the ship remained at anchor for some three to four hours, and I landed to see the port. The Captain had also gone ashore, but he had warned me that the harbour was treacherous and that I should return in good time. It was a very small place. I went to the Post Office and was delighted to see the Indian clerks there, and had a talk with them.

I also saw the Africans and tried to acquaint myself with their ways of life which interested me very much. This took up some time. There were some deck passengers with whom I had made acquaintance, and who had landed with a view to cooking their food on shore and having a quiet meal. I now found them preparing to return to the steamer, so we all got into the same boat. The tide was high in the harbour and our boat had more than its proper load.

The current was so strong that it was impossible to hold the boat to the ladder of the steamer. It would just touch the ladder and be drawn away again by the current. The first whistle to start had already gone. I was worried. The Captain was witnessing our plight from the bridge. He ordered the steamer to wait an extra five minutes. There was another boat near the ship which a friend hired for me for ten rupees. This boat picked me up from the overloaded one.

The ladder had already been raised. I had therefore to be drawn up by means of a rope and the steamer started immediately. The other passengers were left behind. I now appreciated the Captain's warning. After Lamu the next port was Mombasa and then Zanzibar. The halt here was a long one eight or ten days and we then changed to another boat.

The Captain liked me much but the liking took an undesirable turn. He invited an English friend and me to accompany him on an outing, and we all what the outing meant. And little did the Captain know what an ignoramus I was in such matters. We were taken to some Negro women's quarters by a tout. We were each shown into a room. I simply stood there dumb with shame. Heaven only knows what the poor woman must have thought of me. She saw my innocence. At first I felt very much ashamed, but as I could not think of the thing except with horror, the sense of shame wore away, and I thanked God that the sight of the woman had not moved me in the least. I was disgusted at my weakness and pitied myself for not having had the courage to refuse to go into the room. This in my life was the third trial of its kind. Many a youth, innocent at first, must have been drawn into sin by a false sense of shame. I could have credit if I had refused to enter that room. I must entirely thank the All-merciful for having saved me.

The incident increased my faith in God and taught me, to a certain extent, to cast off false shame. As we had to remain in this port for a week, I took rooms in the town and saw a good deal by wandering about the neighbourhood. Only Malabar can give any idea of the luxuriant vegetation of Zanzibar. I was amazed at the gigantic trees and the size of the fruits. The next call was at Mozambique and thence we reached Natal towards the close of May.

SOME EXPERIENCES

The port of Natal is Durban also known as Port Natal. Abdulla Sheth was there to receive me. As the ship arrived at the quay and I watched the people coming on board to meet their friends, I observed that the Indians were not held in much respect. I could not fail to notice a sort of snobbishness about the manner in which those who knew Abdulla Sheth behaved towards him, and it stung me. Abdulla Sheth had not got used to it. Those who looked at me did so with a certain amount of curiosity. My dress marked me out from other Indians. I had a frock- coat and a turban, an imitation of the Bengal pugree. I was taken to the firm's quarters and shown into the room set apart for me, next to Abdulla Sheth's. He did not understand me. I could not understand him. He read the papers his brother had sent through me, and felt more puzzled. He thought his brother had sent him a white elephant. My style of dress and living struck him as being expensive like that of the Europeans. There was no particular work then which could be given me. Their case was going on in the Transvaal. There was no meaning in sending me there immediately.

And how far could he trust my ability and honesty? He would not be in Pretoria to watch me. The defendants were in Pretoria, and for aught he knew they might bring undue influence to bear on me. And if work in connection with the case in question was not to be entrusted to me, what work could I be given to do, as all other work could be done much better by his clerks? The clerks could be brought to book, if they did wrong. Could I be, if I also happened to err? So if no work in connection with the case could be given me, I should have to be kept for nothing. Abdulla Sheth was practically unlettered, but he had a rich fund of experience. He had an acute intellect and was conscious of it. By practice he had picked up just sufficient English for conversational purposes, but that served him for carrying on all his business, whether it was dealing with Bank Managers and European merchants or explaining his case to his counsel.

The Indians held him in very high esteem. His firm was then the biggest, or at any rate one of the biggest, of the Indian firms. With all these advantages he had one disadvantage: he was by nature suspicious. He was proud of Islam and loved to discourse on Islamic philosophy. Though he did not know Arabic, his acquaintance with the Holy Koran and Islamic literature in general was fairly good. Illustrations he had in plenty, always ready at hand. Contact with him gave me a fair amount of practical knowledge of Islam. When we came closer to each other, we had long discussions on religious topics. On the second or third day of my arrival, he took me to see the Durban court. There he introduced me to several people and seated me next to his attorney.

The Magistrate kept staring at me and finally asked me to take off my turban. This I refused to do and left the court. So here too there was fighting in store for me. Abdulla Sheth explained to me why some Indians were required to take off their turbans. Those wearing the Musalman costume might, he said, keep their turbans on, but the other Indians on entering a court had to take theirs off as a rule. I must enter into some details to make this nice distinction intelligible. In the course of these two or three days I could see that the Indians were divided into different groups. One was that of Musalman merchants, who would call themselves 'Arabs.' Another was that of Hindu, and yet another of Parsi, clerks. The Hindu clerks were neither here nor there, unless they cast in their lot with the 'Arab.' The Parsi clerks would call themselves Persians. These three classes had some social relations with one another. But by far the largest class was that composed of Tamil, Telugu and North Indian indentured and freed labourers.

The indentured labourers were those who went to natal on an agreement to serve for five years, and came to be known there as girmitiyas from girmit, which was the corrupt form of the English word 'agreement'. The other three classes had none but business relations with this class. Englishmen called them' coolies' and as the majority of Indians belonged to the labouring class, all Indians were called 'coolies,' or 'samis'. 'sami' is a Tamil suffix occurring after many Tamil names, and it is nothing else than the Samskrit Swami, meaning a master. Whenever, therefore, an Indian resented being addressed as a 'sami' and had enough wit in him, he would try to return the compliment in this wise: 'You may call me sami, but you forget that sami means a master. I am not your master!' Some Englishmen would wince at this, while others would get angry, swear at the Indian and, if there was a chance, would even belabour him; for sami to him was nothing better than a term of contempt. To interpret it to mean a master amounted to an insult! I was hence known as a 'coolie barrister.' The merchants were known as 'coolie merchants.' The original meaning of the word 'coolie' was thus forgotten, and it became a common appellation for all Indians.

The Musalman merchant would resent this and say: 'I am not a coolie, I am an Arab,' or 'I am a merchant,' and the Englishman, if courteous, would apologize to him. The question of wearing the turban had great importance in this state of things. Being obliged to take off one's Indian turban would be pocketing an insult. So I thought I had better bid good-bye to the Indian turban and begin wearing an English hat, which would save me from the insult and the unpleasant controversy. But Abdulla Sheth disapproved of the idea. He said, 'If you do anything of the kind, it will have a very bad effect. You will compromise those insisting on wearing Indian turbans. And an Indian turban sits well on your head. If you wear an English hat, you will pass for a waiter.'

There was practical wisdom, patriotism and a little bit of narrowness in this advice. The wisdom was apparent, and he would not have insisted on the Indian turban except out of patriotism; the slighting reference to the waiter betrayed a kind of narrowness. Amongst the indentured Indians there were three classes: Hindus, Musalmans and Christians.

The last were the children of indentured Indians who became converts to Christanity. Even in 1893 their number was large. They wore the English costume, and the majority of them earned their living by service as waiters in hotels. Abdulla Sheth's criticism of the English hat was with reference to this class. It was considered degrading to serve as a waiter in a hotel. The belief persists even today among many. On the whole I liked Abdulla Sheth's advice. I wrote to the press about the incident and defended the wearing of my turban in the court.

The question was very much discussed in the papers, which described me as an 'unwelcome visitor.' Thus the incident gave me an unexpected advertisement in South Africa within a few days of my arrival there. Some supported me while others severely criticized my temerity. My turban stayed with me practically until the end of my stay in South Africa. When and why I left off wearing any head-dress at all in South Africa, we shall see later.

ON THE WAY TO PRETORIA

I soon came in contact with the Christian Indians living in Durban. The Court Interpreter, Mr. Paul, was a Roman Catholic. I made his acquaintance, as also that of the late Mr. Subhan Godfrey, then a teacher under the Protestant Mission, and father of James Godfery who as a member of the South African Deputation, visited India in 1924. I likewise met the late Parsi Rustomji and the late Adamji Miyakhan about the same time. All these friends, who up to then had never met one another except on business, came ultimately into close contact, as we shall see later. Whilst I was thus widening the circle of my acquaintance, the firm received a letter from their lawyer saying that preparations should be made for the case, and that Abdulla Sheth should go to Pretoria himself or send representative. Abdulla Sheth gave me this letter to read, and asked me if I would go to Pretoria. 'I can only say after I have understood the case from you,' said I. 'At present I am at a loss to know what I have to do there.' He thereupon asked his clerks to explain the case to me. As I began to study the case, I felt as though I ought to begin from the A B C of the subject.

During the few days I had had at Zanzibar, I had been to the court to see the work there. A Parsi lawyer was examining a witness and asking him question regarding credit and debit entries in account books. It was all Greek to me. Book-keeping I had learnt neither at school nor during my stay in England. And the case for which I had come to South Africa was mainly about accounts. Only one who knew accounts could understand and explain it. The clerk went on talking about this debited and that credited, and I felt more and more confused. I did not know what a P. Note meant. I failed to find the word in the dictionary. I revealed my ignorance to the clerk, and I learnt from him that a P. Note meant a promisory note. I purchased a book on book-keeping and studied it. That gave me some confidence. I understood the case. I saw that Abdulla Sheth, who did not know how to keep accounts, had so much practical knowledge that he could quickly solve intricacies of book-keeping.

I told him that I was prepared to go to Pretoria. 'Where will you put up?' asked the Sheth. 'Wherever you want me to,' said I. 'Then I shall write to our lawyer. He will arrange for your lodgings. I shall also write to my Meman friends there, but I would not advise you to stay with them. The other party has great influence in Pretoria. Should any one of them manage to read our private correspondence, it might do us much harm. The more you avoid familiarity with them, the better for us.' 'I shall stay where your lawyer puts me up, or I shall find out independent lodgings. Pray don't worry. Not a soul shall know anything that is confidential between us. But I do intend cultivating the acquaintance of the other party. I should like to be friends with them. I would try, if possible, to settle the case out of court. After all Tyeb Sheth is a relative of yours.' Sheth Tyeb Haji Khan Muhammad was a near relative of Abdulla Sheth. The mention of a probable settlement somewhat startled the Sheth, I could see. But I had already been six or seven days in Durban, and we now knew and understood each other.

I was no longer a 'white elephant.' So he said: 'Y...es, I see. There would be nothing better than a settlement out of court. But we are all relatives and know one another very well indeed. Tyeb Sheth is not a man to consent to a settlement easily. With the slightest unwariness on our part, he would screw all sorts of things out of us, and do us down in the end. So please think twice before you do nothing.' 'Don't be anxious about that,' said I. 'I need not talk to Tyeb Sheth, or for that matter to anyone else, about the case. I would only suggest to him to come to an understanding, and so save a lot of unnecessary litigation.' On the seventh or eighth day after my arrival, I left Durban. A first class seat was booked for me. It was usual there to pay five shillings extra, if one needed a bedding. Abdulla Sheth insisted that I should book one bedding but, out of obstinacy and pride and with a view to saving five shillings, I declined. Abdulla Sheth warned me. 'Look, now,' said he, 'this is a different country from India. Thank God, we have enough and to spare.

Please do not stint yourself in anything that you may need.' I thanked him and asked him not to be anxious. The train reached Maritzburg, the capital of Natal, at about 9 p.m.

Beddings used to be provided at this station. A railway servant came and asked me if I wanted one. 'No,' said I, 'I have one with me.' He went away. But a passenger came next, and looked me up and down. He saw that I was a 'coloured' man. This disturbed him. Out he went and came in again with one or two officials. They all kept quiet, when another official came to me and said, 'Come along, you must go to the van compartment.' 'But I have a first class ticket,' said I. 'That doesn't matter,' rejoined the other. 'I tell you, you must go to the van compartment.' 'I tell you, I was permitted to travel in this compartment at Durban, and I insist on going on in it.' 'No, you won't,' said the official. 'You must leave this compartment, or else I shall have to call a police constable to push you out.' 'Yes, you may. I refuse to get out voluntarily.' The constable came. He took me by the hand and pushed me out.

My luggage was also taken out. I refused to go to the other compartment and the train steamed away. I went and sat in the waiting room, keeping my hand-bag with me, and leaving the other luggage where it was. The railway authorities had taken charge of it. It was winter, and winter in the higher regions of South Africa is severely cold. Maritzburg being at a high altitude, the cold was extremely bitter. My over-coat was in my luggage, but I did not dare to ask for it lest I should be insulted again, so I sat and shivered. There was no light in the room. A passenger came in at about midnight and possibly wanted to talk to me. But I was in no mood to talk. I began to think of my duty. Should I fight for my rights or go back to India, or should I go on to Pretoria without minding the insults, and return to India after finishing the case? It would be cowardice to run back to India without fulfilling my obligation. The hardship to which I was subjected was superficial only a symptom of the deep disease of colour prejudice. I should try, if possible, to root out the disease and suffer hardships in the process. Redress for wrongs I should seek only to the extent that would be necessary for the removal of the colour prejudice.

So I decided to take the next available train to Pretoria. The following morning I sent a long telegram to the General manager of the Railway and also informed Abdulla Sheth, who immediately met the General Manager. The Manager justified the conduct of the railway authorities, but informed him that he had already instructed the Station Master to see that I reached my destination safely. Abdulla Sheth wired to the Indian merchants in Maritzburg and to friends in other places to meet me and look after me. The merchants came to see me at the station and tried to comfort me by narrating their own hardships and explaining that what had happened to me was nothing unusual. They also said that Indians travelling first or second class had to expect trouble from railway officials and white passengers. The day was thus spent in listening to these tales of woe. The evening train arrived. There was a reserved berth for me. I now purchased at Maritzburg the bedding ticket I had refused to book at Durban. The train took me to Charlestown.

MORE HARDSHIPS

The train reached Charlestown in the morning. There was no railway, in those days, between Charlestown and Johannesburg, but only a stage- coach, which halted at Standerton for the night en route. I possessed a ticket for the coach, which was not cancelled by the break of the journey at Maritzburg for a day; besides, Abdulla Sheth had sent a wire to the coach agent at Charlestown. But the agent only needed a pretext for putting me off, and so, when he discovered me to be a stranger, he said, 'Your ticket is cancelled.' I gave him the proper reply. The reason at the back of his mind was not want of accommodation, but quite another. Passengers had to be accommodated inside the coach, but as I was regarded as a 'coolie' and looked a stranger, it would be proper, thought the 'leader', as the white man in charge of the coach was called, not to seat me with the white passengers. There were seats on either side of the coachbox. The leader sat on one of these as a rule. Today he sat inside and gave me his seat. I knew it was sheer injustice and an insult, but I thought it better to pocket it, I could not have forced myself inside, and if I had raised a protest, the coach would have gone off without me. This would have meant the loss of another day, and Heaven only knows what would have happened the next day.

So, much as I fretted within myself, I prudently sat next the coachman. At about three o'clock the coach reached Pardekoph. Now the leader desired to sit where I was seated, as he wanted to smoke and possibly to have some fresh air. So he took a piece of dirty sack-cloth from the driver, spread it on the footboard and, addressing me said, 'Sami, you sit on this, I want to sit near the driver,.' The insult was more than I could bear. In fear and trembling I said to him, 'It was you who seated me here, though I should have been accommodated inside. I put up with the insult. Now that you want to sit outside and smoke, you would have me sit at your feet. I will not do so, but I am prepared to sit inside.' As I was struggling through these sentences, the man came down upon me and began heavily to box my ears. He seized me by the arm and tried to drag me down. I clung to the brass rails of the coachbox and was determined to keep my hold even at the risk of breaking my wristbones.

The passengers were witnessing the scene - the man swearing at me, dragging and belabouring me, and I remaining still. He was strong and I was weak. Some of the passengers were moved to pity and exclaimed: 'Man, let him alone. Don't beat him. He is not to blame. He is right. If he can't stay there, let him come and sit with us.' 'No fear,' cried the man, but he seemed somewhat crestfallen and stopped beating me. He let go my arm, swore at me a little more, and asking the Hottentot servant who was sitting on the other side of the coachbox to sit on the footboard, took the seat so vacated. The passengers took their seats and, the whistle given, the coach rattled away. My heart was beatingfast within my breast, and I was wondering whether I should ever reach my destination alive. The man cast an angry look at me now and then and, pointing his finger at me, growled: 'Take care, let me once get to Standerton and I shall show you what I do.' I sat speechless and prayed to God to help me. After dark we reached Standerton and I heaved a sigh of relief on seeing some Indian faces. As soon as I got down, these friends said: 'We are hereto receive you and take you to Isa Sheth's shop. We have had a telegram from Dada Abdulla.' I was very glad, and we went to Sheth Isa Haji Sumar's shop. The Sheth and his clerks gathered round me. I told them all that I had gone through. They were very sorry to hear it and comforted me by relating to me their own bitter experiences. I wanted to inform the agent of the Coach Company of the whole affair.

So I wrote him a letter, narrating everything that had happened, and drawing his attention to the threat his man had held out. I also asked for an assurance that he would accommodate me with the other passengers inside the coach when we started the next morning. To which the agent replied to this effect: 'From Standerton we have a bigger coach with different men in charge. The man complained of will not be there tomorrow, and you will have a seat with the other passengers.' This somewhat relieved me. I had, of course, no intention of proceeding against the man who had assaulted me, and so the chapter of the assault closed there. In the morning Isa Sheth's man took me to the coach, I got a good seat and reached Johannesburg quite safely that night. Standerton is a small village and Johannesburg a big city. Abdulla Sheth had wired to Johannesburg also, and given me the name and address of Muhammad Kasam Kamruddin's firm there. Their man had come to receive me at the stage, but neither did I see him nor did he recognize me.

So I decided to go to a hotel. I knew the names of several. Taking a cab I asked to be driven to the Grand National Hotel. I saw the Manager and asked for a room. He eyed me for a moment, and politely saying, 'I am very sorry, we are full up', bade me good-bye. So I asked the cabman to drive to Muhammad Kasam Kamruddin's shop. Here I found Abdul Gani Sheth expecting me, and he gave me a cordial greeting. He had a hearty laugh over the story of my experience at the hotel. 'How ever did you expect to be admitted to a hotel?' he said. 'Why not?' I asked. 'You will come to know after you have stayed here a few days,' said he. 'Only we can live in a land like this, because, for making money, we do not mind pocketing insults, and here we are.' With this he narrated to me the story of the hardships of Indians in South Africa. Of Sheth Abdul Gani we shall know more as we proceed. He said: 'This country is not for men like you. Look now, you have to go to Pretoria tomorrow.

You will have to travel third class. Conditions in the Transvaal are worse than in Natal. First and second class tickets are never issued to Indians.' 'You cannot have made persistent efforts in this direction.' 'We have sent representations, but I confess our own men too do not want as a rule to travel first or second. I sent for the railway regulations and read them. There was a loophole. The language of the old Transvaal enactments was not very exact or precise; that of the railway regulations was even less so. I said to the Sheth: 'I wish to go first class, and if I cannot, I shall prefer to take a cab to Pretoria, a matter of only thirty-seven miles.' Sheth Abdul Gani drew my attention to the extra time and money this would mean, but agreed to my proposal to travel first, and accordingly we sent a note to the Station Master. I mentioned in my note that I was a barrister and that I always travelled first. I also stated in the letter that I needed to reach Pretoria as early as possible, that as there was no time to await his reply I would receive it in person at the station, and that I should expect to get a first class ticket.

There was of course a purpose behind asking for the reply in person. I thought that if the Station master gave a written reply, he would certainly say 'No', especially because he would have his own notion of a 'collie' barrister. I would therefore appear before him in faultless English dress, talk to him and possibly persuade him to issue a first class ticket. So I went to the station in a frock-coat and necktie, placed a sovereign for my fare on the counter and asked for a first class ticket. 'You sent me that note?' he asked. 'That is so. I shall be much obliged if you will give me a ticket. I must reach Pretoria today.' He smiled and, moved to pity, said: 'I am not a Transvaaler. I am a Hollander. I appreciate your feelings, and you have my sympathy. I do want to give you a ticket on one condition, however, that, if the guard should ask you to shift to the third class, you will not involve me in the affair, by which I mean that you should not proceed against the Railway Company. I wish you a safe journey. I can see you are a gentleman.'

With these words he booked the ticket. I thanked him and gave him the necessary assurance. Sheth Abdul Gani had come to see me off at the station. The incident gave him an agreeable surprise, but he warned me saying: 'I shall be thankful if you reach Pretoria all right. I am afraid the guard will not leave you in peace in the first class and even if he does, the passengers will not.' I took my seat in a first class compartment and the train started. At Germiston the guard came to examine the tickets. He was angry to find me there, and signalled to me with his finger to go to the third class. I showed him my first class ticket. 'That doesn't matter,' said he, 'remove to the third class.' There was only one English passenger in the compartment. He took the guard to ask. 'Don't you see he has a first class ticket? I do not mind in the least his travelling with me.' Addressing me, he said, 'You should make yourself comfortable where you are.' The guard muttered; If you want to travel with a coolie, what do I care?' and went away. At about eight o'clock in the evening the train reached Pretoria.

FIRST DAY IN PRETORIA

I had expected someone on behalf of Dada Abdulla's attorney to meet me at Pretoria station. I knew that no Indian would be there to receive me, since I had particularly promised not to put up at an Indian house. But the attorney had sent no one. I understood later that, as I had arrived on a Sunday, he could not have sent anyone without inconvenience. I was perplexed, and wondered where to go, as I feared that no hotel would accept me. Pretoria station in 1893 was quite different from what it was in 1914. The lights were burning dimly. The travellers were few. I let all the other passengers go and thought that, as soon as the ticket collector was fairly free, I would hand him my ticket and ask him if he could direct me to some small hotel or any other such place where I might go; otherwise I would spend the night at the station. I must confess I shrank from asking him even this, for I was afraid of being insulted.

The station became clear of all passengers. I gave my ticket to the ticket collector and began my inquiries. He replied to me courteously, but I saw that he could not be of any considerable help.

But an American Negro who was standing near by broke into the conversation. 'I see,' said he, 'that you are an utter stranger here, without any friends. If you will come with me, I will take you to a small hotel, of which the proprietor is an American who is very well known to me. I think he will accept you.' I had my own doubts about the offer, but I thanked him and accepted his suggestion. He took me to Johnson's Family Hotel. He drew Mr. Johnson aside to speak to him, and the latter agreed to accommodate me for the night, on condition that I should have my dinner served in my room. 'I assure you,' said he, 'that I have no colour prejudice. But I have only European custom, and, if I allowed you to eat in the dining-room, my guests might be offended and even go away.' 'Thank you,' said I, 'even for accommodating me for the night. I am now more or less acquainted with the conditions here, and I understand your difficulty. I do not mind your serving the dinner in my room. I hope to be able to make some other arrangement tomorrow.'

I was shown into a room, where I now sat waiting for the dinner and musing, as I was quite alone. There were not many guests in the hotel, and I had expected the waiter to come very shortly with the dinner. Instead Mr. Johnston appeared. He said: I was ashamed of having asked you to have your dinner here. So I spoke to the other guests about you, and asked them if they would mind your having your dinner in the dining-room. They said they had no objection, and that they did not mind your staying here as long as you liked. Please, therefore, come to the dining-room, if you will, and stay here as long as you wish.' I thanked him again, went to the dining-room and had a hearty dinner. Next morning I called on the attorney, Mr. A. W. Baker. Abdulla Sheth had given me some description of him, so his cordial reception did not surprise me. He received me very warmly and made kind inquiries. I explained all about myself. Thereupon he said: 'We have no work for you here as barrister, for we have engaged the best counsel. The case is a prolonged and complicated one, so I shall take your assistance only to the extent of getting necessary information. And of course you will make communication with my client easy for me, as I shall now ask for all the information I want from him through you.

That is certainly an advantage, I have not yet found rooms for you. I thought I had better do so after having seen you. There is a fearful amount of colour prejudice here, and therefore it is not easy to find lodgings for such as you. But I know a poor woman. She is the wife of a baker. I think she will take you and thus add to her income at the same time. Come, let us go to her place.' So he took me to her house. He spoke with her privately about me, and she agreed to accept me as a boarder at 35 shilling a week. Mr. Baker, besides being an attorney, was a staunch lay preacher, He is still alive and now engaged purely in missionary work, having given up the legal profession. He is quite well-to-do. He still corresponds with me. In his letters he always dwells on the same theme. He upholds the excellence of Christianity from various points of view, and contends that it is impossible to find eternal peace, unless one accepts Jesus as the only son of God and the Saviour of mankind. During the very first interview Mr. Baker ascertained my religious views.

I said to him: 'I am a Hindu by birth. And yet I do not know much of Hinduism, and I know less of other religions. In fact I do not know where I am, and what is and what should be my belief. I intend to make a careful study of my own religion and, as far as I can, of other religions as well.' Mr. Baker was glad to hear all this, and said: 'I am one of the Directors of the South Africa General Mission. I have built a church at my own expense, and deliver sermons in it regularly. I am free from colour prejudice. I have some co-workers, and we meet at one o'clock every day for a few minutes and pray for peace and light. I shall be glad if you will join us there. I shall introduce you to my co-workers who will be happy to meet you, and I dare say you will also like their company. I shall give you, besides some religious books to read, though of course the book of books is the Holy Bible, which I would specially recommend to you.' I thanked Mr. Baker and agreed to attend the one o'clock prayers as regularly as possible. 'So I shall expect you here tomorrow at one o'clock, and we shall go together to pray,' added Mr. Baker, and we said good-bye. I had little time for reflection just yet.

I went to Mr. Johnston, paid the bill and removed to the new lodgings, where I had my lunch. The landlady was good woman. She had cooked a vegetarian meal for me. It was not long before I made myself quite at home with the family. I next went to see the friend to whom Dada Abdulla had given me a note. From him I learnt more about the hardships of Indians in South Africa. He insisted that I should stay with him. I thanked him, and told him that I had already made arrangements. He urged me not to hesitate to ask for anything I needed. It was now dark. I returned home, had my dinner, went to my room and lay there absorbed in deep thought. There was not any immediate work for me. I informed Abdulla Sheth of it. What, I thought, can be meaning of Mr. Baker's interest in me? What shall I gain from his religious co-workers? How far should I undertake the study of Christianity? How was I to obtain literature about Hinduism? And how was I to understand Christianity in its proper perspective without thoroughly knowing my own religion? I could come to only one conclusion: I should make a dispassionate study of all that came to me, and deal with Mr. Baker's group as God might guide me; I should not think of embracing another religion before I had fully understood my own. Thus musing I fell asleep.

4

BIOGRAPHY OF JAWAHARLAL NEHRU

Jawaharlal Nehru (1889-1964) was a great Indian nationalist leader who worked for independence and social reform. He became first prime minister of independent India, a position he retained until his death. He initiated India's nonalignment policy in foreign affairs.

Jawaharlal Nehru was born on Nov. 14, 1889, in Allahabad into a proud, learned Kashmiri Brahmin family. His father, Motilal Nehru, was a wealthy barrister and influential politician. Jawaharlal was an only child until the age of 11, after which two sisters were born. The atmosphere in the Nehru home was more English than Indian; English was spoken. It was also a luxurious home, with an impressive stable and two swimming pools. Jawaharlal was educated at home by tutors, most of them English or Scottish. Under the influence of a tutor Nehru joined the Theosophical Society at 13.

At the age of 15 Nehru left for England, where he studied at Harrow and Cambridge and then for the bar in London. He was called to the bar in 1912. His English experience reinforced his elegant and cosmopolitan tastes. As Nehru said of himself at Cambridge, "In my likes and dislikes I was perhaps more an Englishman than an Indian." In London he was attracted by Fabian ideas; nationalism and socialism from this time on provided his intellectual motive force.

EARLY POLITICAL MOVES

Back in India, Nehru began to practice law with his father. It was not until 1917 that Nehru was stirred by a political issue, the imprisonment of Annie Besant, an Irish theosophist devoted to Indian freedom. As a result, Nehru became active in the Home Rule League. His involvement in the nationalist movement gradually replaced his legal practice. In 1916 Nehru was married to Kamala Kaul, of an orthodox Kashmiri Brahmin family. They had one daughter (later Indira Gandhi, third prime minister of independent India).

Apart from his father and Besant, the greatest influence on Nehru politically was Mohandas Gandhi. Gandhi had been educated much like Nehru but, unlike him, remained basically untouched, essentially Indian. A second issue which fired Nehru's nationalism and led him to join Gandhi was the Amritsar massacre of 1919, in which some 400 Indians were shot on orders of a British officer.

The year 1920 marked Nehru's first contact with the Indian kisan, the peasant majority. Nehru was "filled with shame and sorrow ... at the degradation and overwhelming poverty of India." This experience aroused a sympathy for the underdog which characterized many of Nehru's later political moves.

The plight of the peasant was a challenge to his socialist convictions, and he attempted to persuade the peasants to organize. From this time on Nehru's concerns were Indian. He began to read the Bhagavad Gita and practiced vegetarianism briefly. Most of his life he practiced yoga daily.

In 1921 Nehru followed Gandhi in sympathy with the Khilafat cause of the Moslems. Nehru was drawn into the first civil disobedience campaign as general secretary of the United Provinces Congress Committee. Nehru remarked, "I took to the crowd, and the crowd took to me, and yet I never lost myself in it." Nehru here articulated two of his most distinctive traits throughout his career: his involvement with the people and his aloof and lonely detachment.

The year 1921 also witnessed the first of Nehru's many imprisonments. In prison his political philosophy matured, and he said that he learned patience and adaptability. Imprisonment was also a criterion of political success.

INTERNATIONAL INFLUENCES

In 1926-1927 Nehru took his wife to Europe for her health. This experience became a turning point for Nehru. It was an intellectual sojourn, highlighted by an antiimperialist conference in Brussels. Here Nehru first encountered Communists, Socialists, and radical nationalists from Asia and Africa. The goals of independence and social reform became firmly linked in Nehru's mind. Nehru spoke eloquently against imperialism and became convinced of the need for a socialist structure of society. He was impressed with the Soviet example during a visit to Moscow.

Back in India Nehru was immediately engrossed in party conferences and was elected president of the All-India Trades Union Congress. In speeches he linked the goals of independence and socialism. In 1928 he joined the radical opposition to proposals for dominion status by his father and Gandhi. In 1930 Gandhi threw his weight to Nehru as Congress president, attempting to divert radicalism from communism to the Congress.

In 1930 Nehru was arrested and imprisoned for violation of the Salt Law, which Gandhi also protested in his famous "salt march." Nehru's wife was also arrested. From the end of 1931 to September 1935 Nehru was free only 6 months.

During the 1937 elections the Moslem League offered to cooperate with the All-India Congress Committee in forming a coalition government in the United Provinces. Nehru refused, and the struggle between the Congress and the Moslem League was under way. Nehru also established the precedent for economic planning in a suggestion that the Congress form a national planning committee. In 1938 Nehru paid a brief visit to Europe. On his return he was sent briefly as envoy to China until war intervened and made it necessary for him to return.

War in Europe drew India in, together with England. For Indian leaders the question was how an honorable settlement could be reached with England and still allow India to participate on the Allied side. Negotiations toward this end culminated in the Cripps mission and offer of dominion status in March 1942.

Nehru refused to accept dominion status, as did the rest of Congress leadership. There followed the Congress "Quit India" resolution and the imprisonment of Nehru, Gandhi, and other Congress leaders until June 1945. There were nationwide protests, a mass demand for independence.

PRIME MINISTER

In 1945, as Congress president, Nehru was pressed into negotiations with the Moslem League and the viceroy. Congress-Moslem League negotiations were marked by communal killings in Calcutta, followed by sympathetic outbreaks throughout India. Final decisions were reached in conversations between the last British viceroy, Lord Mountbatten, and Nehru, Gandhi, and Mohammad Ali Jinnah. According to the Mountbatten Plan, two separate dominions were created. Nehru became prime minister and minister of external affairs of independent India in 1947.

Following Gandhi's assassination in January 1948, Nehru felt very much alone facing economic problems and the possibility of the Balkanization of India. In 1949 he made his first visit to the United States in search of a solution to India's pressing food shortage.

Free India's first elections in 1951-1952 resulted in an overwhelming Congress victory. Economic planning and welfare were the first claims on Nehru's attention. He inaugurated a diluted version of socialist planning: concentration of public investment in areas of the economy that were free from private interests. The Planning Commission was created in 1950 and launched the First Five-Year Plan in 1951, stressing an increase in agricultural output. Nehru also took pride in the Community Development Program, established to raise the standard of living in the villages. He saw the Third Five-Year Plan operative before his death on May 27, 1964, in New Delhi.

Nehru was the architect of nonalignment in foreign policy. Economic weakness and the Indian tradition were powerful factors in formulating the policy. The other influence on Nehru's foreign policy was his controversial minister of defense, Krishna

Menon. Nehru sought closer relations with nonaligned Asian states, with India in the role of leader.

Nehru's nonalignment policy was criticized by many Westerners and some Indians as giving preference to totalitarian countries rather than to democracies. Some critics believed that nonalignment left India no effective means to deal with China, national defense, the Great Powers, or the underdeveloped community. On the other hand, nonalignment had many Indian defenders, even in the face of the Chinese invasion of Indian border territory in 1962. Some held that nonalignment was a strategy for deterrence and peace, a force for protecting Indian independence and preservation of the international community on ethical grounds. Nevertheless, nonalignment as implemented by Nehru did not prevent the government from resorting to force in Hyderabad, Kashmir, and Goa.

Nehru the man and politician made such a powerful imprint on India that his death on May 27, 1964, left India with no political heir to his leadership. Indians repeated Nehru's own words of the time of Gandhi's assassination: "The light has gone out of our lives and there is darkness everywhere."

5

BIOGRAPHY OF R. K. NARAYAN

Malgudi Days is a collection of short stories by R.K.Narayan that focused on the trial and tribulations of a small Indian town of Malgudi. According to R.K. Narayan, Malgudi is a town "habited by timeless characters who could be living anywhere in the world" and is located on the banks of river Sarayu and surrounded by the Mempi Hills.

BACKGROUND

As an attempt to popularize television, the Government of India undertook several steps to popularize the medium. The 1970s and 1980s saw a boom in television programming as the Ministry of Information and Broadcasting invited independent producers and directors to shoot television serials on a regular basis; Malgudi Days was one such television serial.

The serial was directed by the late Kannada actor and director, Shankar Nag, and was shot entirely near Agumbe in Shimoga District, Karnataka. The music was rendered by L. Vaidyanathan and was produced by T.S. Narasimhan of the Padam Rag Fims. It included many of Narayan's short stories and novels such as "Swami and Friends" and "The Vendor of Sweets".

"Vendor of Sweets" narrated the story of a sweet vendor, Jagan, his business and confrontation with his son who had returned from abroad. The title role was played by Kannada actor, Anant Nag.

"Swami and Friends" revolves around ten-year old Swaminathan, or Swami as he is known by other characters.

Swami portrays the growing pangs of a boy who despises school, as he makes excuses and roams around Malgudi with his friends. Swami's father works in a government office and his mother is a housewife. At home, Swami shares his adventures with his aged granny, who lovingly addresses him as "Chamy." Swami also has two close ιends; Mani and the son of the Police Chief Superintendent, Rajam. Swami's character was enacted by Manjunath, a regular feature in many of Shankar Nag directed movies.

The sketches for the serial were done by Narayan's brother and acclaimed cartoonist, R.K. Laxman. Thirty-nine episodes of "Malgudi Days" were telecast on Doordarshan . Subsequently, it was re-telecast on Doordarshan and later on Sony Entertainment Television. Currently, director Kavitha Lankesh is scripting and directing new 26 episodes of "Malgudi Days" in Hindi based on R.K. Narayan's short stories/novel.

THE LIFE OF R.K. NARAYAN

Narayan's fiction rarely addresses political issues or high philosophy. He writes with grace and humor, about a fictional town Malgudi and its inhabitants; and their little lives. Narayan is a classic teller of tales; an enduring appeal springs from his canvas where common men and women of all times and places are joined in their commonality.

Rasipuram Krishnaswamy Iyer Narayanswamy stood shortened to R.K.Narayan, on Graham Greene's advice. Narayan lived till ninety-five, writing for more than fifty years, and publishing till he was eighty seven. He wrote fifteen novels, five volumes of short stories, a number of travelogues and collection of non-fiction, English translation of Indian epics, and the memoirs "My Days". Yet it is neither the copiousness of output, nor currency of content - or the lack of either - that gives Narayan his place among the finest story-tellers of modern English.

He weaved a world existing nowhere, but striking a chord of perfect reality with readers across the English reading peoples. His books appeal in a quiet, reassuring way and have a remained popular over many decades. His writing is also part of literature coursework in some American universities.

Narayan evokes a diction of unusual freshness and rare ingenuity with the English literary idiom.

Narayan was born at the beginning of the twentieth century, on October 10, 1906 at Chennapatna, near Mysore in southern India. He was one among many siblings, his father a provincial head-master of much repute with the rod. Narayan studied at his father's school and maintained a diligent dislike for studies. The qualifier to the graduate course in Arts proved his nemesis; Narayan failed. In spite of sustained loathing, Physics and Chemistry had stood by him, but English betrayed. He much liked the subject and was already aspiring for a writerly life. But a compromise was never reached with the English pieces in his syllabus. Getting plucked fetched him a year of reprieve from classes; he promised his father he will try the test again.

Narayan started reading in earnest, the classics of English literature, and writing. He read out his pieces to a close band of friends, and after priming the audience with coffee and snacks, asked for their opinion. Such reviews were laudatory, "brilliant" being the unanimous word. His father had his own qualms about institutional education, and encouraged Narayan in literary pursuits. The next year's entrance examination was cleared, Narayan served his time in the university and graduated. Though the repugnance to studies never recouped he queued for the Master of Arts course, viewing the degree as an expedient in job hunting. While walking up the university stairs to submit the form, a friend warned of the privations of M.A. Narayan turned around and came down the steps in a hurry, never to try their ascent again.

He resolved to write for his living and write in English. Reporting for defunct journals, freelancing here and there and similar "literary" odd jobs catered more to the spirits than pockets. He kept on writing and submitting. A few lyrical pieces went to publishers in England, and returned in due or undue time, along with "...cold, callous rejection slips, impersonal and mocking".

Narayan's first published work was the review of a book titled "Development of Maritime Laws of 17th-Century England". He is rather cynical about it and writes, "A most unattractive book, but I struggled through its pages and wrote a brief note on it, and though not paid for, it afforded me the thrill of seeing my words in print for the first time." To better arrange meetings of the proverbial ends, Narayan took up teaching at a government school, and left the job within two days.

In the autumn of 1930, on a sudden spurt of inspiration, writing of his first novel "Swami and Friends" started. It was as if a window had opened, and through it Narayan saw a little town and its rail station, the Mempi Forest and the Nallapa's Grove, the Albert Mission school, Market Road, the River Sarayu. Its inhabitants appeared, and Malgudi was born.

Malgudi is the setting of nearly all of Narayan's work. It is described as being somewhere in southern India. Malgudi has some elements of Hardy's Wessex and perhaps can be pinned on a map as exactly Wodehouse's Blandings has recently been done. But Malgudi is different from either. Its moorings in geography - and also history - seem never an issue; Narayan's space-time bubble bounces in absolute ether.

"Swami and Friends" was completed and sent to publishers. It repeatedly returned. Narayan dispatched it yet another time and gave the return address as one of his friend's in London. He wrote to the friend requesting the manuscript be tied to a brick and thrown into the Thames if it came back. It did.

But the friend took it to his acquaintance Graham Greene, who was already an established author. Narayan received a telegram soon thereafter, "Novel taken. Graham Greene responsible."

"Swami and Friends" was published in October 1935. Greene's suggestion for pruning his never-ending name to something more succinct was readily taken by Narayan.

Thus began Narayan's friendship with Greene; it continued till the latter's death in 1991. They corresponded often but had met only once, in 1964. This association is surprising in its depth and sincerity, given the two's widely varying oeuvres.

"Swami and Friends" had a few enthusiastic reviews but was lost in the deluge of current bestsellers. Throughout his career, Narayan changed publishers often, sometimes publishers changed him; he even dabbled in self-publishing for some of his books.

Narayan's renown as a writer came slowly, almost with a touch of diffidence. He never had the trappings of a high profile author, and stayed scrupulously shy of literary lunches and book signing binges. He was most at home near his characters, somewhere in south India.

Malgudi is a land of fantasy, not as in a dream, colored and brilliant; but the reverie of relaxed awakening, a contemplation of commonness. Life there is reduced, or elevated, to the lowest common denominator of living, which remains the same in nearly all places and times. Small men, smaller means, touched at times by the cares of a larger world, but unruffled, still moving on. The characters yearn for fame and money and virtue and those "real" things, but their longings stand tempered by a subtle sense of limitation, almost comic.

The narrator of one the novels is an archetypal Malgudian: "We were about twenty unrelated families in Kabir Street, each having inherited a huge rambling house stretching from the street to the river and back. .... so comfortably placed, (we) were mainly occupied in eating, breeding, celebrating festivals, spending the afternoons in a prolonged siesta on the pyol, and playing cards all evening. ..... This sort of existence did not appeal to me. I liked to be active, had dreams of becoming a journalist. .... I noticed a beggar woman one day, at the Market Gate, with Siamese twins, and persuaded my friend Jayaraj, photographer and framer of pictures at the Market Arch, to take a picture of the woman, wrote a report on it and mailed it to the first paper which caught my attention at the Town Hall reading room; that was my starting point as a journalist. Thereafter I got into the habit of visiting the Town Hall library regularly to see if my report appeared in print."

Narayan's irony dissembles in humor, and the reader realizes only when hit,

"Excuse me. I made a vow never to touch alcohol in my life, before my mother," said Chandran.

This affected Kailas profoundly. He remained solemn for a moment and said : "Then don't. Mother is a sacred object. It is a commodity whose value we don't realize as long as it is with us. One must lose it to know what a precious possession it is. If I had my mother I should have studied in a college and become a respectable person. You wouldn't find me here. After this where do you think I'm going ?"

"I don't know."

"To the house of a prostitute."

He remained reflective for a moment and said with a sigh:

"As long as my mother lived she said every minute, 'Do this don't do that.' And I remained a good son to her. The moment she died I changed. It is a rare commodity, sir. Mother is a rare commodity." '

Nature remains an abounding presence in the semi-suburban life of Malgudi. Narayan's observation and his felicity with words reveal in passages such as, "It was April. The summer sun shone like a ruthless arc lamp - and all the water in the well evaporated and the road dust became bleached and weightless and flew about like flour spraying off the grinding wheels." Long solitary walks remained a lifelong passion; the world percolated his every pore. "When the monsoon broke out, one could watch dark mountainous clouds mustering, edged with lightning; these would develop awesome pyrotechnics. In June, drizzle and sunshine alternating, leaving gold mohur, flame of the forest, and jacaranda in bloom along the avenues. In July and August the never-ending downpour, grey leaden skies, and damp air blowing."

After Swami and Friends, Narayan was settling into his rhythm; "The Bachelor of Arts" and "The Dark Room" came out in quick succession, each book further cementing Malgudi as the cornerstone of his ccsmos.

In 1939, Narayan's wife Rajam passed away. Their only child, a daughter, was three years old. This bereavement brought about a permanent change in his life. Narayan remained distressed for a long time, out of grief and concerns of single parenthood. His fourth novel, "The English Teacher" is a catharsis of these times, and Narayan has said, "More than any other book, The English Teacher is autobiographical in content, very little part of it being fiction." The wife of the protagonist dies of typhoid. Her illness, the prognosis, the hopes, despair and death are painted with stokes of delicate detachment. And infinite pain. The reader is touched by the narrative, a universal loss echoes.

It was some time before the earlier lightness returned to Narayan's writing. It eventually did, but became nuanced with heightened sensitivity and restraint. His wife's demise also opened certain psychic explorations for Narayan. He was reportedly able to communicate with the departed soul, and the transcendental tête-? -tête continued for a long time. Such assertions leave the reader slightly baffled at times and openly skeptical at others. But Narayan writes about his experiences with as much intensity as grace, "We stood at the window, gazing on a slender, red streak over the eastern rim of the earth. A cool breeze lapped our faces. The boundaries of our personalities suddenly dissolved. It was a moment of rare, immutable joy - a moment for which one feels grateful to Life and Death." Thus ends "The English Teacher" (published in USA as "Grateful to Life and Death") in a description of the deceased wife "visiting" her husband from the great beyond.

The book speaks to me as one of the finest odes to love, rather than an almanac of after-life.

The Rockefeller Foundation selected Narayan for a travel grant. This was his first travel abroad, and he says coyly, "Finally I did break out of the triangular boundary of Madras, Mysore and Coimbatore and left for the United States, in October 1956."

A memorable travelogue, "My Dateless Diary", came out of Narayan's American sojourn. He visited New York, Chicago,

Los Angeles, Washington, the Grand Canyon among other places and met eminent personalities such as Aldous Huxley, John Gunther, Greta Garbo. Garbo was apparently much interested in Narayan's mystic leanings.

In the Hotel Carlton, Berkeley, California, Narayan wrote the most famous of his novels, "The Guide". Sometimes he wrote with a typewriter, sometimes with paper and pen, cooking his own food on a hot plate in the hotel room every day.

Narayan has written, "The Guide attained a certain degree of popularity, which, though pleasant in itself, brought in its wake involvements that turned out to be ludicrous and even tragic." It was made into a film which mutilated the original storyline much to the author's chagrin. A planned Broadway edition was as reckless in its treatment. Narayan had to withhold his permission to present it on stage, even as the adaptation was done by an old friend of his, a former literary editor of the New York Times. As an example of the outrage, Narayan mentions, "For instance, his version managed to abolish the heroine. I objected to his omission and to two irrelevant characters of his own; above all I objected to the hero's turning around and urinating on the stage."

Matters became rather acrimonious over this script and Narayan had to leave New York at a very short notice to avoid being summoned for a subpoena; he found asylum in the Indian consulate before boarding a flight out of the United States. However the script was later revised and "The Guide" opened in Broadway in March 1968. It closed in less than a week.

In his essays and columns, Narayan pokes gentle but stirring fun at himself and the idiosyncrasies of his writing. In a piece titled "Love and Lovers", Narayan contrives an interview between a critic and himself.

" '... Are you going to tell me that you portray the individual in his fullness? There are areas you have neglected. For example, do you deal with man-woman relationship with any seriousness? Aren't you prudish when it comes to sex?'

'Not exactly prudish, only I take the hint. When a couple, even if they happen to be characters in my own novel, want privacy, I leave the room; surely you wouldn't expect one, at such moments, to sit on the edge of their bed and take notes ?'"

In "Reflections cn Frankfurt", Narayan continues in the same vein of easy irresponsibility, "I heard rumors in Frankfurt and then in Paris and London that I was to be awarded the Nobel Prize this year (1986). Some Paris newspapers carried the 'shortlisted' names of these writers in the Third World, as the committee had decided to award the Prize to the Third World this year to overcome the charge of being biased in favor of American and European writers. I was greeted and congratulated here and there."

He did not win the Prize and has speculated on what might have tripped him. Here is his reflection on the committee's deliberations,"...His writing is too simple, and too readable, requiring no effort on the part of the reader. ...He has created a new map called Malgudi in which his characters live and die. Story after story is set in the same place, which is not progressive, a rather stagnant background..... We hope some day Narayan will develop into a full-fledged writer deserving our serious consideration."

The recurrent motifs in Malgudi's saga are irrelevance and irreverence.

Narayan's oeuvre never syncs with the contemporary, never means to. His writing career spanned the second half of the twentieth century, arguably the most happening phase of human history. Both the world at large and the world at small witnessed upheavals; technology leaped, politics changed and morals mutated. Yet, all this is alien to Malgudi's denizens. Life there might have stood still, or may have been always moving in a cosmic continuum, from primal past to fathomless future. The Malgudi men and the women and children, go on about their lives, as they have always done, and always will. Narayan often invokes the current as a backdrop, perhaps to show how meaningless it is for Malgudi. "Waiting for the Mahatma" (1955) is set amid the final years of India's freedom struggle, and Mahatma Gandhi appears in the novel, complete in his loincloth and moral exhortations. But the characters are just brushed by the tension of the times, not swayed. They remain very much themselves; so does Malgudi. Narayan does bring in change, perhaps inevitably, towards the later part of his career. Here his dexterity stretches very thin, and a hint of absurdity creeps in at times. In one of these stories a Malgudi man returns from the US with a Korean wife and a story-writing machine; the humor seems slightly affected and the precision of earlier touch, sadly amiss.

Narayan has been irreverent in his Malgudi tales; to institutions, individuals and inclinations. There is not a hint of stridency, he makes fun supremely poised and assured. His characters fall in love, and then out of it, promises are made and broken, youths converted to causes, and then exorcised by nubile females. Married men indulge peccadilloes and prayers, sages in shenanigans and married women in gossips and fantasy. People die of disease or dotage, and survivors get on with the game, insignificant as ever.

Readers are left with a search for meaning in all this. Narayan never intrudes with interpretations.

But the greatest point about Narayan's writing is its use of language. His talent goes beyond mere aptitude with words or a maverick Malgudi. Narayan stands for the immense flexibility, adaptability and élan of English; he uses the language of Bible, Shakespeare and American Constitution to an amazing effect while dealing in subjects vastly removed. His creatures squat on the floor for meals, wear dhoti with a coat, read the Ramayana, regard mothers as sacred, rebel against fathers, marry for love over money, and aspire for eternal life. The author writes all this without a single footnote, without any discernible twang of the foreign, with a sense of disarming familiarity.

Narayan represents the synthesis that is English, a language evolving through the synergy of civilizations, known and unknown; a language in continual quest.

R.K.Narayan passed away on May 13, 2001. Malgudi lives on. And so does his writing.

6

BIOGRAPHY OF KAMALA DAS

`My story` is an autobiographical story by Kamala Das. The title is self-explanatory as it reveals the authors own life story.

Born on March 31, 1934 Kamala Das is known as one of India`s foremost poets. She was in Malabar in Kerala. Nalapat Narayan Menon who was a prominent writer was her great uncle. Her love of poetry began at an early age through his influence. Das remembers watching him work from day and night and that attracts her a lot.

Das was also deeply affected by the poetry of her mother, Nalapat Balamani Amma, and the sacred writings kept by the matriarchal community of Nayars. She was privately educated until the age of 15. at that time she was married to K. Madhava Das. At the age of 16 her first son was born. But then she was not so matured. Her husband often played a fatherly role for both Das and her sons.

Because of the great age difference between Kamala and her husband, he often encouraged her to associate with people of her own age. Das says that he was always very understanding and loving husband. When Das wished to begin writing, her husband supported her decision. One of the main reasons behind this was to increase the family`s income.

Since das was a woman she could not enjoy the morning-till-night work schedule. She would wait until nightfall after her family had gone to sleep and would write until morning: she used to write in the kitchen table. This rigorous work also affected das` health. Talking about her illness optimistically she once told in an interview that her illness gave her more time at home and thus more time to write. At her later age in 1999 the author was converted to Islam and take the name of Kamala Surayya.

Synopsis:

`My story` is an autobiography by the poet writer Kamala Das. Her outspoken autobiography is a source of controversy. It contains the clear picture of her life. Her multiple affairs, her strained relationship with her husband and so many hidden facts of her life. She had a natural flair fot both Malayalam and English. The book faced different controversies as it contains some frank discussion of author about her quest of love inside and outside the marriage. She writes about the society as well as the traditional conservativeness in which she lives. She possess a clear vision about relationship. My Story, shocked mainstream Kerala with its candid accounts of her encounters with men. As an artist, her paintings included nudes. In this piece of work of Kamala Das she clearly depicts the intensely personal experiences including her growth into womanhood, her unsuccessful quest for love in and outside marriage, and her living in matriarchal rural South India after inheriting her ancestral home. While at home, the rich families try to kill her with magic because they fear that her writing will reveal their immorality in. She was very honest and never felt scared of anything.

Published by Ind-Us in 1977 `My story` is a controversial autobiography by Kamala Das where she seized the control of the society`s own cultural codes, particularly those formed by dominant religious ideologies.

`My story` is a masterpiece by Kamala Das. She raised many topics here in this novel, which are still under cover. She was downtrodden, with a sense of sincerity and urgency. His novels, belonging to the genre of social realism, include Untouchable (1935), Coolie (1936), Two Leaves and A Bud (1936), The Village (1939), and The Big Heart (1945). Private Life of an Indian Prince (1953)deals with a totally different class of characters. Untouchable is a great milestone in Indian

English literature, as a work of social realism and as the first Dalit novel. Besides being a novelist and short-story writer, Mulk Raj Anand is also an astute art critic who edited Marg, an art magazine, for quite some time. Anand is also known for his beautiful story The Lost Child.

OTHER EMINENT WRITERS

Raja Rao (b. 1909) alongwith Mulk Raj Anand and R. K. Narayan constitutes the great trio of the Indian English novel. Of his five novels, Kanthapura (1938), The Serpent and the Rope (1960) and The Cat and Shakespeare (1965) were critically acclaimed. The Serpent and the Rope won the Sahitya Akademi Award and The Chessmaster and His Moves, the first of a trilogy, the prestigious Neustadt International Prize for literature. Raja Rao's famous short stories have been collected in The Cow of the Barricades (1947) and The Policeman and the Rose (1977).

G. V. Desani (b. 1909) worked as a newspaper correspondent, lecturer and broadcaster in England for more than two decades, before shifting to America where he has been teaching Philosophy since 1970. All About H. Hatterr, a highly experimental work of fiction is his only novel.

Manohar Malgaonkar (b. 1913), a prominent Indian English novelist, has written the majority of his novels with a historical perspective. His works are a testimony to his narrative skill and his penchant for historical themes of epic dimensions. Distant Drum (1960), Combat of Shadows (1962), The Princes (1963), A Bend in the Ganges (1964) and The Devil's Wind (1972) show him to be a novelist who artistically presents the historical and social milieu, primarily of pre-Independence days and the early years of Independence.

Khushwant Singh (b. 1915), apart from being a novelist and a short-story writer, is also a reputed editor, columnist and a Sikh historian. Born at Hadali in Western Punjab (now in Pakistan), he was educated in Delhi, Lahore and London. Khushwant Singh first came into public spotlight as the editor of the Illustrated Weekly of India. Though he has over thirty books to his credit, Train to Pakistan remains his best known work of fiction. His other works are Delhi and I Shall Not Hear The Nightingale. He is also known for his voluminous and authoritative History of the Sikhs.

Kamala Markandaya (b. 1924) was born in India and educated at the University of Madras. Apart from her first novel, Nectar in a Sieve, which has been compared with Pearl S. Buck's The Good Earth, she has published Some Inner Fury (1954), A Silence of Desire (1961), Possession (1963), A Handful of Rice (1966), The Coffer Dams (19690 and Two Virgins (1973). Her depiction of the quintessential aspects of the life of the Indian peasantry in a novel like Nectar in a Sieve, are rendered authentic by the sense of empathy and sincerity that she exudes.

Nissim Ezekiel (b. 1924) is probably the most influential poet of the post-Independence era which witnessed the birth of modernism in Indian English poetry. A teacher by profession, he is not only a poet but a poet's poet, who has painstakingly nurtured most of the budding talents in Mumbai. Dom Moraes, Adil Jussawalla and Gieve Patel are among those who benefited from Ezekiel's creative inputs. Ezekiel was primarily instrumental in ushering Modernism in the country, with the publication of his first collection of poems titled A Time to Change (1952). His other major works include Sixty Poems (1955); The Third (1958), The Unfinished Man (1960); The Exact Name (1965); Hymns in Darkness (1976); Latter-Day Psalms (1982); and Collected Poems (1989). His poetry is specific, concentrated, made up of 'the ordinariness of most events', and questioned social mores.

A. K. Ramanujan (1929-1993) is one of the finest Indian English poets to grace the Indian literary horizon. An Imagist poet, a true disciple of William Carlos Williams, Ramanujan's poetry is essentially the petry of 'seeing', of perception. His principal works include his collections of poetry, The Striders, Relations, Second Sight, Selected Poems and his creative translations from ancient Tamil and medieval Kannada poems, The Interior Landscape (1967), Speaking of Shiva (1973), Hymns for the Drowning (1981) and Poems of Love and War (1985).

He has also translated some poems of Gopalakrishna Adiga, Song of the Earth and Other Poems (1968) with M. G. Krishnamurthy and U. R. Ananthamurthy's novel, Samskara (1976). His last work, Folk Tales from India (1990) is a piece of brilliant transcreation. A bilingual writer, Ramanujan has published three major collections of poems, a novel and some interesting stories in Kannada.

Arun Kolatkar (b. 1932), belongs to a group of new Indian English poets who made their presence felt in the 1970s. Also a major poet in Marathi, Kolatkar has shaped a vibrant poetic idiom that blends the searching tone of medieval Bhakti (devotional) poetry with the imagistic precision of modernist poetry. He has penned a volume of poems in Marathi titled Kolatkaranchya Kavita. Jejuri, a poetic sequence of 31 poems in English, won him the Commonwealth Poetry prize for 1977.

Kamala Das (b. 1934) is perhaps the best-known Indian woman poet writing in English at present. Nowhere can we see the intensity and genuineness of the artist in her more clearly than in her poetry. Her principal works include Summer in Calcutta (1965); The Descendants (1967), The Old Playhouse and Other Poems (1973); My Story (Autobiography, 1974); Manas (1975); and Alphabet of Lust (1976) (both novels). Among all the Indian English poets of her generation, male or female, she maintains the shortest interval between emotion and expression. Unlike most of other Indian English poets, Kamala Das has not received any academic education or training in poetry writing.She is a bilingual writer, writing short fiction in Malayalam, her mother-tongue, under the pseudonym 'Madhavikutty'.

Anita Desai (b.1937) is a popular Indian English novelist with a number of novels and collections of short stories to her credit. The all-pervading theme of her works is the contemporary Indian woman, her loneliness and frustration. Clear Light of Day is considered to be the best of her novels, to date. Other works include The Accompanist.Fire on the Mountain (Heinemann, 1978), Games at Twilight (Heinemann, 1979), In Custody (Heinemann, 1984), Baumgartner's Bombay (Heinemann, 1988), and Journey to Ithaca.

Kiran Nagarkar (1949): married, based in Bombay, Kiran Nagarkar works in an advertising agency. His first novel--in Marathi--Saat Sakkam Trechalis (or Seven Sixes are Forty Three) is a landmark in Marathi literature. His first English novel, Ravan and Eddie, appeared last year. Cuckold is his latest novel

Vikram Seth (b. 1952) created a furore in the US literary world in 1986, when he published The Golden Gate, the first Indian English novel in verse. Apart from his second novel, A Suitable Boy (1993) his other works include five collections of poetry- Mappings, All You Who Sleep Tonight, The Humble Administrator's Garden, Beastly Tales from Here and There, Three Chinese Poets: Translations and a travelogue titled From Heaven Lake. Seth has also won the Commonwealth Writer's prize.

Upamanyu Chatterjee (1956): Upamanyu Chatterjee graduated from St Stephen's, and joined the IAS. Married, with two children, he is chief officer, Bombay Slum Improvement Board. His debut novel, English August: An Indian Story attracted instant notice, and has been made into an award winning film. He has published another novel The Last Burden.

Shashi Tharoor (1956): Shashi Tharoor studied in Calcutta, Bombay and Delhi. Graduating from St Stephen's, where he excelled at virtually everything, he joined the UN High Commission for Refugees in 1978 and is now at the UN headquarters in New York. He is married, with twin sons. His first novel The Great Indian Novel won the Commonwealth Award. He has since published Show Business and The Five Dollar Smile, a collection of short-stories.

Amitav Ghosh (b. 1956) graduated from Delhi University and is a social anthropologist with a D. Phil. from Oxford. He has worked with the Indian Express and taught at the Delhi School of Economics, University of Virginia and Columbia University. His first novel, The Circle of Reason (1986) written in the modernist mode of magical realism was highly acclaimed and has been translated into several European languages.The Circle of Reason won the Prix Medici Estranger, a top French literary award; The Shadow Lines won the Sahitya Akademi award; His latest novel In An Antique Land (1992) is a fascinating amalgam of field notes and historical imagination, wherein Ghosh's academic discipline, extensive travel and creative mastery find full play. Calcutta Chromosome is his recent novel.

Arundhati Roy: Her first novel, The God of Small Things, which won the Booker Prize for the year 1997 become an international literary sensation and a bestseller as soon as it came out.. Roy, was paid a total of 5,00,000 pounds in advances by 18 publishers worldwide thereby creating history in the publishing field. Brought up in Kerala, Roy, trained as an architect in New Delhi, where she still lives with her film-maker husband, Pradeep Kishen. She wrote screenplays for television and films, her most successful feature film being Electric Moon, before locking herself away to write The God of Small Things. Drawn from experiences in Roy's life, it tells the tragic story of a Syrian Christian family from Aymenem, in Kerala, riven by internal jealousies and divided by social prejudices. Its unique structure and lyrical prose makes for an brilliant debut.

7

Indian English Literature: In Search of a Name

When one thinks of Indian English Literature, one cannot but think of the complexity and difficulty in choosing a name for it. The following names been given with different interpretations suggesting different nuances and shades of meaning.

1. Anglo-Indian Literature
2. Indo-Anglian Literature
3. Indo-English Literature
4. Indian writing in English
5. Indian-English writing
6. Indian English Literature

It's true that the literary nomenclatures are never fully resolved to the best satisfaction of all. To start with it was referred to as an Anglo-Indian Literature (to think of Edward Farley Oaten's prize-winning essay with that title) and it covered the writings of Englishmen in Indian on Indian themes but the word Anglo-Indian also refers to a race, a microscopic minority in India and it somehow acquired a pejorative dimension. But the Indian creative writing in English needs to be referred by a name. The phrase Indian Literature, on the analogy of American Literature or Australian Literature is not suitable here, for in America and in Australia, English is the only language (may be with different dialects or creolized English as it happens to be in the case of Black-American Literature) and the spoken medium of people. But in India the case is different. Indian Literature would mean, any literature in any Indian language, hence the difficulty.

It's said that J.H.Cousins coined the term Indo-Anglian literature in 1883 and later it was given currency by Sreenivasa Iyengar, the pioneer in this field. But Iyengar himself feels that the phrase 'Indo-Anglian' is not much too happy an expression and this phrase was used by him as a title for his handbook on Indian writing in English, brought out by PEN- (All India Centre).

In this book he makes a reference to the phrase 'Indo-Anglian' and how it was misprinted as Indo-Anglican by mistake and how he had to send an answer when he was chastised for this odd expression by 'Autolycus'. He feels that people prefer 'Indo-English' to 'Indo-Anglian', though 'Indo-Anglian' can be used both as an adjective and substantive. Referring to this body of literature he recalls Bottemley's phrase 'Matthew Arnold in Sari' - not so an appalling apparition, perhaps after the passage of 150 or more years. Iyengar likens this body of literature to legendary Sakuntala who was disowned by her parents and feels that it is a tributory and an off-shoot of English Literature which he refers to as a new mutation.

The more surprising thing is two distinct streams flow together simultaneously; one, the other Indian language classical works getting translated into English and the other creative works in English. V.K.Gokak prefers the phrase Indo-English to refer to the former work and the latter is termed as Indo-Anglian. Surjit Mukherjee in his essay 'Indo-English Literature' refers to works like 'Geetanjalai' (works translated by the authors themselves into English) not merely as translations and like to call them as trans-creations. Referring to 'Geetanjali' he says, "Its unique quality was the result of the author endeavouring to be his own translator, in which process, he went beyond the bounds of translations and achieved something which may be called 'trans-creation'". And he refuses to categorize 'Geetanjali' under either Indo-English or Indo-

Anglian. For that matter any creative work is a trans-creation, for, that in the sub-conscious is brought out as creation. It's a creative transformation.

It's understandable that a distinction is kept between these two types of translations;- one ,a work put into English by others, (other than the author) two, a work translated into English by the author himself. The former is considered under Indo-English writing and the latter is considered under Indo-Anglian or Indian English Literature (a phrase coined by Dr.M.K.Naik for his critical survey of this body of literature and accepted by Sahitya Akademi and gained currency now for the simple reason that it scores over other names, for it can widely cover the entire body of Indian creative writing in English).

Amarjit Singh feels that "The appellation 'Indo-English' or even the less felicitous 'Indo-Anglian' suggests only a part of the difficulty in trying to place the literature produced by Indians in English within clear, national, regional or linguistic boundaries."

Mulk Raj Anand - himself an established writer- prefers the phrase 'Indian- English writing' and says." I feel that Indian-English writing has come to stay as part of world-literature". But somehow the phrase Indian-English has not yet coughed off its pejorative colouring. Also Indian-English cannot be considered as pidgin- English, for it is nothing short of degradation, for Indian-English is almost on par with English barring a few irregularities in speech, nor can it be considered as creolized English as seen in some parts of the world.

In this connection, the remarks of M.K.Naik are quite appropriate. Referring to the origins he says "Indian English Literature began as an interesting by-product of an eventful encounter in the eighteenth century between a vigorous and enterprising Britain and a stagnant and chaotic India". Later, almost coining a phrase, he explains it thus: "The Sahitya Akademi has recently accepted 'Indian English Literature' as the most suitable appellation for this body of writing. The term emphasizes two significant ideas: first, that this literature constitutes one of the many streams that join the great ocean called Indian Literature, which though written in different languages, has an unmistakable unity; and secondly that it is an inevitable product of the nativization of the English Literature appears to be more acceptable than the other phrases discussed earlier.

Indian-English Literature has acquired a new identity as much identity as American and Austrian literature have acquired which of course is quite distinct from Indian English. The efforts by writers like Raja Rao in Indianizing English language cannot be ignored though it is very difficult to express the Indian sensibility in English.

I am reminded of my own remarks in this connection: "to clothe the very Indianness in English tongue - though it has gone into the very system of our life - without making it appear bizarre is yet another difficulty for the cloth which sometimes is either too long or too short which makes one prefer the naked majesty itself. A rapprochement is somehow wrought between Indianness and the English tongue and sometimes vice verse".

People feel that Indian writing English at the moment is more an illusion than of reality and more a promise and less an achievement. It's too early to pass such a judgment. While dealing with this mass of literature, the Carlylean approach of dealing with the literary biography as a first-phase in tracing literary history is needed but it is not all, for "Indian writing English produced over the last hundred odd years does not reveal a homogenous continuity, but rather a critical cyclical continuity."

The role of a literary historian in tracing this great unwieldy mass of Indian English Literature is a no mean task. The early writers and their immediate demandings followed by the next successive phases and writers before and after Independence present a much too complex picture to analyse. The pioneering efforts of Sreenivasa Iyengar followed by the pursuing efforts of professors like M.K.Naik and C.D. Narasimhaiah in this direction, deserve not only complaints but even commendation.

THE AUTOBIOGRAPHY OF AN UNKNOWN INDIAN

The Autobiography of an Unknown Indian is an autobiographical work of one of the most controversial writers of India -- Nirad C. Chaudhuri, the last imperialist. He wrote this when he was around fifty and records his life from his birth at 1897 in Kishorganj, a small town in present Bangladesh. The book relates his mental and intellectual development, his life and growth at Calcutta, his observations of Vanishing Landmarks, the connotation of this is dual -- changing Indian situation and historical forces that was making exit of British from India an imminent affair.

Nirad, a self-professed Anglophile, is in any situation an explosive proposition and in the book he is at his best in observing as well as observing-at-a-distance and this dual perspective makes it a wonderful reading. His treatment of his childhood, his enchantment, disillusionment and gratitude to the colonial capital Calcutta is highly factual as well as artistic to the extent highly readable.

Arguably, his magnum opus considering his literary output that he could generate as late age as ninety years, Autobiography is not a single book, it is many. Consciously or unconsciously he has left traces of all his erudition, his spirit and learning. Declaring himself a cartographer of learning, the book is also a cartographic evidence of the author's mind and its varied geographies, of the map as well as of the mind.

The dedication of the book runs thus:

To the memory of the British Empire in India,

Which conferred subjecthood upon us,

But withheld citizenship.

To which yet every one of us threw out the challenge:

"Civis Britannicus sum"

Because all that was good and living within us

Was made, shaped and quickened

By the same British rule.

Who's the most authentic of them all? - II

It's perfectly all right to write about people who are not the norm in the society they are placed. One of the thumbrules of good fiction writing is to make interesting things happen to interesting people. Usually, in the effort to make a character interesting, he also becomes unusual (though the real skill of the writer comes out when he makes the usual interesting).

But, but...

With the growing body of IWE writers, one would naturally expect that the subject of writing follows a normal scattered distribution. If some writers are not comfortable using typical characters and settings and rely on the uncommon, then there should be some who should be comfortable. But in actuality, statistics appear to be skewed in favour of the uncommon.

What I mean is that most books by IWE writers are about people who might be interesting as individuals, but do not strike the reader as being typical of a class of people. The character is not representative.

Or at best, he or she may be representative of a niche class. Say, books about bored or repressed housewives: about an individual who can be seen as a symbol for group of people in similar conditions. But there would be few novels dealing with, say, the masses below the poverty line. If at all, the protagonist would be looking at the situation from the outside in. A story seen and told by a person belonging to that strata, facing the problems and concerns that people in that strata face, would be a rarity (I would be glad if someone apprised me of exceptions to this).

Even more so in modern times. Earlier, a Mulk Raj Anand could write a Coolie, or an Untouchable (though there are criticisms that even they weren't truly authentic). These days, hardly anyone even attempts--either due to the lack of a market, or because IWE writers are not capable of writing from such a character's viewpoint.

It is this point which lends maximum credence to M. Prabha's thesis of IWE being the waffle of the toffs. A major reason behind this (as has been discussed before) is that English is not the lingua franca of the country; it is not the language of the masses. This automatically implies their exclusion from IWE, or the absence of authentic IWE writing about the hoi polloi from within.

Another aspect of authenticity to be considered is the bone of contention between the native and the NRI IWE writers. When the NRI tries to be authentic by typifying his Indian setting, he is accused of exoticising. (Vikram Chandra has devoted an essay to this debate.) Writers from both sides need to have a balanced perspective. If a writer describes a cuckoo singing, or the process of making dal, it doesn't necessarily mean he is exoticising. He could honestly be laying out an Indian scene.

At the same time, when Indian keywords like mangoes, curries, tamarind, sarees, and so on populate the titles themselves, the charge of exoticising doesn't sound baseless.

As is the practice, we will not conclude without reaching a conclusion. The question we were grappling with: is Indian Writing in English authentic?

One of our conclusions was authenticity does not depend on numbers. Say, I am an abstruse poet and you are a ragpicker. My problem is not finding the right level of symbolism to portray in my blank verses, and your problem is not finding enough glass bottles in the grabage given the prevalence of plastic these days. I have a problem in my life and so do you. Mine is as real as yours. (Seriousness? Ah, that's another matter. Perhaps the soldier on the Kashmir border has more serious problems than the ragpicker's or the poet's.)

Now if I am the only poet, and there are a ninety-nine other ragpickers, does it make my problem less authentic and the ragpicker's, more? My reality and authenticity is as real and authentic as yours.

Are numbers to be simply ignored, then? Not quite. Consider another analogy. There's a big box. It is divided into two sections, one of them ten times as large as the other. Both the sections are filled with multi-coloured balls. The IWE writer delves into the smaller section and picks out ball after ball, examining and describing each in detail, reching deeper and deeper. The contents of the small section become well known to all.

The big section, ten times bigger, lies untouched and unknown... The IWE writer doesn't reach into it.

The full answer: the IWE writer is authentic in a limited setting.

Mirror, mirror on the wall, who's the most authentic of them all?

Authenticity, we have seen, is the first weapon that comes to hand when one body of writers attacks another. Whether it is regional writers vituperating IWE writers, or native IWE writers criticising the NRI ones, the frontal line of attack is on their authenticity.

It's time to take the bull by the horns. What exactly is this authenticity which results in such a hullabaloo?

Authenticity is about reality; at the same time it is not about realism carried to extremities, describing each and every minute detail as it exists. Reproduction of life exactly as it exists is not art: photography cannot replace painting, nor can a tape recorder replace a singer.

We say a work of fiction is authentic when we feel that what it portrays is likely to have occurred in a certain setting in a certain period. It need not have actually happened as it is described word to word, but there is nothing in the book that precludes the chances of it ever happening. In fiction, the writer tries to portray only the most interesting and eventful things, and characters speak dialogues rich in meaning which bring out their characters and personalities. Certainly, real life will never be that interesting at a stretch.

Authenticity then, lies in the typicality of characters and their lives. How likely is such a fictional character's existence? And if he does, how likely is it that he will talk in such and such a manner, think such and such thoughts and do such and such deeds?

Authenticity is about generalizing and typifying people in a unique way (sounds self-contradictory but therein lies the skill of the writer. Without the uniqueness, we get stereotypes.).

It takes all kinds of people to make the world. A writer can always retort that maybe his character is not all that typical, but what is the guarantee that there is no such person in some corner of the world whose behaviour would be similar to that particular character? Possible, but then that writer gets a low score in authenticity.

If we use the typicality of a work as the measure of its authenticity, then we better know how to measure that typicality. Is it in numbers? If Author A writes about a poet, and Author B writes about a peasant, by dint of sheer numbers Author B always scores over Author A in authenticity (assuming that in India, the number of peasants of the kind as described by Author B will always be much greater than the number of poets of the kind described by Author A).

The question that arises is whether we are caught in a class equation. Are books with intellectual or billionaire protagonists always less authentic than books with the farmer protagonist? Do we give our approval only to socialist fiction that deal with class and society as a whole and not individuals? That is dangerous, and our answer ought to be no.

The core of fiction has to be individualistic. There's nothing unauthentic about having neurotic lonely women protagonists (think Anita Desai) or intellects philosophising in English, Sanskrit and French with equal ease (think Raja Rao) as long as the rest of such character's behaviour falls in line with the personality sketched out for them. The demerit lies in the fact that such a character is atypical; the reader has nothing to judge the character by; everything the author writes about the character has to be accepted by the reader as being typical of that particular character.

For such characters, their problems and concerns are intensely personal. It hardly touches even the fictional world outside the character, leave alone the reader's world.

THE NATIVE VERUS THE NRI WRITER

Seen against the body of regional writers, we considered the body of IWE writers as a unified whole. Peering closer into the latter, we find there exists the boundary between the native writer (meaning IWE writer based in India) and the NRI one (meaning the Non-Resident Indian IWE writer). The divide is yet another facet of the all-pervading issue of authenticity.

What the regional writer wields as a weapon against IWE as a whole, the native IWE writer wields against the NRI. The thrust of his argument is how can someone not living in India write and present authentic stories about India. To the native writer, the NRI writer is as good as a foreigner. He is not aware of the ground-level problems to the extent a person living in that society is. All he gets is information filtered through the media, and he has to make his assumptions and judgments based on that.

The second point of accusation against the NRI writer is that he presents a deliberately erroneous picture of India. He exoticises. Not having a feel for existing realities because of distance is one thing, but creating and contorting a stereotypical "reality" is another. This he does by focussing by and large to the picture of India that already exists in the western mind: progressing from snake-charmers and elephants, to rajahs and maharajahs, arranged marriages, gender oppression, exploitative and casteist society, spices, saris and so on. He panders to the West, and is hence, a sell-out.

He wants to have the best of both worlds: live in the comfort of the West, and present himself as a portrayer of India (that's the only thing he is allowed to portray). When someone has the best of both worlds, there must be something unethical involved.

Notice the strong parallels between the regional v/s the IWE and the native v/s the NRI cases. Just like the regional writer, the native IWE writer considers himself to be on relatively higher moral ground vis-a-vis his proximity to authentic India. He stands in long queues, is compelled to pay bribes to find his way through government offices, knows the inside-out of political developments, and thus knows India first-hand unlike the NRI. Rebuttals by the NRI writers flow in from various fronts. Looking in from the outside enables them to take in the big picture of India. This, they say, is not possible for someone living in the midst of it all. You have to be at a certain distance to make out what is happening in the overall scheme of things, and they are better equipped than the native writer to do this.

He is not a sell-out. He is based abroad (mainly UK, US or Canada) mainly due to business reasons. The bigtime publishers, the markets, the readership, literary agents are there. Publishing is an organized profession there, unlike in India, where things are haphazard. The native writer is against the NRI precisely because he does not enjoy these advantages. In other words, he is plain jealous of the NRI's success.

So the responses also, are almost on the same track as that of IWE writers to the regional writers. Even the commenators. Rushdie's dismissal of Indian vernacular writing finds an echo in Dalrymple's assessment that the future of IWE lies in the hands of the NRI writer.

Our Conclusions?

Again, we have a mixture of truths and untruths. There are few places purely black or white; the world is all the shades of grey. The NRI writer cannot be called a fraud simply because he has a New York or a London or a Montreal address. There is some validity to their claim of an outsider looking in. A writer should be judged by his book, not by his address. If he is not authentic, if he doesn't have a true picture of India in his mind, it will show on the pages of his book. And if he is, that will show too. On the other hand, the accusation of exoticising India also holds true--for some writers.

I am instantly on my guard when I come across titles containing masala, tamarinds, chilis, memsahibs, arranged marriages, cuckoos and saris. It is like putting baseball or stars and stripes in the title to indicate this is a book about USA. In most such cases, you get the feeling of mediocre writers trying to cash in on the publishing fad of exotic India, making hay while the sun shines, so to speak. For a writer serious about his claim to fame and wealth, it makes good sense to be based in the West; the route to being published there is easier, or at least, more organized. A book well-received in the US or UK, is almost certain to do well in India, but the vice versa is not true.

A true writer will sound true no matter where he is based. Amitav Ghosh, Amit Chaudhuri or Vikram Seth are never blamed of exoticising because they don't. Lesser writers do. While every NRI writer cannot be a fake, neither is it true that none of them are. But it takes an exceptional writer to be based abroad and yet sound true. The onus of proving their authenticity seems to lie with the NRI rather than the native writer as if by virtue of being native, he is automatically authentic.

Back again to the minefield of authenticity. Next time, we will gingerly step into that minefield.

Regional Literature versus IWE

In the last couple of posts, we saw authenticity (call it realism or genuineness if you will) as a millstone that IWE has to carry around its neck wherever it goes. We also touched upon a few topics with authenticity at the heart of the issue : regional or vernacular writing v/s IWE (the topic of the current discussion), Indian IWE v/s NRI IWE writer, and what is authenticity actually.

It looks like there has to be a "versus" in the relationship between regional writing and IWE. Using an innocent conjunction like "and" would probably give an incorrect picture. To reiterate our conclusions from previous discussions, the English language enjoys (or suffers) a different status with respect to India's regional languages. And that different status is primarily due to the none-too-flattering inter-related tags of colonialism and elitism.

This otherness of English creates a state of friction instead of cohesion in the body of Indian writing as a whole. We are compelled to say "Indian Writing in English", but we sound ridiculous saying "Indian Writing in Hindi or Bengali". The status of these regional languages as Indian is unquestionable, while that of English continues to be questioned (mostly in nationalist rhetoric. Practically, English seems to be entrenched firmly in India for a long, long time to come.)

Officially, India has twenty-odd recognized national languages which more or less map to individual states (whether dividing the nation into states on a linguistic basis was a sound idea is an argument that has kept many a people awake all night). There are around 2000 dialects, so talking about literatures in terms of dialects is absurd. Regional literature thus refers to writing in those twenty-odd national languages.

From the perspective of regional writers, their writing is rooted to Indian realities, and hence much more authentic when compared to IWE. Their problems are essentially Indian, the settings Indian, and their characters talk in the same language as they would if they were real. Their works (many serialized through periodicials) are immediately accessible and open to appraisal by readers who can judge its authenticity at once (and thus decide a writer's success).

This claim of regional writers is irrefutable. IWE, as we saw, is twice-born fiction, while vernacular writing is once-born. There's not much an IWE writer can do setting things right here because this weakness is inherent in IWE; it's bigger than an individual writer.

The other charge of regional writers against IWE is that the big money and publicity accompanying English writing is strangling regional writing. Glamour and limelight is the lot of the IWE writer (underservedly), while obscurity (except within a state) and almost no money to speak of is the fate of the regional writer. (If writing is an art and has nothing to do with material success, then regional writers have nothing to complain of on this count!)

This again is a charge IWE writers can't do much about (apart from refusing his share of fame, which doesn't really help anyone). Publicity and big money come to an IWE writer only if he is backed by a reputed publishing house in the US/UK. Those IWE writers depending on only an Indian readership hardly earn anything as the English readership in India is minuscule (a sale of 5000 copies implies a bestseller). The big numbers (and money) come from a worldwide readership.

For the regional writers, their readership starts and ends with the people who speak that particular language: geographically limited to one or a few states of India at the most. There are simply are not enough numbers that can bring about big money-publicity-glamour et al.

IWE writers bristle at the accusation that they are not authentic enough, but the range of Indian subjects they can portray realistically is limited. Some IWE writers like Rushdie dismiss vernacular literature as having little value and widen the chasm between the two bodies.

As both the charges--lack of authenticity and profusion of wealth and fame in IWE--don't have a feasible solution (at least I can't think of any... unless India becomes an English-speaking country, or regional languages gain a worldwide readership), the chasm is likely to remain. It is unlikely that both IWE and regional literature will be clubbed in a seamless category of Indian literature. IWE will continue to be looked upon as a bastard child of Indian literature (regional literature being the legitimate offspring), a wealthy, pompous and snobbish bastard at that.

Dream within a Dream - II

Carrying on with the discussion on whether IWE makes sense.

The English language in India carries with it a connotation of elitism, as opposed to native languages which are seen as being down to earth, belonging to the people proper. Or as opposed to French literature in France, or English in America, which are the native languages in those nations. Perhaps French spoken in the Czar's court in Russia, or the use of Italian in operas in Germany in the past had a similar tag of elitism that English has in India today.

The English-speaking population in India has grown since, say, the era of Independence, and it is certainly not as exclusivist today as it was then. But the English language has a terribly long way to go before it reaches the acceptance-level of another British legacy: cricket. Seen objectively, both English and cricket are imports of the Raj. Then why should one have a colonial taint attached to it (indeed many movements in India have viewed the continued use of English post-Independence as a continuation of mental slavery), while the other has practically replaced the national game of hockey, is baffling. (And one would think that the knowledge of English has done more for India than the pursuit of cricket.)

No IWE writer can ever dream of approaching Sachin Tendulkar's iconic status. But then writing could hardly have the mass appeal that cricket has. And writing in English, impossible. The point to note is that Sachin's cricketing genius makes him a national hero, but an IWE writer, however great he is, will carry an elitist tag with him, maybe even one of pandering to foreign tastes.

The vernacular writer thus, considers himself, closer to reality and hence more authentic than the IWE writer. (IWE versus the vernacular writer will be a separate topic for discussion later.) The IWE writer based in India considers himself more authentic than the NRI IWE writer. (India-based versus NRI IWE writers is another topic too!)

According to an extreme criticism of IWE in Waffle of the Toffs (the title says it all, a rough and alliterative translation of which reads: the pointless prattle of pretentious people), only those belonging to the poorer strata of society are fit to write the real stuff (what is real for whom is--you guessed it--another topic). In India, an IWE writer is almost certain not to belong to that strata, and as a corollary, no one in that strata will write in English. So whatever is a genuine subject for literature, can never get written in English in India. That's the extreme stand.

Fictive writing, as everybody knows, is not real. The tacit understanding between a writer and a reader is that the writer has created a dream, and the reader lives that dream as if it were real, though knowing fully well that it is not. (We don't really believe Amitabh Bachchan beating up a dozen armed baddies, do we?) This agreement is termed the "willing suspension of disbelief". The writer's part of the contract is that he will make the dream as real as he possibly can.

And when the IWE writer's Indian characters all talk and think in English, he is asking the reader for another indulgence, for a higher degree of suspension of disbelief. The reader needs to accept that not only are the characters and their story real, but also their language. That's why IWE is also called twice-born fiction, or a dream within a dream (some also call it the waffle of the toffs).

So where does all this discussion lead? The question we started with still hangs fire. Does IWE make sense?

Such a subjective question merits a subjective conclusion too; a simple true/false answer is incomplete. It is true that IWE suffers from handicaps that other literatures don't. The IWE writer has to labour under additional constraints, work doubly hard or take recourse to literary sleight of hand in order to maintain an air of authenticity. A few modern writers like Rushdie recognize that traditionally realistic IWE is not possible, and hence instead of creating a semblance of reality, deliberately make their fiction as fantastic as possible (so that the reader is compelled to follow only the rules the writer lays down).

One cannot deny that IWE has an extra layer of artificiality built within it. This is not due to the inadequacies of IWE writers, but a congenital weakness. The reader of fiction is fully aware that he is sharing a dream, living within a bubble, while he is reading a novel. Does it then matter, whether that bubble is inside another bubble?

If a reader is strict about having only one bubbly layer between him and the world, then IWE does not make sense to him. If another reader considers a two-layered bubble as good as a single-layered one, then IWE makes sense to him. Ultimately, it is upto the reader to decide whether he wants to carry on with his dream, or burst the bubble. He could dismiss fiction in any genre or form as unreal if he were that strict... and find pleasure in reading only newspapers.

IWE: Dream within a Dream?

Does IWE make sense? Why this doubt that questions the very foundation of the whole edifice? Nobody asks such a question of British or American literature, or for that matter even Tamil literature. Then why single out IWE?

One fault line runs through the foundation of IWE, but is absent among other literatures. (Perhaps it exists in other colonial literatures, especially of the sub-continent. I don't know the situation in Africa.)

The fault line's name is authenticity. The starting point of most critics of IWE is its authenticity. Authenticity of a work, as I understand, is its closeness to reality, or its truthfulness in the represenation of a ground reality. Usually, such fidelity is expected only from realistic literary fiction (other genre fiction such as sci-fi, fantasy, romance, mystery, etc. do not make claims about realism). As there is hardly any genre fiction in IWE, the question of IWE's authenticity is legitimate.

There are mainly two lines of questioning:

- How representative are the writers and their subjects?
- How representative is English as the medium of writing?

Writers and subjects: The major accusation against writers of IWE is that they are elitist. They are said to live in ivory towers cut-off from ground realities, and what is worse, they don't really care about being cut-off. The only reality they know is that which exists in their high circles, but which constitutes at best a minuscule fraction of the populace.

As a result, even when they do write about issues that affect the masses, it is already a second-hand experience to them (filtered through the glasses of the media or elsewhere), and percolates to the reader at third-hand.

Even a renowned writer like Mulk Raj Anand whose novels deal with social issues of caste inequality and untouchability is not writing about what he has gone through or seen, but what he thinks must have been happening in a strata of society isolated from his own.

The (modern) writers don't care, the accusations continue, because they are busy exoticising their subject to appeal to a Western readership (only a large Western readership can translate into large sales).

If not exoticising, if a writer is honest about writing what he can relate to, then he ends up writing about characters whose individual concerns can only belong to an exclusive society. A possible example could be Anita Desai.

An IWE writer writes from the outside trying to look in; seldom does he write from the inside trying to reach out.

English as Medium: The English-speaking fraction of the population is a pretty small number (I will desist from providing statistical sounding figures like 2.45%). English readership consequently, would be a fraction of that pretty small number, and English writers a fraction of that fraction. So if we are talking of the representativeness of IWE in India, it must be clear where we stand. Forget writing, even reading or speaking English in India puts one in an elite club.

A charge of elitism can be argued against, but what is undeniable is that the moment you put an English-speaking character on a page, you are asking the reader for a lot. It is a daunting task to make such a character believable. A writer is faced with limited choices:

1. For the utmost seriousness and authenticity, use characters who are fluent in English. That means, you are bound to give up on any kind of representativeness.
2. Try to be more inclusive of the other strata of society by using characters who are not fluent in English. But you cannot show characters talking in the vernacular in an English novel (not for pages, surely). So you perhaps differentiate by showing the difference in fluency, but using broken English for long usually results in caricature and loses seriousness.
3. Not much choice is left. If you want both representativeness and seriousness, then you will have to rely on narrative description for characterization.

More of telling, than showing. That's one reason you will find most IWE writers making abundant use of description, but miserly in using dialogue (unless it is the "non-representative" novel).

What is IWE

Cramming a definition from a textbook of which you don't understand half the terms is one thing, and coming up with your own definition is another.

The objective here is to come up with some criteria, or a set of rules with minimal haziness, to judge what is IWE and what is not. This definitiveness is needed to avoid applying this term haphazardly and inconsistently to all and sundry. More important is the need to bring some structure and organization to the study of this emerging corpus of writing.

The set of words Indian Writing in English sounds innocent enough; at least you don't have to try to explain words like antidisestablishmentarianism. Ignoring the preposition "in" (which even Google ignores while searching), you have three words left: Indian, writing, and English.

Let's read them right to left (rather an Arabic than an English way to go about it). (All right, let me confess right at the outset, before it becomes obvious, that I am partial to parentheses. I can't indulge in them while writing fiction, being the equivalent of the archaic "asides" in plays, but I do mean to indulge myself on this blog. Parentheses help you in making smart alec comments.)

English

- This should be simple and self-explanatory. Any writing originally in English automatically qualifies to become a superset for IWE (confession #2: I am an engineer by background, so mathematical terms tend to creep into my writing surreptitiously.)
- Translations from any other language into English do not count, unless the translation is also done by the original author himself (I am not going to beat myself

into a frenzy replacing every "him" with a "her" in order to sound politically correct. When I say "him" it means "him", "her" and even "it" if you please.)

That means, bilingual writers like Kamala Das or Kiran Nagarkar belong to IWE. At least that part of their oeuvre written in or translated to English belongs to IWE, while someone like Premchand whose works have been translated to English will not, because he wrote only in Hindi. (Nothing disparaging against regional languages is to be inferred from this. IWE versus IW in the vernacular will be discussed later.)

Writing

- The primary rule is that literature is the sole constituent of IWE. So this excludes technical or scientific writing, or news reporting and journalisting writing, or management, spiritual and chicken-soup inspirational writing. IWE then consists of all writings in prose (plays included) or verse, particularly those of an imaginative character.

What about non-fiction, like half the works of V. S. Naipaul, or the socio-political essays of Arundhati Roy? There is subjectivity in play here, and a stand needs to be taken.

Leeway is given to writers who write in both fiction and non-fiction forms, and if they are known primarily as writers, and not through any other profession. So V. S. Naipaul and Arundhati Roy (treading a fine line, writing only essays after The God of Small Things, but well, a Booker winner is a Booker winner) come under IWE, but Amartya Sen, renowned as an economist, will not qualify for IWE via The Argumentative Indian (unless he writes a novel or a book of poetry!). Neither does Sunil Gavaskar for his Sunny Days.

Indian: The most subjective of the three. What does Indian in IWE stand for? Does it refer to a person from India (akin to a Frenchman, or an Englishman) who writes in English, or does it refer to the cultural aspect of India (Indian writing, akin to French cuisine, or the British stiff upper lip) in the sense that IWE is writing about India? Is this ambiguity purposeful or unintentional? Or is this an exercise in hair-splitting? Whether by design or by accident, the ambiguity turns out to be useful because we will rely on both the possible interpretations to formulate our rule.

The Writer as an Indian: OK, this is going to break open a 5-litre jerrycan of worms. How do you define an Indian writer?

The answer is straightforward if the writer is an Indian by birth, and is/was an Indian citizen based in India. Unfortunately, perhaps less than half of IWE writers can be classified as easily as say, R. K. Narayan or Mulk Raj Anand. Many of the well-known IWE writers are based abroad, mainly in USA, UK or Canada.

There could be any number of permutations: whether a writer is holding an Indian citizenship, or has relinquished it; whether he is an Indian by origin, but not by birth; by birth and not by origin (?); Indian family but living abroad for generations; parents of mixed nationalities, ad nauseum. Tracking and classifying writers based on these myriad factors would be on the same scale of cleaning the Augean stables.

So instead of trying to unravel the nuances of NRI-ship, we adopt a simple and easily deterministic approach: that of race. This approach could be on the verge of political incorrectness, but there is some factor that links Rabindranath Tagore, Salman Rushdie and Nissim Ezekiel (as disparate a group as can be) but excludes Rudyard Kipling (in spite of the Indian setting of his works).

And that distinguishing factor is what we use to determine whether a writer is Indian or not. For this reason, we will not call William Dalrymple's White Mughals or E. M. Forster's A Passage to India as part of IWE.

In the odd case where the writer's parentage is of mixed nationalities, the subject of that writer's works will decide the issue of Indian-ness. For instance, if a particular writer is a second- or third-generation American-Indian, and yet writes about his feeling of being caught in a cross-cultural divide, of living as an outsider, then that writer belongs to IWE. If, otherwise, his writing has nothing to do with India, then he does not belong to IWE.

The Writing as Indian: The cultural aspect is relatively easy to judge. Almost all India-based writers' theme is India Also of those who are based abroad and whose Indian origin is not that apparent. If it were not, they would not qualify to be called IWE writers in the first place. I cannot think of anyone based in India whose subject is never India. Writers like Vikram Seth and Amitav Ghosh are at ease in international settings, but they also have many works with a purely Indian setting. It isn't unheard of, for an IWE writer to claim he does not want to be pigeonholed in a category called IWE. He belongs to the globalized world, he says; judging him as part of IWE smacks of provincialism. If a writer is truly global, then he doesn't have to depend on an Indian theme to set him apart from other writers. To extract your themes from India, and depend on your view of Indian-ness to set you apart from other writers, and then claim you are not part of IWE is hypocritical As far as we are concerned, we don't give two hoots whether a writer wishes to be included in IWE or not, as long as he meets our criteria.

Circle of Fame: Yes, there is a fourth point to consider too, possibly trivial, but it needs to be stated. We have formulated rules for language, literature, nationality and culture. Suppose a writer qualifies in all of them, does he then automatically become a part of IWE? What if nobody has heard of him?

Obviously, all men are not equal. All writers, even less so. To quote the immortal Bard, "Some are born great, some achieve greatness, and some have greatness thrust upon them." Appending to it, "some have greatness withheld from them, while some achieve it posthumously."

One definition for literature is that it should be permanent; it should stand the test of time. The writer himself may fade away, but he should live through his works. Few writers achieve that kind of immortality, and if that criterion is strictly applied to IWE, hardly a handful would qualify.

The extent of fame, again, is a subjective issue. It is perhaps unfair to apply the condition of international fame for IWE. National fame should suffice. The writer and his work should have a reasonable number of references in newspapers and magazines (usually showing up on Google). Writers like Arun Joshi or Rama Mehta, who were active before the age of book promos, but won major literary awards like the Sahitya Akademi, and are critically mentioned, definitely merit inclusion in IWE. Of course the conditions are loaded in favour of the current crop of writers in this age of publicity and information. Equally meritorious writers of earlier years run the risk of getting excluded simply due to lack of information, but the only option is to live with it.

Self- or vanity-published unknown writers will not be considered. Fame is not always a manifestation of talent; examples abound of unworthy writers becoming world famous while great writers are swallowed by obscurity. Yet, in the overall scheme of things, it is reasonable to expect a talented writer to be recognized by and by. As for those untalented hacks who have greatness thrust upon them... well, nobody said we live in a fair world.

8

INDIANS WRITING IN ENGLISH

The greatest gift of the British Raj to the Indian Subcontinent was probably the English language and its rich, varied literature. During the British regime, Indians (natives) ves had to learn the language for the purpose of education as well as to earn their livelihood by securing a government job. The Indian intelligentsia and men (also women) of letters who had sufficient mastery over the language, thought differently. They tried their hand at poetry, prose and fiction. It was a unique combination: The Indian litterateurs describing their environs and social milieu in a strange language that belonged to a faraway land As part of the Indians' interactions with the Europeans, and the British, individuals from the affluent classes went abroad for their education, married foreign women, spoke English better than their mother tongues, lived in and toured the Continent, several times. Their progeny enjoyed tremendous advantage both in terms of exposure and language skills.

Nirad. C. Chaudhuri (1897 - 1999) devoted his life to study India's relationship with Britain. Chaudhuri gained critical acclaim and was one of the most successful writers of Indian origin, in English. His remarkable Bengali prose pieces were "Atmoghaati Bangali" (Suicidal Bengali) and "Bangali Jivone Ramani" (Women in Bengali Life). A conservative at heart, he eulogized the 19th century Britain, for which he was derided on many occasions by Indian critics. He was a fellow of the Royal Literary society of England and was conferred an Honorary Commander of the British Empire (CBE) by the Queen. He was also presented with Honorary degree of Doctor of Letters by both Oxford and Stirling (in Scotland) universities. His other famous literary works are Continent of Circe, Three Horsemen in the New Apocalypse and Autobiography of an Unknown Indian (his own). At the age of 90 he added another volume in his autobiography, "Thy Hand, Great Anarch".

R. K Narayan (1906 - 2001) this patriarch of Indian literature in English highlighted the imaginary little town of Malgudi- a microcosm of life in southern India, during the early 20th century. The most outstanding of all the characters, portrayed by Narayan is the little Swaminathan-so full of mischief and yet aspiring to make it big, someday.

Mulk Raj Anand (1905 - 2004) hailed as the Munshi Premchand of Indian English writing, vividly and powerfully depicts the sordid lives of the lowest strata of the society in his novels, viz Coolie, The Untouchable etc.

Kamala Markandaya (1924 - 2004) is best remembered for her novel Nectar in a Sieve, published in early 50s. It is a touching account of the life of an Indian peasant woman, Rukmani, her struggle for survival and her abiding love for her husband. They also reflect the changing times and society.

Nayantara Sehgal (1927 -) from the famous Nehru clan is a feminist writer, advocating women's emancipation. She is a child of the tradition, where the women are deified as an epitome of power (Shakti). Her novels try to highlight the independent existence of women and their efforts to thwart attempts to isolate them from the centre-stage of human existence.

Anita Desai's (1937 -) works appearing in the 60's are aptly classified under Post-colonial literature. Published more than a decade after Markandaya, her Voices of the City is a story about three siblings, and their divergent viewpoints on life in Calcutta. Fire on the Mountain, set in Kasauli, focuses on three women and their complex experiences in life.

About the same time, faraway in the islands of Trinidad & Tobago, V. S. Naipaul (1932 -) a writer of Indian descent, started writing prolifically eventually bagging a Nobel, years later, for his literary masterpieces. He deals with specific themes:

the loss of home in Post-colonial Britain, the loss of the past that is a consequence of these forced migrations, and the yawning void that still remains behind. The Mystic Masseur, The Suffrage of Elvira and A House for Mr. Biswas are widely read.

Shashi Deshpande (1938 -) hails from Karnataka. A journalist by profession, she started at a very early age, publishing her first short story in 1970. To start with her stories were published in magazines like "Femina", "Eve's Weekly", etc. "Legacy" her first collection of short stories was published in 1978, followed by her first novel, "The Dark Holds No Terrors" in 1980. She is a winner of the Sahitya Akademi Award for the novel, "That Long Silence."

Sasthibrata (1939 -) appeared on the Indian literary scene in the late 1960's with My God Died Young, an autobiography. Its unassuming style and youthful angst addressed an entire generation, and the book was an instant success. In this explicit and irreverent autobiography, Sasthibrata mainly deals with the social milieu he was born into, the experiences which left him shattered and disillusioned and isolated. Alternately tender and brutal, he exposes the double standards and hypocrisies of the tradition-bound society in India as well as in the West with his no-holds-barred honesty and astonishing insight and understanding.

Bharati Mukherjee (1940 -) who describes herself as an American of Bengali Indian origin too falls in this cadre. She deals with the themes of the Asian immigrants in North America, and the change taking pace in South Asian Women in a new World. The Tiger's Daughter, Jasmine and The Wife are her landmarks.

Though fictional works will remain forever popular; the reading trends today have slightly tilted towards non-fiction. There is of course no dearth of eminent writers in this category. If we go back a little, we find how in the 60s Gita Mehta (1943 -) based her creative writing on the theme of the country's struggle for freedom and finally the achievement of freedom independence, as is evident in Snakes and Ladders , Karma Cola and many more...

Salman Rushdie (1947 -) one of the numerous "Midnight's Children" (Those who were born at midnight of 14th August 1947) has suitably captured this epoch-making incident in his novel "Midnight's Children". His controversial novel The Satanic Verses won him a death warrant from the global Islamic community, if not anything else. Other famous books by him include The Moor's Last Sigh, and The Ground Beneath Her Feet. Rushdie's novels are replete with symbolism, powerful imagery, allegory and a vivid narrative style. The language is a trifle queer with Hindi words phrases and colloquial expressions smoothly incorporated into English.

Shobha De (1947 -) writes racy thrillers, with urban India as their backdrop and these are invariably bestsellers. The erotic content of her novels has been somewhat controversial, with some reviewers being contemptuous of her work while others feel that she is blowing away the taboos adhered to, by many women writers. Her novels include Starry Nights, Sisters, Socialite Evenings, to name a few. The speeding up of the sexual revolution in India with her sensuous novels and Western outlook may largely be attributed to her.

Uma Vasudev joined the bandwagon of non-fictional writers with her three exhaustive biographies of Smt. Indira Gandhi- Courage under Fire, Revolution in Restraint and Two Faces of Indira Gandhi. However she also has two novels - Shreya of Sonagarh and The Story of Anusuya to her credit.

In the writing of Vikram Seth (1952 -) whose famous novels include The Golden Gate, A Suitable Boy and An Equal Music, we find a reflection of the post-independent, contemporary life, that we ourselves are a part of. Seth's profound knowledge of western classical music, his romanticism, his welter of emotions, all come through very effectively.

Shama Futehally (1952 - 2004) was an academician by profession. She lived in Mumbai, Ahmedabad and finally Delhi. She has two anthologies of short stories to her credit, and her first novel, Tara Lane, won great critical acclaim. Her other novel Reaching Bombay Central is written with astonishing economy; it is an elegant and heart-warming novel. In pared down, poetic prose, Shama writes about the fears and hopes of an individual life which bring into sharp focus the larger realities of contemporary India.

Manjula Padmanabhan (1953 -) is an author playwright and artist. Her books include "Hot Death, Cold Soup" (1996), a collection of short stories and "Getting There" (1999) a travel memoir. "Harvest", her fifth play, won first prize in the 1997 Onassis Prize (The foundation has its headquarters in Greece) for theatre. "Kleptomania" (2004), a collection of short stories, was published in 2004. She has illustrated 23 books for children including, most her own two novels for children, "Mouse Attack" and "Mouse Invaders".

Gita Hariharan (1954 -) is a journalist by profession and based in New Delhi. Her first book, The Thousand Faces of Night won the Commonwealth Prize for the best first novel. Her other works include The Art of Dying (a collection of stories), The Ghosts of Vasu Master, When Dreams Travel (both novels) A Southern Harvest and In Times of Siege. She has also co-edited Sorry, Best Friend, a collection of stories for children.

Manju Kapur is a professor of English at the prestigious Miranda House in Delhi. Her first novel, Difficult Daughters, received the Commonwealth Award for the Eurasian region. The book is set during India's independence struggle and is partially based on the life and experiences of the author's own mother. Her other novel A Married Woman is a seductive story of love, set at a time of political and religious upheaval within the country. Narrated with sympathy and intelligence, it is the story of an artist whose canvas challenges the constraints of middle-class existence.

Indian born Amitav Ghosh (1956 -) demonstrates the blend and interstitial nature of diverse cultures, in his writings. Ghosh has already bagged several prestigious awards for his works. Some of these awards are Prix Medicis Etranger for The Circle of Reason (1986), the Sahitya Akademi Award for The Shadow Lines (1988), the Arthur C. Clarke Prize for science fiction for The Calcutta Chromosome (1996), the Pushcart Prize for his essay, "The March of the Novel through History: My Father's Bookcase".

Dr. Shashi Tharoor (1956 -) is the celebrated, award-winning author of several novels, as well as hundreds of articles in reputed international publications like The New York Times, the Washington Post, the Los Angeles Times, the International Herald Tribune, Time, Newsweek and The Times of India. His most famous work is The Great Indian Novel (1989) which is included in various curricula as a fine example of post-colonial literature; Riot (2001), a searing examination of Hindu-Muslim violence in contemporary India, and Show Business (1992) which received a front-page accolade in the New York Times Book Review, and has since been made into a motion picture, "Bollywood". Shashi Tharoor's books have been translated into French, German, Italian, Malayalam, Marathi, Polish, Romanian, Russian and Spanish.

Chitra Bannerjee Divakaruni (1956 -) s works are partly autobiographical, with most plots set in the Bay Area of California (where she lives). She also deals with the immigrant experience, an important issue in the contemporary world. Arranged Marriage is a collection of short stories, about women from India caught between two worlds. The protagonist of The Mistress of Spices, Tilo, provides spices, not only for cooking, but also for the homesickness and alienation of the Indian immigrant clients d frequenting her shop. She writes to unite people, fiercely breaking down all kinds of barriers.

Delhi-based bureaucrat Upamanyu Chatterji (1959 -) made his debut on the Indian literary scenario with his novel "English August-An Indian Story" centering on the bizarre experiences of a young IAS officer, who is sent to the remote, nondescript town of Madna, for training. The language is colloquial Indian English with generous dosages of Hinglish.

Pico Iyer (1957 -) based in the U.K and the U.S.A is one of the most revered and respected travel writers today. His essays, reviews, and other writings have appeared in Time, Conde Nast Traveler, Harper's, the New Yorker, Sports Illustrated, and Salon.com. His books include Video Night in

Kathmandu, The Lady and the Monk, Cuba and the Night, Falling off the Map, Tropical Classical, and The Global Soul. These have been translated into several languages and published across several continents.

Arundhati Roy (1960 -) whose God of Small Things fetched her the prestigious Booker, probes deep into the obscure, insignificant, inconsequential things in our mundane world.

Jhumpa Lahiri (1967 -) the Bostonian, is a true-blue Bengali. In spite of having lived all her life in the U.K and the USA, she knows the subtle nuances of typical Bengali life and culture, like the back of her hand. While her Pulitzer- winning collection of stories Interpreter of Maladies is mainly based on her experiences in Kolkata, her novel Namesake powerfully depicts the angst, the disillusionment of the Bengali immigrants to the US, whose children grow up rootless - aliens to the culture of their country of origin, not completely comfortable in the society in which they actually live.

Hari Kunzru (1969 -) is a young author of English and Kashmiri descent, who shot into fame with his novels The Impressionist and Transmission. Having grown up in Essex, he studied English at Wadham College, Oxford University, then gained an MA in Philosophy and Literature from Warwick University.He has worked as a travel journalist since 1998, writing for such newspapers as The Guardian and The Daily Telegraph, and Time Out magazine. He has also published a short story collection "Noise". Moreover Kunzru was named by Granta magazine as one of twenty 'Best of Young British Novelists'.

Kiran Desai (1971 -), currently based in the U.K is the daughter of a celebrated mother, author Anita Desai. Her first novel Hullabaloo in the Guava Orchard, was published in 1998 and won appreciation from renowned literary figures including Salman Rushdie. It also won the Betty Trask Award, presented by the Society of Authors for the best new novels by citizens of Commonwealth of Nations under 35. Her second book The "Inheritance of Loss" published in 2006, has already won wide acclaim throughout Asia, Europe and the United States and won the 2006 Booker Prize.

AMITAV GHOSH

Amitav Ghosh is one of the most widely known Indians writing in English today. His books include The Circle of Reason, The Shadow Lines, In An Antique Land, Dancing in Cambodia, The Calcutta Chromosome, and most recently, The Glass Palace.

Amitav Ghosh was born in Calcutta in 1956. He studied at St. Stephens College, Delhi; St. Edmund Hall, Oxford; and the Faculty of Arts, University of Alexandria. He worked for the Indian Express newspaper in New Delhi and he earned his doctorate in Oxford before he wrote his first novel.

The Circle of Reason won the Prix Medici Etranger, one of France's top literary awards, and The Shadow Lines won the Sahitya Akademi Award , India's most prestigious literary prize.

The Calcutta Chromosome won the Arthur C. Clarke Award for 1997 and The Glass Palace won the Grand Prize for Fiction at the Frankfurt International e-Book Awards in 2001.

Amitav Ghosh was the winner of the 1999 Pushcart Prize, a leading literary award, for an essay that was published in the Kenyon Review.

He lives with his wife, Deborah Baker and their children, in Brooklyn, USA.

Synopsis : In between the sea and the plains of Bengal, on the easternmost coast of India, lies an immense archipelago of islands. Some of these islands are vast and some no larger than sandbars; some have lasted through recorded history while others have just washed into being. These are the Sundarbans - the beautiful lands. Here there are no borders to divide fresh water from salt, river from sea, even land from water.

The tides reach more than two hundred miles inland, and every day thousands of acres of mangrove forest disappear only to re-emerge hours later. For hundreds of years, only the truly dispossessed and the hopeless dreamers of the world have braved the man eaters and the crocodiles who rule there, to eke a precarious existence from the unyielding mud.

The settlers of the Sundarbans believe that anyone who dares venture into the vast watery labyrinth without a pure heart, will never return. It is the arrival of Piyali Roy, of Indian parentage but stubbornly American, and Kanai Dutt, a sophisticated Delhi businessman, that disturbs the delicate balance of settlement life and sets in motion a fateful cataclysm. Kanai has come to visit his widowed aunt and to review some writings left behind by her husband, a political radical who died mysteriously in the aftermath of a local uprising. He meets Piya on the train from Calcutta and learns she has come to the Sundarbans in search of a rare species of river dolphin. When she hires Fokir, an illiterate, yet proud local fisherman to guide her through the mazelike backwaters, Kanai becomes her translator. From this moment, the tide begins to turn.

Amitav Ghosh has discovered yet another new territory, summoning a singular place from its history, language and myth and bringing it to life. Yet the achievement of The Hungry Tide is in its exploration of a far darker and more unknowable jungle, the human heart. It is a novel that asks at every turn: what danger resides there, and what delusion? What man can take the true measure of another?

The Hungry Tide is a whirlwind work of the imagination, every bit as epic in scope and ambition as his beloved and bestselling work, The Glass Palace.

IMAM AND THE INDIAN

There are about seven-eight essays that hinge around Amitav Ghosh's experiences in Egypt as researcher in early 80s. The title essay "The Imam and the Indian" brings out the pathos of two "superceded civilizations" - one of ancient Egypt and other of India - "vying with each other to lay claim to the violence of the West." In "The Relations of Envy in an Egyptian Village," Ghosh, like an astute anthropologist, works out the relation of Evil Eye practices with conditions of production in rural economy of Egypt. In another essay, "Categories of Labour and the Orientation of the Fellah Economy," the notion of labour as mere performance of a technically necessary technical function is dispensed with. Ghosh investigates into the history and metaphysics of labour as it manifests itself in various forms in rural set-up. These essays are more or less corollaries to the writer's travelogue entitled In An Antique Land (1992)- an account of Egypt, which is reckoned most authentic even by the Egyptians themselves. Its in these essays that Amitav Ghosh approximates Clifford Geertz ideal of 'author as anthropologist.'

Amitav Ghosh is not a professional academic critic, yet at times he is simply impelled to write about writers that overwhelm him. The essay on Agha Shahid Ali's poetry, "The Ghat of the Only World," is lyrical and analytical at the same time; it is obituary and critique at one go. Another highlight of Amitav's critical methodology is the simultaneous presence of various timeframes and cultural contexts that he employs to understand the implications of a work of art in the larger civic context. Ghosh has the flexibility to invoke Cervantes to understand Babar's Babur-nama. He has the range to discuss writers as different as Michael Ondaatje, Agha Shahid Ali, Shyam Sevadorai in the larger context of civil strife and ethnic violence all across the subcontinent.

Spice-encounter at the beginning of the colonial period becomes a cultural correlative of Oil-Encounter in 70s. But despite all his anthropological, academic and activist predilections, it is ultimately Amitav Ghosh, the writer of fine literary sensibili who excels. A rural landscape is described thus: "a maze of low mud huts huddled together like confectionery on a tray." The singing of the bride is likened to the "the bloom of pomegranate." "An Egyptian in Baghdad" is more a tragic short story of Egyptian migrants to Iraq who send money towards the building of their pucka houses back home but never come back to occupy them. "The Slave of MS.H6" has the trappings of an anthropological detective fiction. The essays which deal with the ethnography of the UN peacekeeping force in Combodia, the non-institutional character of Indian diaspora, the fundamentalist challenge in the Post-Cold War period are equally remarkable for their analytical rigour and poetical vigour. The self-critical, perceptive title essay relates an incident from his time doing fieldwork in Egypt. He argues with an intolerant village imam over the relative merits of cremating the dead, as Indian Hindus do, and the Egyptian Muslim practice of burying them. The imam calls the Hindu custom "primitive" and argues that the "advanced" West doesn't burn dead bodies.

Ghosh, soon incensed, lashes out, saying that even Western countries burn their dead: "They have special electric furnaces meant just for that." Both sides are stung. The imam accuses Ghosh of lying, with the logic that the West cannot be so ignorant, as they "have guns, tanks and bombs". Ghosh retorts that India not only has those heavy armaments but also nuclear weapons: a response that shocks Ghosh himself. "So there we were," Ghosh concludes, "the imam and I, delegates from two superseded civilizations vying to lay claim to the violence of the West." This subtle, all encompassing worldview is vintage Ghosh. His historian's eye takes in the breadth of peoples' experiences, and his anthropologist's mind makes connections between their religions, wars, cultures and ways of life. Above all, he describes these complex connections with simple profundity - with the skill of the novelist that he is.

Ghosh can be jocular, too, without being trite. His essay "Four Corners" about a road trip in the US illustrates his keen observational powers and ability to relate the commonplace to history. America's recreational vehicles (RVs), are, in his words, "if not quite palaces, then certainly midtown condos on wheels". He notices their curious names, Native American words like Winnebago and Itasca. "The names of the dispossessed tribes of the Americas hold a peculiar allure for marketing executives of automobile companies. Pontiac, Cherokee - so many tribes are commemorated in modes of transport," Ghosh observes. And then, as always, the summing up: "It is not a mere matter of fashion that so many of the cars that flash past on the highways carry those names, breathing them into the air like the inscriptions on prayer wheels. This tradition of naming has a long provenance: Did not Kit Carson himself, the scourge of the Navajo, name his favorite horse Apache?" Why doesn't Ghosh come off as a know-it-all? With disarming frankness, he acknowledges that he doesn't have all the answers, or even explanations, for the fascinating quirks of culture he describes.

In a short essay about a New York fundraising party for Tibet, for instance, Ghosh confesses that as an undergraduate, he and his friends would get drunk when they went to eat Tibetan food at a Tibetan refugee camp in Delhi. "You couldn?t help doing so - it was hard to be in the presence of so terrible a displacement." As Ghosh muses thus in the trendy Manhattan restaurant, he catches the eye of the sole monk at the gathering and finds that "... his smile seemed a little guilty: the hospitality of a poor nation must have seemed dispensable compared to the charity of a rich one."

Or perhaps he was merely bewildered, Ghosh continues. "It cannot be easy to celebrate the commodification of one's own suffering." Despite the mysterious omission of Ghosh's marvelous essays on Cambodia The Imam and the Indian is one collection that should be on the bookshelves of all who call themselves readers. The 18 essays in The Imam and the Indian were written over a 16-year time span - from 1986 to 2002. Which partly explains the eclecticism of this collection. A translation of Tagore's "Kshudhita Pashan", two essays on the social anthropology of an Egyptian village, an elegy to the Kashmiri poet, Agha Shahid Ali, a travel piece on the Four Corners, some incidental pieces like "A Tibetan Dinner" and "The Ghosts of Mrs Gandhi" - the diversity of genres, subjects, dictions would seem much too heterogenous for compilation in a single volume.

But for Amitav Ghosh, "connections are of greater importance than disjunctions" in the imaginative sphere.One of these "connections", very obviously, is the fact that the pieces were written in the gaps between the novels and hence trace the evolution of the author's interest and ideas that later were transmuted into fiction. Those familiar with Ghosh's fictional career will run into many familiar themes, motifs and characters here. But more notable is Ghosh's fixation with "encounters" between cultures and the modes of thought they embody. It could result, at times, in scepticism - the Imam's suspicion of the doctor al-Hindi, who comes from the land where cows are worshipped and the dead are burnt. Or, it could give rise to conflict like the one between the Navajos and the early settlers in North America. In most cases, the humans caught up in the clash of cultures are unaware of its historical import. Look at Babur's near dislike for the kingdom that he won in the battle of Panipat and which was to earn him a place in history. In the modern world, however, such encounters are almost always violent and throw up a detritus in the form of an uprooted populace. Like the Tibetan monk Ghosh encounters at a New York charity dinner for the Tibetan cause. Some, like Nabeel, are lost to friends and relations forever. Others, like the Sylheti UN peace-keeper entrusted with clearing the Khmer Rouge's mines in Cambodia, learn to cope as best as they can and soon become inured to the brutality around them. And most touchingly, Agha Shahid Ali, a resident of "the country without a pos-office" - Kashmir - who must die of cancer in Northampton, denied the right to go back to his homeland in his last days. What comes in the way of peaceful coexistence between two peoples?

And what happens to the people caught in the midst of war or civil violence? Are their any alternative patterns of relations between different cultures - one that does not lead to strife? In the present global scenario, the artist cannot but state which side of the political fence he is on. Thus art itself is a political stratagem. As Ghosh writes in The Shadow Lines, "Every word I write...is the product of a struggle with silence." And memories of violence, experienced or heard of, a weapon of defiance that helps to destroy the "thickening crust of awareness that is both a sign and a reminder of our unwitting complicity in the evolution of violence". Which is why all fundamentalist regimes consider the destruction of literature and art - a way of ordering memory and human values - an article of faith. As every Kashmiri would say with Shahid: "Your history gets in the way of my memory / I am everything you lost. Your perfect enemy."

Reviews

The Imam and the Indian written over a 16-year time span (1986-2002), is a fascinating compilation of Amitav Ghosh's articles, lectures and translations spanning over two decades where the author's deceptively gentle style conceals cavernous depths of imagination and erudition. The book comprises a translation of Tagore's "Kshudhita Pashan", two essays on the social anthropology of an Egyptian village, an elegy to the Kashmiri poet, Agha Shahid Ali, a travel piece on the Four Corners, some incidental pieces like "A Tibetan Dinner" and "The Ghosts of Mrs Gandhi" - the diversity of genres and issues would seem too diverse for compilation in a single volume. But for Amitav Ghosh, "connections are of greater importance than disjunctions" in the imaginative scheme of things.

The author digs out lost lives from centuries past and he explicitly portrays how the metaphysical is contained within the mundane. With subtlety, Ghosh hints that a critique of the Enlightenment need not lead directly to nativism if such critiques are grounded in meticulous research. He is continually thoughtful, vivacious, responsible rather than rakish.

One of his essays titled, The Slave Of MS.H.6, is indeed a quest for the subaltern. Ghosh's search for an individual who lived in the 12th century, wrote nothing about himself and thus left behind no records of his life. Ghosh depicts the slave as a phantom, who appears only coincidentally in a set of letters exchanged between two 12th century merchants. But this unknown slave may have witnessed the Crusades and his life might provide important clues about the fact that "slavery" was not slavery as we comprehend it today but a quasi-professional relationship between groups unrelated by blood. Ghosh indulges in ghost-hunting and finally finds the spirit of "Bomma the Slave," hiding eerily in a research institute.

In The Ghosts of Mrs Gandhi, Ghosh vividly narrates the endless tragedies (read riots) that gripped the Capital following the murder of Indira Gandhi in 1984. With sensitivity he describes how an elderly Sikh couple in desperation to save their lives clambered over a wall into their neighbours' welcoming South Delhi home. In other words, the author displays with alacrity of how the stories of every act of violence conceal the civil response to them.

Ghosh's brilliance and his nostalgic memories of his stint in Egypt are rekindled in the books' first essay, The Imam and the Indian. Ghosh gives a sparkle to the thematic element in this essay through an argument between an Indian student (himself) and the imam of an Egyptian village. The author opines, "two delegates of superseded civilisations vying with each other to lay claim to the violence of the West".

And in yet another essay, Ghosh answers the call of the desert. Travelogues, the author opines, are an integral part of Bengali literature- Fluent in Arabic, he reflects on the romanticism associated with the adventures of a Bengali traveller.

Meanwhile, in the modern world, encounters are often violent and throw up debris in the guise of an uprooted populace. Like the Tibetan monk, Ghosh encounters at a New York charity dinner for the Tibetan cause. Some, like Nabeel, are lost to friends and relations forever. Others, like the Sylheti UN peace-keeper entrusted with clearing the Khmer Rouge's mines in Cambodia, learn to cope as best as they can and soon become accustomed to the brutality around them. And most touchingly, Agha Shahid Ali, a resident of "the country without a post-office" - Kashmir - who must die of cancer in Northampton, is denied the right to go back to his homeland in his last days.

Above all, Ghosh remains fascinated by the mysticism within whose periphery the written word leaves its mark on earth. The author, also the exponent of the dilemmas between the physical and the metaphysical, the tangential oddities between the erudite and the earthy in the Imam and the Indian, exploresand discusses various issues with remarkable sensitivity and precision.

The Glass Palace

The Glass Palace is a masterful novel of love, war and family and presents us with a band of memorable characters, spread across Burma, Malaya and India, and across three generations - before the door to Burma closes behind them, and the glittering light of that civilisation seems extinguished.

Starting in Mandalay at the time of the exile of King Thebaw and Queen Supayalat, THE GLASS PALACE is compelling historical fiction that tells the story of three families during a time of transition for India and its people. Politics, business, love, and war intertwine with unforgettable characters to immerse you in the story of a land and its people.

Rajkumar is a poor orphan boy stranded in Mandalay while the sampan on which he's working gets repaired. While working for a food vendor, he meets Saya John and his son, Matthew, who is a few years younger than he.

The locals loot the palace during the unsettled days of the King and Queen's disposition. While there, Rajkumar sees the most beautiful girl he's ever seen, the youngest of the Queen's maids. Rajkumar only has time to learn her name before the approaching soldiers force the looters to leave. He sees Dolly once more when the Royal Family is being led to the boat that will bring them to their home in exile. Years later, he'll go in search of the gi rl he cannot forget.

After the King and Queen are forced to leave, Mandalay is like a ghost town. The food vendors can no longer afford to stay open, leaving Rajkumar without a job. Rajkumar again goes to Saya John to find employment.

The Royal Family is exiled to Ratnagiri where they become the responsibility of the District Collector, a member of the Indian Civil Service, who ruled Britain's Indian possessions. In 1905, an Indian District Collector is appointed who brings with him his wife Uma. She becomes a lifelong friend of Dolly's and a voice for India's independence.

Ties between the orphan Rajkumar, Dolly, Saya John's family, and Uma's family span generations; their story is woven into the history of Burma, India, and Malaya. One generation works within the British-ruled system to build their dynasty, harvesting teak and rubber using slave labor. The next generation confronts a rising consciousness of Indian independence, which is intensified during World War II. Indians in the British Indian Army confront racism within their army as well as in the Indian National Army fighting for India's freedom.

Editorial Reviews

Ghosh's epic novel of Burma and Malaya over a span of 115 years is the kind of "sweep of history" that readers can appreciateDeven loveDdespite its demands. There is almost too much here for one book, as over the years the lives and deaths of principal characters go flying by. Yet Ghosh (The Calcutta Chromosome; Shadow Lines) is a beguiling and endlessly resourceful storyteller, and he boasts one of the most arresting openings in recent fiction: in the marketplace of Mandalay, only the 11-year-old Indian boy Rajkumar recognizes the booming sounds beyond the curve of the river as English cannon fire. The year is 1885, and the British have used a trade dispute to justify the invasion and seizure of Burma's capital. As a crowd of looters pours into the fabled Glass Palace, the dazzling throne room of the nine-roofed golden spire that was the great hti of Burma's kings, Rajkumar catches sight of Dolly, then only 10, nursemaid to the Second Princess. Rajkumar carries the memory of their brief meeting through the years to come, while he rises to fame and riches in the teak trade and Dolly travels into exile to India with King Thebaw, Burma's last king; Queen Supayalat; and their three daughters. The story of the exiled king and his family in Ratnagiri, a sleepy port town south of Bombay, is worth a novel in itself, and the first two of the story's seven parts, which relate that history and Rajkumar's rise to wealth in Burma's teak forests, are marvelously told. Inspired by tales handed down to him by his father and uncle, Ghosh vividly brings to life the history of Burma and Malaya over a century of momentous change in this teeming, multigenerational saga. (Feb. 6) Forecast: Novels by Indian authors continue to surge in popularity here, and this title not only ranks among the best but differs from the pack for its setting of Burma rather than India

From Library Journal

In an industry not known for risk-taking, the publisher is to be congratulated for offering Ghosh (The Calcutta Chromosome) a contract on his as-yet-unwritten novel. Set primarily in Burma, Malaya, and India, this work spans from

1885, when the British sent the King of Burma into exile, to the present. While it does offer brief glimpses into the history of the region, it is more the tale of a family and how historical events influenced real lives. As a young boy, Rajkumar, an Indian temporarily stranded in Mandalay, finds himself caught up in the British invasion that led to the exile of Burma's last king. In the chaos, he spies Dolly, a household maid in the royal palace, for whom he develops a consuming passion and whom years later he tracks down in India and marries. As their family grows and their lives intersect with others, the tangled web of local and international politics is brought to bear, changing lives as well as nations. Ghosh ranges from the condescension of the British colonialists to the repression of the current Myanmar (Burmese) regime in a style that suggests E.M. Forster as well as James Michener.

DANCING IN CAMBODIA AND AT LARGE IN BURMA

Synopsis : Dancing in Cambodia, At Large in Burma (1998) is made up of three parts: the two longish travel-essays of the book's title and a shorter Cambodian piece, "Stories in Stones". Ghosh's capacity to find patterns in apparently unconnected events is at its best in "Dancing in Cambodia", which links the 1906 visit of Cambodia's King Sisowath, his entourage, and a troupe of Cambodian classical dancers, to France, with the recent history of the country decimated by the Khmer Rouge Revolution. Ghosh interviews a number of figures who provide living testimony to the interconnectedness of these two narratives. They include a famous dancer, Chea Samy, who has first-hand knowledge of King Sisowath and his daughter Princess Soumphady as a result of having been taken to the royal palace in 1925, at the age of six, to be trained in classical dance under the supervision of the Princess. She is also - and the matter-of-fact manner in which Ghosh records this makes the revelation all the more chilling - Pol Pot's sister-in-law. Palace revolution and the French connection are motifs that run throughout the essay.

Pol Pot was himself taken into the palace at the age of six. Pol Pot appears to have been radicalized during his time as a student in Paris. He particularly admired Robespierre, basing the ideological purity of his genocidal regime on the French revolutionary's belief in the virtue of Terror. Similarly, the grandson of King Sisowath's Palace Minister, Thiounn, becomes a central figure to a generation of Cambodian students in Paris and one of his prote'ge's is Pol Pot. For the most part Ghosh documents these connections neutrally, but lest they be missed, he does comment at one point that coups usually begin in the courtyards of the palace. King Sisowath and Pol Pot may seem polar opposites, but with their common experience of palace life and their enthusiasm for certain, albeit different, aspects of French culture, they emerge as curiously twinned.

In the period of reconstruction after Pol Pot's fall, the return to normalityis associated with an art form that has palace associations: Cambodian classical dance. The text represents dancing as far more than a traditional Cambodian performance art; it becomes a trope for the indestructibility of the middle-class culture threatened with extinction during the Pol Pot era. The essay ends with an "epiphany" in Phnom Penh in 1988, a moment when grief and joy commingle, as classical music and dance are performed once again for the first time. On this occasion, then, the humanist conclusion is not so much championing subaltern survival, but the resilience of an educated class threatened with extinction by a Western-inspired regime, which has declared war on the intelligentsia. "Stories in Stones" considers the iconic significance of Angkor Wat, reputedly the largest religious edifice in the world, as a symbol of Cambodian identity. The essay wryly reflects that its omnipresence as a talismanic object pervades virtually every area of the nation's life - except religion.

Ghosh's illustrationof the proliferation of images of the Wat in a range of commercial contexts is not, however, simply evidence of the extent to which tradition and modernity overlap; it is a striking instance of a modern appropriation of an older tradition, which he sees as eroding the humanist possibilities of earlier belief-systems. "At Large in Burma" provides insights into an Asian country that has been particularly isolated from the outside world in recent years, again doing so through the medium of individual stories. Here the central figure is the leader of the country's democratic movement and winner of the 1991 Nobel Peace Prize, Aung San Suu Kyi, whom Ghosh first met while a student in Oxford in 1980 and whom he now interviews during two visits in 1995 and 1996. At one point he mentions having been brought up to believe that the public and the private should be kept separate, with the corollary that it is wrong to reduce political movements to their leaders, but he finds Aung San Suu Kyi the personification of Burmas democratic resistance.

So, in addition to providing a window on one of the world's more closed societies, the essay becomes another instance of Ghosh's characteristic historiographic method of illuminating national and communal issues through personal stories, though, as in "Dancing in Cambodia", it departs from his earlier focus on subaltern experience. "At Large in Burma" also contains a section in which Ghosh travels to the Thai border in an attempt to understand the independence struggle of one of Burma's many minorities, the Kanenni. Naipaulian ironies emerge when tourists visit refugee camps to see the Kanneni's long-necked giraffe woman, oblivious of their history of oppression and displacement and unaware that they are commodified versions of the rural simplicity they supposedly represent.

Ghosh's own perspective is, of course, much more complicated and again centrally concerned with the impact of modernity. His main interest lies in trying to assess what freedom means to the Kanneni and whether the utative nations around Burma's borders would be better off as separate states. His consideration of this issue revisits the central motif of The Shadow Lines and he once again comments on the arbitrariness of borders drawn by colonial officials and the inevitable artificiality of nations. His conclusion in the case of the Kanneni, and the sixteen or so other potential nation states around multi-ethnic Burma's borders, is that they would not benefit from being separate countries.

So, like so much of Ghosh's work, this part of the essay presents a self-contained micro-history of a group, which can also be read as a metonym for a larger global debate. It holds a mirror up to late twentieth-century cultural theory on the nation state, which both reflects and reverses commonly held assumptions when it suggests that in the case of the Kanneni the historical borders are probably best left unaltered.

The Calcutta Chromosome

Synopsis : This novel has been described as "a kind of mystery thriller" (India Today). It brings together three searches: the first is that of an Egyptian clerk, Antar, working alone in a New York apartment in the early years of the twenty-first century to trace the adventures of L. Murugan, who disappeared in Calcutta in 1995; the second pertains to Murugan's obsession with the missing links in the history of malaria research; the third search is that of Urmila Roy, a journalist in Calcutta in 1995 who is researching the works of Phulboni, a writer who produced a strange cycle of "Lakhan stories" that he wrote in the 1930s but suppressed thereafter.

In An Antique Land

Amitav Ghosh

Synopsis : The cover proclaims IAAL "History in the guise of a traveller's tale," and the multi-generic book moves back and forth between Ghosh's experience living in small villages and towns in the Nile Delta and his reconstruction of a Jewish trader and his slave's lives in the eleventh century from documents from the Cairo Geniza. In the 1980s Amitav Ghosh moved into a converted chicken coop. It was on the roof of a house in Lataifa, a tiny village in Egypt. During the day he poured over medieval letters sent to India from Cairo by Arab merchants. In the evenings hc shut out the bellowing of his fat landlord by turning up the volume of his transistor radio and wrote stories based on what he had seen in the village. The story of Khamees the Rat, the notorious impotent (already twice married); of Zaghloul the weaver determined to travel to India on a donkey; of one-eyed Mohammad, so obsessed with a girl that he spent nights kneeling outside her window to listen to the sound of her breathing; of Amm 'Taha, part-time witch, always ready to cast a spell for a little extra money; and, of course, the story of Amitav Ghosh himself, known in the village as the Indian doctor, the uncircumcised, cow-worshipping kaffir who would not convert to Islam. This book is the story of Amitav Ghosh's decade of intimacy with the village community. Mixing conversation and research, imagination and scholarship, it is also a charged, eccentric history of the special relationship between two countircs, Egypt and India, through nearly ten centuries of parochialism and sympathy, bigotry and affection.

The Shadow Lines

Synopsis : His second novel focuses on the narrator's family in Calcutta and Dhaka and their connection with an English family in London. A boy conjures up a picture of London so vivid in his imagination that he recognizes it when he visits years later and learns that real places can be invented inside your head. From Dhaka to London, this novel contains a wealth of characters and colour.

The Circle of Reason

Synopsis : A saga of flight and pursuit, this novel chronicles the adventures of Alu, a young master weaver who is wrongly suspected of being a terrorist. Chased from Bengal to Bombay and on through the Persian Gulf to North Africa by a bird-watching police inspector, Alu encounters along the way a cast of characters as various and as colorful as the epithets with which the author adorns them. The reader is drawn into their lives by incidents tender and outrageousand all compellingly told. Ghosh is as natural a weaver of words as Alu is of cloth, deftly interlacing humor and wisdom to produce a narrative tapestry of surpassing beauty.

Indian authors writing in English have conquered the world. These eminent writers have won coveted national and international Literary Awards, attracted vast media attention and made the publishing industry breath afresh. With a rising readership, they are the centre of critical attention, scholarly works and research activities of International academia. Showcased here are the brief biographical details of these eminent authors, along with their noteworthy works and critical response.

A. K. RAMANUJAN

Attipat Krishnaswami Ramanujan or A. K. Ramanujan, as he is known, was born in Mysore, India in 1929. He was a transitional figure in the history of Indian English Literature, and also a trans-disciplinary scholar, working as a poet, translator, linguist, and folklorist. Although he wrote primarily in English,

he was fluent in both Kannada and Tamil, the language of his family. Ramanujan received his BA and MA in English language and literature from the University of Mysore. He then spent some time teaching at several universities in South India before getting a graduate diploma in theoretical linguistics from Deccan University in Poona in 1958. He went to the U.S. in 1959. In 1962, he became an assistant professor at the University of Chicago, where he was affiliated throughout the rest of his career. The following year, he went to Indiana University where he got a Ph.D. in linguistics in 1963. He taught at several U.S. universities, including Harvard, University of Wisconsin, University of Michigan, University of California at Berkeley, and Carlton College. At the University of Chicago, Ramanujan was instrumental in shaping the South Asian Studies program. He worked in the departments of South Asian Languages and Civilizations, Linguistics, and with the Committee on Social Thought. In 1976, the government of India awarded him the honorific title "Padma Sri," and in 1983, he was given the MacArthur Prize Fellowship. Ramanujan breathed his last in Chicago on July 13, 1993.

Contributions to South Asian Studies

Ramanujan was a major figure in shaping South Asian studies. According to him, the Indian way of thinking is "context-sensitive" as opposed to "context-free." Context-sensitive is, he suggests, the more appropriate term for what others have taken for an Indian tendency toward inconsistency and hypocrisy, as well as, perhaps tolerance and mimicry.

Ramanujan cites Said's Orientalism here, suggesting a European source for these stereotypes created out of a necessity to essentialize and exoticize the Eastern world. These terms, he takes from linguistics, in which they refer to different kinds of grammatical rules.

In applying them to cultures or ways of thinking, Ramanujan relies primarily on a text-based analysis. He cautions that they are "overall tendencies." "Actual behavior may be more complex, though the rules they think with are a crucial factor guiding the behavior". Context-free thinking, which he attributes to Euro-American culture, gives rise to universal testaments of law, such as in the Judeo-Christian tradition and in the European philosophical tradition, e.g. Hegel. Context-sensitive thinking, on the other hand, gives rise to more complicated sets of standards such as the Laws of Manu, by which appropriateness depends on various factors, especially factors of identity and personhood, such as birth, occupation, life stage, karma, dharma, etc. Ramanujan stresses that this difference in philosophical outcome is not a symptom of irrationality, but a different kind of rationale.

Sociolinguistic Theory

Ramanujan's work in sociolinguistics also speaks to the critique of Sanskritic Indology. As shown in his 1964 essay with W. Bright, Sociolinguistic Variation and Language Change, Ramanujan opposes those who would conceive a monolithic standard grammar for Indian languages. Rather, he seeks to legitimize the vast variety of linguistic dialects. Specifically, here, Ramanujan and Bright compare a Brahmin Tamil dialect with a non-Brahmin Tamil dialect. The Brahmin dialect, they found, was much more inflected with Sanskrit loan words and styles, whereas the non-Brahmin dialect tended to shift by innovation on existing phonologic and morphologic features rather than by foriegn adoption. Ramanujan and Bright do not address the political and economic implication of this differential grammatical shift. However, their point, in 1964, was only to acknowledge and legitimize linguistic innovation as it occurs in various social groups in India.

Folklore Studies

In Ramanujan's writing about Indian folklore and classic poetry, the theme of context-sensitivity reappears. In Where Mirrors are Windows (1989) and in Three Hundred Ramayanas (1991), he discusses the "intertextual" nature of written and oral Indian literature. By this, he means that Indian stories refer to one another and sometimes to other versions of the very story being told. He says, "What is merely suggested in one poem may become central in a 'repetition' or an 'imitation' of it. Mimesis is never only mimesis, for it evokes the earlier image in order to play with it and make it mean other things". It is important for Ramanujan to note that these intertextual influences do not occur in a unidirectional pattern. He emphasizes that the oral and written traditions, the Sanskritic and local traditions are in dialogue with and mutually influence one another.

Translation Works

Ramanujan worked to make non-Sanskritic Indian literature acknowledged in the realm of South Asian studies through the translation of works in the South Indian languages Kannada and Tamil. His translation works include Interior Landscapes: Love Poems from a Classical Tamil Anthology (1967), Speaking of Siva (1973), Hymns for the Drowning (1981), and A Flowering Tree and Other Oral Tales from India. In The Interior Landscape (1967), Ramanujan covers another sense of intertextuality which lies in the symbolic evocation common in Tamil poetry. Here, he discusses the highly stylized symbol system of Tamil poetry in which different landscape features evoke emotional tones, meanings and relational qualities. Necessary to understanding any Tamil poem is knowledge of the symbolic context and tradition in which it was written.

Ramanujan's Poetry

Ramanujan wrote poetry almost entirely in English. The poet is known for his rather atavistic poetic arguments - arguments which disrupt common expectations. Ramanujan is not a poet of easy moral expectations. Where conventional morality collapses, poetry takes off. In Ramanujan's quirky universe, excellence in human affairs is more a product of one's compulsions or handicaps rather than one's innate genius. Reviewer Bruce King called Ramanujan one of the "Indo-Anglian harbingers of literary modernism". This description highlights several characteristics of Ramanujan's poetry, perhaps less common in other transcultural poetry. Characteristics of his modernist style include an almost jarring realism and hints at a kind of confessional style. Themes of hybridity and transculturation are also highlighted in his poetry.

Abha Dawesar

"Fun Fearless Female" - is how Abha Dawesar has been crowned by Cosmopolitan, a monthly magazine of India. Femina magazine in India named her one of India's 12 remarkable women and one of India's leading national English language newspapers, The Hindustan Times, included Dawesar with a list of eleven other authors in its Next Big Things for 2005. New York's weekly magazine Time Out listed Dawesar as one of 25 People to make their mark in 2005. This young and promising author was born in New Delhi in 1974. She graduated with a degree in political philosophy from Harvard University after writing an honors thesis examining the conception of human greatness in Nietzsche's On the Genealogy of Morals. She currently works in Business Development for a software company in New York. She is the receipient of the New York Foundation of the Arts Fellowship in Fiction for 2000.

Dawesar's debut novel Miniplanner was chosen as a "Season's best pick" by the NY publication LGNY. It was also published in India by Penguin Books under the title The Three of Us and hailed as "a coming-of-age of Indian diaspora writers."

Babyji, her second novel, is the winner of the American Library Association's Stonewall Award for 2006. The novel was also named one of the ten best books of fiction for 2005 by the Boston Phoenix. It was reviewed nationally and internationally in the US media, India, Italy, Germany, and Spain.

That Summer in Paris is Abha Dawesar's third novel and it is to be released on 20th June, 2006.

AKHIL SHARMA

AKHIL SHARMA was born in Delhi, India, in 1971. He grew up in Edison, New Jersey.

His stories have appeared in the Best American Short Stories anthology, the O. Henry Award Winners anthology, The Atlantic Monthly, and The New Yorker. He is a winner of The Voice Literary Supplement's Year 2000 "Writers on the Verge" Award. A portion of An Obedient Father was excerpted in the debut fiction issue of The New Yorker in June 2000.

Sharma lives in New York City, where he is an investment banker at a major Wall Street firm.

Recent reviews...

"Sharma's sharply realistic fiction effortlessly interweaves one man's life, one family's history, and one country's fate into a compelling debut novel ... Sharma allows his fiction to unfold through wonderfully rich details. From Karan's cajoling of bribes from a school principal to his memories of his childhood in Beri to the minutiae of his sad domestic life with his daughter, the facts of this novel fascinate the reader. Combine this with Karan's greedy, comic, petty, and ultimately horrifying voice, and the result is a tale that haunts us long after we've finished it. A remarkable first novel." -Booklist, starred review

"A supernova in the galaxy of young, talented Indian writers, Sharma debuts with a bold and shocking novel that casts a mesmerizing spell. Ram Karan is a widower whose widowed daughter, Anita, and eight-year-old granddaughter, Asha, live with him in a tiny apartment in one of Delhi's poorer sections. Nominally a functionary in the physical education department of the city's schools, Ram is in fact 'Mr. Gupta's moneyman'; that is, he coerces bribes for his boss, who funnels the money to the Congress Party.

At first, Ram's candid admissions of 'general incompetence and laziness' are perversely endearing, but when the real cause of his self-hatred comes to light, the reader's perceptions begin to change. In a moment of temptation, Ram commits a furtive sexual act with his unwitting granddaughter - and his downfall begins. Twenty years ago, he had repeatedly raped Anita, who now becomes unhinged at the thought that her daughter may be in peril. Anita's bizarre revenge will result in Ram's complete degradation; ironically, the repercussions of her obsessive need for disclosure cause even more emotional damage to everyone involved. Concurrent with these personal tragedies and the breakdown of one family, Sharma draws an acid-etched picture of modern Indian society, in which the corrupt political system victimizes all citizens ... Sharma's depiction of a society riddled with graft, violent religious prejudice, male chauvinism and bigoted cultural attitudes is a cautionary tale about what happens to the individual spirit when poverty, superstition, racial tension and general hopelessness are exacerbated by the absence of judicial morality. This caustic yet darkly comic story resonates powerfully, as the reader comes to sympathize with fallible human beings trapped in circumstances that corrupt the soul."

AMIT CHAUDHURI

Born in Calcutta, India, in 1962, Amit Chaudhuri was brought up in Bombay. He graduated from University College, London, and was a research student at Balliol College, Oxford. He was later Creative Arts Fellow at Wolfson College, Oxford, and received the Harper Wood Studentship for English Literature and Poetry from St John's College, Cambridge. He has contributed fiction, poetry and reviews to numerous publications including The Guardian, the London Review of Books, the Times Literary Supplement, the New Yorker and Granta magazine.

His first book, A Strange and Sublime Address (1991), a novella and a number of short stories, won the Betty Trask Prize, the Commonwealth Writers Prize (Eurasia Region, Best First Book) and was shortlisted for the Guardian Fiction Prize. His second novel, Afternoon Raag (1993), won both the Southern Arts Literature Prize and the Encore Award (for best second novel of the year). The novel adopts the metaphor of Indian classical music, the raag, to evoke the complex emotions displayed by the narrator, a young Indian student at Oxford.

It was followed by Freedom Song (1998), set in Calcutta during the winter of 1992-3 against a backdrop of growing political tension between Hindus and Muslims. The US edition of Freedom Song won the Los Angeles Times Book Prize (Fiction) in 2000. A New World (2000) is the story of Jayojit Chatterjee, a divorced writer living in America, and the visit he makes with his son Vikram to his elderly parents' home in Calcutta. His latest book, Real Time (2002), includes a number of short stories set in Bombay and Calcutta, some of which have been published in the London Review of Books, the Times Literary Supplement and the New Yorker, as well as 'E-minor', a memoir written in verse. D. H. Lawrence and 'Difference': Postcoloniality and the Poetry of the Present, exploring Lawrence's position as a 'foreigner' in the English canon, was published in 2003.

Amit Chaudhuri lives in Calcutta with his wife and daughter. He is editor of The Picador Book of Modern Indian Literature, published in 2001. His most recent book is St. Cyril Road and Other Poems (2005).

Bibliography of Amit Chaudhuri

A Strange and Sublime Address Heinemann, 1991

Afternoon Raag Heinemann, 1993

Freedom Song Picador, 1998

A New World Picador, 2000

The Picador Book of Modern Indian Literature (editor) Picador, 2001

Real Time Picador, 2002

D. H. Lawrence and 'Difference': Postcoloniality and the Poetry of the Present (with foreword by Tom Paulin) Oxford University Press, 2003

St. Cyril Road and Other Poems Penguin, 2005

Prizes and awards

1991 Betty Trask Prize A Strange and Sublime Address

1991 Guardian Fiction Prize (shortlist) A Strange and Sublime Address

1992 Commonwealth Writers Prize (Eurasia Region, Best First Book) A Strange and Sublime Address

1993 K. Blundell Trust Award

1993 Southern Arts Literature Prize Afternoon Raag

1994 Encore Award Afternoon Raag

2000 Los Angeles Times Book Prize (Fiction) Freedom Song: Three Novels (US edition)

2003 Sahitya Akademi Award A New World

AMITAVA KUMAR

AMITAVA KUMAR was born in Ara, Bihar, and grew up in the nearby town of Patna, famous for its corruption, crushing poverty and delicious mangoes.

Kumar's writings have appeared in The Nation, Harper's, New Statesman, Transition, American Prospect, Toronto Review, Colorlines, Biblio, Outlook, Frontline, India Today, The Hindu, Himal, Herald, The Friday Times, The Times of India, and other publications. He has also been a literary columnist at Tehelka.com.

Kumar is the author of Passport Photos (University of California Press and Penguin-India, 2000) and Bombay-London-New York (Routledge and Penguin-India, forthcoming in 2002). Passport Photos was the winner of an "Outstanding Book of the Year" Award from the Myers Program for the Study of Bigotry and Human Rights in North America. Kumar is also the scriptwriter and narrator of the prize-winning documentary, Pure Chutney (1997).

He has been awarded a Barach Fellowship at the Wesleyan Writers Festival and a SAJA prize in 2001 for op-ed writing. He has won fellowships from the NEH, Yale University, SUNY-Stony Brook, Dartmouth College, and University of California-Riverside. Kumar is a professor in the English department at Penn State University. He and his wife live in State College, only a few blocks away from three equally bad Indian restaurants.

AMULYA MALLADI

Amulya Malladi was born and raised in India. She graduated with a bachelor's degree in engineering from Osmania University, Hyderabad, India and received a master's degree in journalism from The University of Memphis, Tennessee, USA.

After living in the United States for several years, Amulya now lives in Copenhagen, Denmark with her husband and two sons.

Amulya's fourth novel, Song of the Cuckoo Bird was released by Ballantine Books on December 27, 2005. She is currently working on her fifth novel, tentatively titled, The Sound of Language, which is set in Denmark.

ANITA DESAI

Anita Desai was born in Mussoorie, a hill station north of Delhi, as the daughter of a D.N. Mazumdar, a Bengali businessman, and the former Toni Nime, of German origin. She grew up speaking German at home and Bengali, Urdu, Hindi and English at school and in the city streets. She has said that she grew up surrounded by Western literature and music, not realizing until she was older that this was an anomaly in her world where she also learned the Eastern culture and customs. She married a businessman at twenty-one and raised several children before becoming known for her writing. Her first book, Cry,the Peacock was published in England in 1963, and her better known novels include In Custody (1984) and Baumgartner's Bombay (1988). She once wrote: "I see India through my mother's eyes, as an outsider, but my feelings for India are my father's, of someone born here" (Griffiths).

She never considered trying to first publish in India because there was no publisher in India who would be interested in fiction by an Indian writer (Jussawalla) and it was first in England that her work became noticed. U.S. readers were slower to discover her, due, she believes to England's natural interest in India and the U.S.'s lack of comprehension regarding the foreignness of her subject.

But Desai only writes in English. This, she has repeatedly said,was a natural and unconscious choice for her: "I can state definitely that I did not choose English in a deliberate and conscious act and I'd say perhaps it was the language that chose me and I started writing stories in English at the age of seven, and have been doing so for thirty years now without stopping to think why "(Desai).

She is considered the writer who introduced the psychological novel in the tradition of Virginia Woolf to India. Included in this, is her pioneer status of writing of feminist issues. While many people today would not classify her work as feminist, she believes this is due to changing times: "The feminist movement in India is very new and a younger generation of readers in India tends to be rather impatient of my books and to think of them as books about completely helpless women, hopeless women. They find it somewhat unreal that the women don't fight back, but they don't seem to realize how very new this movement is" (Jussawalla).

Also, she says, her writing is realistic: "Women think I am doing a disservice to the feminist movement by writing about women who have no control over their lives. But I was trying, as every writer tries to do, even in fiction, to get at the truth, write the truth. It would have been really fanciful if I had made [for example, in Clear Light of Day] Bim and Tara modern-day feminists "(in Griffiths).

Desai considers Clear Light of Day, her most autobiographical book, because she was writing about her neighborhood in Delhi, although the characters are not based on her brothers and sisters. What she was exploring in this novel, she has said, was the importance of childhood and memories as the source of a life. She had wanted to start the book at the end and move backwards, into the characters' childhood and further, into the childhood of their parents etc., but in the end: "When I had gone as far back as their infancy the book just ground to a halt; it lost its momentum. It told me that this was done, that I couldn't carry it further. But I still have a sense of disappointment about that book, because the intention had been different" (Jussawalla). The character of Raja is identified with her in the sense that he is so immersed in all different types of literature and culture, and is so concerned with protecting the multicultural heritage of India. His worries about the Muslim neighbor family is not just about them particularly, but rather worry about the loss of all that the Muslim culture and literature contributes to India.

While Desai has taught for years at Mount Holyoke and MIT, and spends most of the year outside of India, she does not consider herself part of the Indian Diaspora. Although she does not fit in the Indian box anymore (Griffiths) as she said, she considers herself lucky for having not left India until late in her life, because she feels that she has been drifting away from it ever since: "I can't really write of it with the same intensity and familiarity that I once had." Yet she cannot feel at home in any other place or society (Griffiths).

ANITA RAU BADAMI

Anita Rau Badami was born in 1961, in the town of Rourkela in ,Orissa, India. Her father, a mechanical engineer who designed trains, was transferred every two or three years, so that she had a mobile childhood. She grew up in a household where English was the primary language spoken and attended Catholic schools in India, because, as she explains, until around twenty years ago, these were the good schools in India .

At age 18, Anita Rau Badami borrowed money from her father to buy novels at a book fair in Chennai, India. To pay him back she took her first writing assignment, an article in a local newspaper, and earned 75 rupees. She holds degrees in Communication Media, English Literature, and Journalism from universities in Bombay and Madras. Badami began her career as a freelance writer in India with regular features in The Hindu, The Deccan Herald, and Indian Express.

She worked as a copywriter for advertising agencies in Bombay, Bangalore and Madras, and wrote stories for children's magazines. She married in 1984, had a son in 1987, and moved to Calgary in 1991. In 1995, she graduated from the University of Calgary where she received an M.A. degree in English. She submitted her first work to Penguin Books. Penguin published her work, and soon Badami was touring North America, reading from her best-selling debut novel Tamarind Mem.

Several of her short stories appeared in Canadian literary journals such as The Malahat Review, Event, Toronto Review of Contemporary Fiction among others. The Hero's Walk was the winner of the Marian Engel Award for excellence in fiction for a body of work; a Finalist in the 2000 Kiriyama Pacific Rim Prize for fiction; and on the longlist for the 2002 Orange Prize for Fiction.

The Hero's Walk was nominated for the 2002 International IMPAC Dublin Literary Award. The Hero's Walk also won the Commonwealth Best Book Prize in the Canada/ Caribbean region, as well as the Washington Post Best Book of 2001. Ms. Badami has taught writing at University of British Columbia.

Since moving to Montreal two years ago when her husband, Madhav, got a job teaching at McGill University, she has been working quietly on her third novel. A year ago, she received a call from Concordia offering her the position.

It was in Vancouver that she began working on her third novel, Can You Hear the Night Bird Sing, to be published next fall. She has been contacted by her publishers in India and England to republish her children's stories, and she has had an idea for book number four. The working title is The Guest.

ANJANA APPACHANA

Anjana Appachana was born in India, received her education and also worked there for a few years before moving to USA. She has degrees from Delhi University, Jawaharlal Nehru University, and in Creative Writing from Pennsylvania State Univeristy.

One of her short stories Sharmaji was included in the anthology on 50 years of Indian writing (by Salman Rushdie and Elizabeth West). Her focus, as evinced by the theme of her novel Listening Now is the experience of the ordinary Indian woman: her dreams and passions frustrated and realised, through and in spite of the mundane, repetitive and domestic pattern of her life.

Anjana Appachana is the recipient of an O. Henry Festival Prize and a National Endowment for the Arts Creative Writing fellowship. She lives in Tempe, Arizona.

ANURAG MATHUR

Anurag Mathur was born in Delhi and educated at Scindia School, Gwalior, St Stephen's College, Delhi, and the University of Tulsa, Oklahoma, USA. He is a journalist in the print and electronic media and loves reading, music, eating out and tennis. His published books include the best-selling novels The Inscrutable Americans and Making the Minister Smile.

ARUNDHATI ROY

Arundhati Roy is known as an award winning author and also as a social activist and inspiration to all those who seek to support the poor and oppressed. Roy came in the limelight in 1997 when her book The God of Small Things fetched the coveted Booker Prize. This down-to-earth girl-next-door whisked off a whirlwind of controversy through her pen and her association with various social movements and activities. And this year again she is back in the public eye having been awarded the prestigious Sahitya Akademi Award (2005) for her collection of Essays The algebra of infinite justice. Arundhati Roy - the multifaceted talent - is In Focus this week.

Life : Born in 1961 in Bengal, Arundhati Roy grew up in Kerala, the Indian state where The God of Small Things is set.

The tale is based on twin children battling with the caste structures in India. Roy, herself, is the product of an inter-caste marriage. Her father is from a Hindu family of Bengal while her mother is a Christian. From the time she was very young, she knew in her heart that she wanted to be a writer. She studied architecture and taught aerobics but once Roy began writing screenplays, her writing career took off. Roy's debut novel, The God of Small Things, was published in 1997. It became an international bestseller, and in October 1997 won the coveted Booker Prize. Roy has since involved herself in causes such as the anti-nuclear movement and the Narmada Bachao Andolan and has written several essays in support of the causes she so strongly believes in. Arundhati is a towering intellect with a poetic fluency with words delivered in a soft modulated voice. She is also a dog-lover and her past times are writing and running.

ASHOK BANKER

Ashok Kumar Banker (born 1964) is a novelist and short story writer born and living in Mumbai, India. He has written professionally since his early teens, and has worked as a print journalist, columnist, scriptwriter for television series and documentaries, and in advertising.

Banker has published in several genres, ranging from contemporary fiction about urban life in India to multi-volume mythological epics, as well as science fiction, fantasy, and cross-genre works. His first three novels to be published were crime thrillers, claimed to be the first written by an Indian novelist in English. They gained him widespread attention and a reputation for being a crime novelist that has clung to him despite his not having written crime novels since [1], though he has written short crime fiction, some of which involves characters from the novels [2]. The stories of his "Devi" series are short works featuring avatars of the Hindu goddess Devi, and have appeared in various science fiction, fantasy, and horror magazines.

Bibliography

The Ramayana series:

- The Prince of Ayodhya (2003)
- Siege of Mithila (2003)
- Demons of Chitrakut (2004)
- Armies of Hanuman (2005)
- Bridge of Rama (2005)
- King of Ayodhya (2006)

The Mahabharata series:

- The Seeds of War (2006)

His other novels include:

- The Iron Bra (1993)
- Murder & Champagne (1993)
- Ten Dead Admen (1993)
- Vertigo (1993)
- Byculla Boy (1994)
- The Missing Parents Mystery (1994)
- Beautiful Ugly (forthcoming)

BALAJI VENKATESWARAN

Balaji Venkateswaran grew up in India and moved to the US to earn his master's degree. He is an engineer by training and manages engineering operations for a software company in the San Francisco Bay area, where he lives with his wife and two children. His stories and book reviews have appeared in Himal, India West, Indian Review of Books, Weber Studies, India Currents, etc. Rage is his first novel.

BHARATI MUKHERJEE

Bharati Mukherjee was born on July 27, 1940, to an upper-middle class Hindu Brahmin family in Calcutta, India. The second of three daughters of Sudhir Lal, a chemist, and Bina (Banerjee) Mukherjee, she lived with 40 or 50 relatives until the age of eight.

Born into an extraordinarily close-knit and intelligent family, Mukherjee and her sisters were always given ample academic opportunities, and thus have all pursued academic endeavors in their careers and have had the opportunity to receive excellent schooling. In 1947, her father was given a job in England and he brought his family to live there until 1951, which gave Mukherjee an opportunity to develop and perfect her English language skills.

Mukherjee earned a B.A. with honors from the University of Calcutta in 1959. She and her family then moved to Baroda, India, where she studied for her Master's Degree in English and Ancient Indian Culture, which she acquired in 1961. Having planned to be a writer since childhood, Mukherjee went to the University of Iowa in 1961 to attend the prestigious Writer's Workshop. She planned to study there to earn her Master's of Fine Arts, then return to India to marry a bridegroom of her father's choosing in her class and caste. Finally fed up with Canada, Mukherjee and her family moved to the United States in 1980, where she was sworn in as a permanent U.S. resident. Continuing to write, in 1986 she was awarded a National Endowment for the Arts grant. After holding several posts at various colleges and universities, she ultimately settled in 1989 at the University of California-Berkeley. Because of the distinctly different experiences she has had throughout life, shc has been described as a writer who has lived through several phases of life. First, as a colonial, then National subject in India. She then led a life of exile as a post-colonial Indian in Canada. Finally, she shifted into a celebratory mode as an immigrant, then citizen, in the United States. She now fuses her several lives and backgrounds together with the intention of creating a "new immigrant" literature.

Bibliography

- Desirable Daughters (2002)
- The Holder of the World (1993)
- Jasmine (1989)
- The Middleman and Other Stories (1988)
- "Immigrant Writing: Give Us Your Maximalists!" New York Times Book Review (28 August 1988), 28-29.
- The Sorrow and the Terror: The Haunting Legacy of the Air India Tragedy, with Clark Blaise (1987)
- Days and Nights in Calcutta, with Clark Blaise (1986)
- Darkness (1985)
- Wife (1975)
- The Tiger's Daughter (1971)

BHARATI MUKHERJEE

I swam to where the river was a sun-gold haze. I kicked and paddled in a rage. Suddenly my fingers scraped the soft waterlogged carcass of a small dog. The body was rotten, the eyes had been eaten. The moment I touched it, the body broke in two, as though the water had been its glue. A stench leaked out of the broken body, and then the pieces quickly sank.

That stench stays with me. I'm twenty-four now, I live in Baden, Elsa County, Iowa, but every time I lift a glass of water to my lips, fleetingly I smell it. I know what I don't want to become. --Jasmine

Biography / Criticism

Bharati Mukherjee was born on July 27, 1940, to an upper-middle class Hindu Brahmin family in Calcutta, India. The second of three daughters of Sudhir Lal, a chemist, and Bina (Banerjee) Mukherjee, she lived with 40 or 50 relatives until the age of eight. Born into an extraordinarily close-knit and intelligent family, Mukherjee and her sisters were always given ample academic opportunities, and thus have all pursued academic endeavors in their careers and have had the opportunity to receive excellent schooling. In 1947, her father was given a job in England and he brought his family to live there until 1951, which gave Mukherjee an opportunity to develop and perfect her English language skills.

Mukherjee earned a B.A. with honors from the University of Calcutta in 1959. She and her family then moved to Baroda, India, where she studied for her Master's Degree in English and Ancient Indian Culture, which she acquired in 1961. Having planned to be a writer since childhood, Mukherjee went to the University of Iowa in 1961 to attend the prestigious Writer's Workshop. She planned to study there to earn her Master's of Fine Arts, then return to India to marry a bridegroom of her father's choosing in her class and caste.

However, a lunch break on September 19, 1963, changed that plan, transferring Mukherjee into a split world, a transient with loyalties to two cultures. She impulsively married Clark

Blaise, a Canadian writer, in a lawyer's office above a coffee shop after only two weeks of courtship. She received her M.F.A. that same year, then went on to earn her Ph.D. in English and comparative literature from the University of Iowa in 1969.

In 1968, Mukherjee immigrated to Canada with her husband and became a naturalized citizen in 1972. Her 14 years in Canada were some of the hardest of her life, as she found herself discriminated against and treated, as she says, as a member of the "visible minority." She has spoken in many interviews of her difficult life in Canada, a country that she sees as hostile to its immigrants and one that opposes the concept of cultural assimilation. Although those years were challenging, Mukherjee was able to write her first two novels, The Tiger's Daughter (1971) and Wife (1975), while working up to professorial status at McGill University in Montreal. During those years she also collected many of the sentiments found in her first collection of short stories, Darkness (1985), a collection that in many sections reflects her mood of cultural separation while living in Canada.

Finally fed up with Canada, Mukherjee and her family moved to the United States in 1980, where she was sworn in as a permanent U.S. resident. Continuing to write, in 1986 she was awarded a National Endowment for the Arts grant. After holding several posts at various colleges and universities, she ultimately settled in 1989 at the University of California-Berkeley. Because of the distinctly different experiences she has had throughout life, she has been described as a writer who has lived through several phases of life. First, as a colonial, then National subject in India. She then led a life of exile as a post-colonial Indian in Canada. Finally, she shifted into a celebratory mode as an immigrant, then citizen, in the United States. She now fuses her several lives and backgrounds together with the intention of creating a "new immigrant" literature.

Known for her playful and developed language, Mukherjee rejects the concept of minimalism, which, she says, is "designed to keep anyone out with too much story to tell."(New York Times Book Review) Rather, she considers her work a celebration of her emotions, and herself a writer of the Indian diaspora who cherishes the "melting pot" of America. Her main theme throughout her writing discusses the condition of Asian immigrants in North America, with particular attention to the changes taking place in South Asian women in a new world. While the characters in all her works are aware of the brutalities and violence that surround them and are often victimized by various forms of social oppression, she generally draws them as survivors. Mukherjee has oft been praised for her understated prose style and her ironic plot developments and witty observations. As a writer, she has a sly eye with which to view the world, and her characters share that quality. Although she is often racially categorized by her thematic focus and cultural origin, she has often said that she strongly opposes the use of hyphenation when discussing her origin, in order to "avoid otherization" and the "self-imposed marginalization that comes with hyphenation." Rather, she prefers to refer to herself as an American of Bengali-Indian origin.

The Tiger's Daughter is a fictionalized story drawing from Mukherjee's own first years of marriage and her return home for a visit to a world unlike the one that lives in her memory. The protagonist, Tara Banerjee, returns to India after marrying an American and faces a different India than the one she remembers leaving. This first novel addresses Mukherjee's personal difficulties of being caught between two worlds, homes and cultures and is an examination of who she is and where she belongs. Similarly, Days and Nights in Calcutta, co-authored with her husband, is a shared account of the first trip the couple took to India together after being married. Each offers a different India through their separate journals, and ultimately, the two tell the tale of a relationship that faces the daily difficulties of cultural barriers that have been drawn and separate pasts that linger.

Mukherjee's second novel, Wife, is a more distant story that sees Dimple, a young, naive Indian woman, trying to reconcile the Bengali ideal of the perfect, passive wife with the demands of her new American life. As a young woman who was raised to be passive, Dimple lacks the inner strength and resources it takes to cope in New York City as the young wife in an arranged marriage. Again in this novel, Mukherjee deals with the complications that come from being thrown between two worlds and the strength and courage it takes to survive and, ultimately, live. Wife was often dismissed because its heroine fails to make the transition from one world to another, and was often judged to be "weak." Although both of Mukherjee's first books weave complex tales, they lack the strength of storytelling that her later works are more successful at capturing.

Darkness, her first collection of short stories, focuses on natives of South Asia who crave success and stability, but are burdened by their histories and face the difficulties of prejudice and misunderstanding. This collection was a transitional work for Mukherjee, who was reflecting back on her difficult years in Canada and cherishing the opportunity to establish herself in the United States.

In 1988, Mukherjee had a major public breakthrough that lifted her into the top ranks of all writers. She was awarded the National Book Critics Circle Award for Fiction for The Middleman and Other Stories. In this collection, Mukherjee becomes a valuable middleman linking disparate worlds. She tells her tales from many perspectives, with a keen eye for the concept of self within a larger society. She wrote this collection in a lighter, more celebratory tone, with characters who are adventurers and explorers, rather than refugees and outcasts, and are a part of a new, changing America.

Jasmine, Mukherjee's most popularly read novel, was generally received enthusiastically, but there was some criticism that it was too short and its plot too contrived to be a really successful work of fiction. It is a novel that stems from an earlier short story from The Middleman and Other Stories and was expanded to a story of a young widow who uproots herself from her life in India and re-roots herself in search of a new life and the image of America. It is a story of dislocation and relocation as the title character continually sheds lives to move into other roles, moving further westward while constantly fleeing pieces of her past. In it, Mukherjee rejoices in the idea of assimilation and makes it clear that Jasmine needs to travel to America to make something significant of her life, because in the third world she faced only despair and loss. What Mukherjee hoped that people would read in the story is not only Jasmine's story and change, but also the story of a changing America.

While Mukherjee has been received favorably by many critics and academics, she has also faced a good deal of criticism, particularly from East Indian scholars and critics. It has been said that she often represents India in her fiction as a land without hope or a future. She has also been criticized for a tendency to overlook unavoidable barriers of caste, education, gender, race and history in her tales of survivors, particularly within Jasmine, giving her characters more opportunities than their social circumstances would realistically allow.

Mukherjee is currently a Distinguished Professor of English at the University of California-Berkeley. Her husband, with whom she shares a "literary marriage," teaches at the University of Iowa and they have two sons together, Bart Anand and Bernard Sudhir. Mukherjee has established herself as a powerful member of the American literary scene, one whose most memorable works reflect her pride in her Indian heritage, but also her celebration of embracing America. As she said in an interview in the Massachusetts Review, "the immigrants in my stories go through extreme transformations in America and at the same time they alter the country's appearance and psychological make-up." And so we are given a writer whose voice tells the tales of her own experiences to demonstrate the changing shape of American society.

Selected Bibliography

Works by the Author

- Desirable Daughters (2002)
- The Holder of the World (1993)
- Jasmine (1989)
- The Middleman and Other Stories (1988)

- "Immigrant Writing: Give Us Your Maximalists!" New York Times Book Review (28 August 1988), 28-29.
- The Sorrow and the Terror: The Haunting Legacy of the Air India Tragedy, with Clark Blaise (1987)
- Days and Nights in Calcutta, with Clark Blaise (1986)
- Darkness (1985)
- Wife (1975)
- The Tiger's Daughter (1971)

Works about the Author

- Alam, Fakrul. Bharati Mukherjee. New York: Twayne, 1996.
- Ed. Nelson, Emmanuel S. Bharati Mukherjee: Critical Perspectives. New York: Garland, 1993.
- Bahri, Deepika. "Always Becoming: Narratives of Nation and Self in Bharati Mukherjee's Jasmine." Women, America, and Movement: Narratives of Relocation. Ed. Susan L. Roberson. Columbia: University of Missouri Press, 1998.
- Bonnie, Fred. "An Interview with Bharati Mukherjee." AWP Chronicle 28.2 (1995).
- Brewster, Anne. "A Critique of Bharati Mukherjee's Neo-Nationalism." SPAN: Journal of the South Pacific Association for Literature and Language Studies (SPAN) vol. 34-35 (1992-1993).
- Byers-Pevitts, Beverley. "An Interview with Bharati Mukherjee." Speaking of the Short Story: Interviews with Contemporary Writers. Ed. Farhat Iftekharuddin, Maurice Lee, and Mary Rohrberger. Jackson: University Press of Mississippi, 1997.
- Carb, Alison B. "An Interview with Bharati Mukherjee." The Massachusetts Review 29.4 (1988): 645-654.
- Chua, C.L. "Passages from India: Migrating to America in the Fiction of V. S. Naipaul and Bharati Mukherjee." Reworlding: The Literature of the Indian Diaspora. Ed.

Emmanuel S. Nelson. Westport, Conn.: Greenwood Press, 1992.

- Connell, Michael, Jessie Grearson, and Tom Grimes. "An Interview with Bharati Mukherjee." Iowa Review 20.3 (1990): 7-32.
- Hancock, Geoff. "An Interview with Bharati Mukherjee." Canadian Fiction Magazine 59 (May 1987).
- Kehde, Suzanne. "Colonial Discourse and Female Identity: Bharati Mukherjee's Jasmine." International Women's Writing: New Landscapes of Identity. Ed. Anne E. Brown and Marjanne E. Gooze. Westport: Greenwood, 1995.
- Koshy, Susan. "The Geography of Female Subjectivity: Ethnicity, Gender, and Diaspora." Diaspora 3:1 (1994).
- Leong, Liew-Geok. "Bharati Mukherjee." International Literature in English: Essays on the Modern Writers. Ed. Robert L. Ross. New York: St. James Press, 1991.
- Pandya, Sudha. "Bharati Mukherjee's Darkness: Exploring the Hyphenated Identity." Quill 2.2 (1990).
- Vignisson, Runar. "Bharati Mukherjee: An Interview." SPAN: Journal of the South Pacific Association for Commonwealth Literature and Language Studies (SPAN), vol. 34-35 (1992-1993).
- Wickramagamage, Carmen. "Relocation as Positive Act: The Immigrant Experience in Bharati Mukherjee's Novels." Diaspora: A Journal of Transnational Studies 2. 2 (1992)

BAPSI SIDHWA

Bapsi Sidhwa was born in Karachi - a city in Pakistan. She has taught in several International Universities and presently resides in Houston, Texas. A vocal proponent of women's rights in South Asia, she has also infused her works with strong female characters. She is also the recipient of many awards, including the Sitara-e-Imtiaz, Pakistan's highest honor. Sidhwa's novel, Cracking India, (1991, U.S.; 1992, India; originally published as Ice Candy Man, 1988, England), is the basis for Deepa Mehta's 1998 film, Earth. This story is set in Lahore in the time period directly before and during the partition of India in 1947 and is told from the point of view of a young Parsi Zoroastrian girl.

Bapsi Sidhwa began her writing career at the age of 26 after visiting the Karakoram mountain-area of Pakistan with her husband. She was touched by a tragic story of a young girl who had been brought to one of the area's tribes as a bride. After being there for a short time, the girl ran away from her husband's home.

The tribals considered this a highly dishonourable act. Some of the men hunted her down and murdered her. Sidhwa first wrote a couple of short articles about the beauty of the Karakoram Mountains. However, feeling compelled to tell the girl's story, she decided to make her first attempt at fiction writing and sat down to write a short story which turned into her first novel, The Bride (also in print as The Pakistani Bride). It is a work of fiction based on the events from the tribal girl's life. Her second novel, Crow Eaters, was a lively and humorous story about the Parsi community of Pakistan.

Success didn't come to Bapsi Sidhwa without a lot of hard work. She wrote her first two novels in Pakistan where no one was publishing in English at the time. So, after receiving many rejections, Sidhwa decided to self-publish and self-distribute Crow Eaters. In 1980, after receiving a copy of Sidhwa's self-published Crow Eaters, Britain's Jonathon Cape decided to publish it. the first two novels brought her recognition, it was her third novel, Cracking India (also published as Ice-Candy Man), that earned Bapsi Sidhwa international acclaim and acceptance as one of the most promising English novelists from South Asia, placing her among the likes of Kushwant Singh, Anita Desai, and R.K. Narayan. Cracking India won the Liberator Prize in Germany.

Her works include :

- City of Sin and Splendour : Writings on Lahore (2006, U.S.)

- Water: A Novel Based on the Film by Deepa Mehta (2006, U.S.)
- Bapsi Sidhwa Omnibus (2001, Pakistan)
- An American Brat (1993, U.S.; 1995, India)
- Cracking India (1991, U.S.; 1992, India; originally published as Ice Candy Man, 1988, England)
- Pakistani Bride (1990, U.S.)
- The Bride (1982, England; 1983, U.S.;1984, India)
- The Crow Eaters (1978, Pakistan; 1979 &1981, India; 1980, England; 1982, U.S.)

CAUVERY MADHAVAN

Cauvery Madhavan (b.l962) was born and educated in India. As an army officer's daughter she attended ten schools, always run by nuns, and retains an abiding horror of needlework. She graduated with a First in Economics from Stella Maris College, University of Madras and then worked in a variety of marketing jobs. She got her first taste of writing whilst working at an ad agency. Cauvery married her childhood sweetheart, a newly qualified doctor and moved to Ireland in 1987 arriving on St. Valentine's Day. Despite the Irish weather she has been in love with the country ever since. A keen cook, she now lives with her husband and three children in County Kildare.

Chetan Bhagat was born on born 22 April 1974. He studied at The Army Public School, Delhi (1978-1991) and graduated from IIT Delhi (1991-1995). He completed his post-graduate studies from IIM Ahmedabad (1995-1997). At IIM Ahmedabad, he received a medal for the 'best outgoing student award'. He has been working in Hong Kong with Goldman Sachs, an investment bank, since 1999.

His first novel Five Point Someone relives his own days in IIT through the light-hearted story of three IITians who do not live up to others' academic expectations. The book, with its humorous narrative and contemporary Indian student argot, achieved a sort of cult popularity and has topped national bestseller lists.

Chetan Bhagat won the Society Young Achiever's award in 2004 and the Publisher's recognition award in 2005. .

His Work

- Five Point Someone
- One night @ the call center

CHITRA BANERJEE DIVAKARUNI

Chitra Banerjee Divakaruni was born Calcutta and spent the first nineteen years of her life in India. She moved to the United States to continue her studies, getting a Master's degree from Wright State University in Dayton, Ohio, and a Ph.D. from the University of California at Berkeley, both in English. For several years she has been interested in issues involving women, and has worked with Afghani women refugees and women from dysfunctional families, as well as in shelters for battered women. Since 1991 she has been president of MAITRI, a South Asian women's service which she helped found in the San Francisco area. She has written several books of poetry, and her work has been included in over 30 anthologies. Her book of short stories, Arranged Marriage, which has won critical acclaim and the 1996 American Book Award, the Bay Area Book Reviewers and PEN Oakland awards for fiction. She has two published novels: The Mistress of Spices and Sister of my Heart.

DAVID DAVIDAR

David Davidar (b. 1959) was born in Kerala into a military family. He is a graduate of Madras University. In his mid-twenties, he moved to Bombay to pursue journalism, before changing over to publishing. He completed a course in publishing from Radcliffe/Harvard. David Davidar is best known as the head of Penguin India, who turned around its publishing program from a mere six titles in 1987 to 150 titles annually. In 2004, he relocated to Penguin Canada and is now based in Toronto.The House of Blue Mangoes is his debut novel, a voluminous work chronicling multiple generations set in deep southern India.

His Work

- The House of Blue Mangoes.

The House of Blue Mangoes is sweeping, epic and an ambitious tome which chronicles three generations of the Dorai clan. It covers the period 1899-1947, a momentous period that witnessed the fall of the British Raj, the turmoil of caste wars, the rise of Gandhi, and the culmination of independence.

The story focuses on the Dorai men, and the inescapable conflicts between father and son that tragically play out each generation, from Solomon to Daniel to Kannan. Passionate affairs, assassinations, caste wars, and household acrimony are inextricably linked to the Dorai family home-the house of blue mangoes of the title-in the seaside village of Chevathar. No matter how far members of the clan may travel, they are always drawn back to their ancestral land.

DILIP CHITRE

Dilip Chitre was born in 1938 in Baroda, Gujarat, India. He is a poet, translator, painter, filmmaker and editor. His collected Marathi poems published in three volumes--- Ekoon Kavita--I, II, and III- contain all of his published and unpublished poems since 1954. He has a collection of short stories, a collection of four novellas, four collections of essays, one volume of critical writings, and two plays among his Marathi opus. He has published an anthology of contemporary Marathi poetry in translation.

His other books of translations include: Says Tuka (Penguin), Anubhavamrut (Sahitya Akademi), and Virus Alert. His English poetry books and chapbooks are: Travelling in a Cage, Ambulance Ride, The Mountain, and No Moon Monday at the River Karha.. His English poems are included in every major anthology of Indian poetry, including, most recently, Post Climactic Love Poem (Aark Arts). He has won the Sahitya Akademi Award for Ekoon Kavita-I and the Sahitya Akademi Translation Prize for Says Tuka.

He was a Fellow of the International Writing Program of the University of Iowa and a writer-in-residence at the Villa

Waldberta, Munich. His feature film, Godam, won the Jury's Special Prize at the Festival des Trois Continents, Nantes, France. He is the editor of New Quest , A Quarterly Journal of Participative Inquiry. Chitre lives with his wife Viju in Pune, Maharashtra.

DOM MORAES

Dom Moraes was born was born in Bombay (now Mumbai) to Beryl and Frank Moraes, former editor of Indian Express. He published nearly 30 books. He spent eight years in Britain, living in London and Oxford (where he studied at the university and was a member of Jesus College), but spent most of his life in Mumbai, a city he detested. He married the Indian actress Leela Naidu and then separated from her.He had a life long battle with alcoholism.

He edited magazines in London, Hong Kong and New York. He became the editor of The Asia Magazine in 1971. He scripted and partially directed over 20 television documentaries for the BBC and ITV. He was a war correspondent in Algeria, Israel and Vietnam. In 1976 he joined the United Nations.

Dom Moraes was an alumnus of St. Mary's High School(ISC), Mazagoan, Mumbai.Moraes conducted one of the first interviews of the Dalai Lama after the Tibetan spiritual leader fled to India in 1959. The Dalai Lama was then 23 and Moraes was 20.He ended his writing career writing books in collaboration with Sarayu Srivatsa.

EUNICE DE SOUZA

Eunice de Souza was born in Pune, India in 1940, and educated there. She received an MA from Marquette University in Wisconsin and a PhD from Bombay in 1988. She is now a lecturer in English in St Xavier's College, Bombay. Apart from writing extensively on contemporary literature and culture, she has written four books for children, and was the co-editor of Statements (1976), an anthology of Indian prose in English. Her collections of verse are Fix (1979), Women in Dutch Painting (1988), and Ways of Belonging: New and Selected Poems (1990); the last of these was a Poetry Book Society Recommendation.

GITA MEHTA

Gita Mehta was born in Delhi in 1943 to a family extremely active in the struggles for Indian liberation from Britain. She is the daughter of Biju Patnaik, a famous Indian freedom fighter who later became the major political leader of the Eastern state of Orissa. At her birth, Mehta's grandmother demanded that she be named Joan of Arc, as a child born into a community of freedom fighters who were often forced to go underground as a result of their political actions. But instead, she was named Gita (translated "song"), as in song of freedom. Only several weeks after Mehta's birth, her father was imprisoned for his political activity. Growing up, she was surrounded by her parent's active struggle for Indian liberation. At the age of three, she and her brother were sent to a boarding school while her mother followed her father from one jail to the next.

Mehta was educated in India and the United Kingdom. While attending Cambridge University, she met fellow student Ajai Singh Mehta. The two married and have one son. Mehta and her husband "Sonny," the president of Alfred A. Knopf publishing house, currently maintain residences in New York, London and Delhi, spending at least three months of every year in India. As a result of Sonny Mehta's prominent position in New York's publishing industry, the couple are a central figure in New York's literary publishing world.

HARI KUNZRU

Hari Kunzru was Born in 1969. He is the British author of The Impressionist and Transmission. Of mixed English and Kashmiri Pandit ancestry, he grew up in Essex. He studied English at Wadham College, Oxford University, then gained an MA in Philosophy and Literature from Warwick University.

He has worked as a travel journalist since 1998, writing for such newspapers as The Guardian and The Daily Telegraph, and was travel correspondent for Time Out magazine. In 1999 he was named The Observer Young Travel Writer of the Year. From 1999-2004 he was also music editor of Wallpaper* magazine and since 1995 he has been a contributing editor to

Mute, the culture and technology magazine. He won the Betty Trask Award and the Somerset Maugham Award for The Impressionist. Transmission, his second novel, was published in the summer of 2004. In 2005 he published the short story collection "Noise".

In 2003, Hari Kunzru was named by Granta magazine as one of twenty 'Best of Young British Novelists'. Although he was also awarded The John Llewellyn Rhys prize for writers under 35, the second oldest literary prize in the UK, he turned it down on the grounds that it was backed by the Mail on Sunday whose "hostility towards black and Asian people" he felt was unacceptable. In a statement read out on his behalf, he stated "As the child of an immigrant, I am only too aware of the poisonous effect of the Mail's editorial line.... The atmosphere of prejudice it fosters translates into violence, and I have no wish to profit from it." He further went on to recommend that the award money be donated to the charity Refugee Council (UK). He sits on the executive of English PEN.

IMTIAZ DHARKER

Imtiaz Dharker' is a Pakistani-British poet and documentary film-maker. She was born in Lahore in 1954 to Pakistani parents, but she was brought up in Glasgow where her family moved to during her teens. She currently lives in Mumbai with her Hindu husband, but spends time in London also.[1] She has written three books of poetry, conceived as sequences of poems and drawings. The main themes of her poetry are home, freedom, journeys, geographical and cultural displacement, communal conflict and gender politics. She is a prescribed poet on the AQA GCSE English syllabus. Her poems 'Blessing' and 'This Room' are in AQA Anthology, Different Cultures, Cluster 1 and 2 respectively. She is also an artist and documentary-maker. In 1980, she won an award for a short film.

INDU SUNDARESAN

Indu Sundaresan is an American author. She was born and raised in India, and migrated to the United States for graduate school. Trained as an economist, her short fiction has appeared in The Vincent Brothers Review and on iVillage.com. She lives in the Seattle, Washington area.

One of the novels Indu Sundaresan has written is The Twenthieth Wife which is about how a girl named Mehrunissa becomes Empress of the Mughal Empire. Another is The Feast of Roses, the sequel to The Twentieth Wife.

JHUMPA LAHIRI

Jhumpa Lahiri was born in London, England in July 1967, and brought up in South Kingstown, Rhode Island. Her parents, a teacher and a librarian, taught her about her Bengali heritage from an early age. Lahiri received her B.A. in English literature from Barnard College in 1989. She then received multiple degrees from Boston University: an M.A. in English, an M.A. in Creative Writing, an M.A. in Comparative Literature and a Ph.D. in Renaissance Studies. She took up a fellowship at Provincetown's Fine Arts Work Center, which lasted for the next two years (1997-1998).

In 2001, she married Alberto Vourvoulias-Bush, a journalist who was then Deputy Editor of Time Latin America. Lahiri currently lives in Brooklyn with her husband and two children. She has been a Vice President of the PEN American Center since 2005.

KAMALA DAS

Kamala Das was born on March 31, 1934 in Malabar in Kerala, India. She is the daughter of V.M. Nair, a former managing editor of the widely-circulated Malayalam daily Mathrubhumi, and Nalappatt Balamani Amma, a renowned Malayali poetess. In 1984, she was short-listed for the Nobel Prize for Literature along with Marguerite Yourcenar, Doris Lessing, and Nadine Gordimer. Kamala Das is probably the first Hindu woman to openly and honestly talk about sexual desires of Indian woman, which made her an iconoclast of her generation.

Kamala Das, is a well-known female Indian writer writing in English as well as Malayalam, her native language. She is considered one of the outstanding Indian poets writing in English, although her popularity in Kerala is based chiefly on her short stories and autobiography. Much of her writing in Malayalam came under the pen name Madhavikkutty

KAMALA MARKANDAYA

Kamala Markandaya was born in 1924. He was a pseudonym used by Kamala Purnaiya Taylor, an Indian novelist and journalist. A native of Mysore, India, Markandaya was a graduate of Madras University; and afterwards published several short stories in Indian newspapers. After India declared its independence, Markandaya moved to Britain, though she still labeled herself an Indian expatriate long afterwards.

Known for writing about culture clash between Indian urban and rural societies, Markandaya's first published novel, Nectar in a Sieve, was a bestseller and named a noteable book of 1955 by the American Library Association. Other novels include A Silence of Desire, A Handful of Rice, The Nowhere Man, Two Virgins, The Golden Honeycomb, and Pleasure City. Markandaya died in London on May 16, 2004.

KEKI DARUWALLA

Keki N Daruwalla was born in Lahore, now in Pakistan. His education was at Ludhiana. He joined the Indian Police Service in 1958 and, on retirement, he lives in Delhi. A recipient of Sahitya Akademi Award (1984) and Commonwealth Poetry Award, Keki N. Daruwalla has published several books, consisting of mostly poems and a couple of fictional works.

His works of poetry include Under Orion (1970), Apparition in April (1971), Crossing of Rivers (1976), Winter Poems (1980), The Keeper of the Dead (1982), Landscapes (1987), A Summer of Tigers (1995), Night River (2000) and The Map-maker (2002). Swords and Abyss (1979) and The Minister for Permanent Unrest & Other Stories (1996) are his works of fiction. He also edited Two Decades of Indian Poetry. The Library of Congress has all his books.

KESHAV MALIK

Keshav Malik was born on 5 November 1924 in Miani (Punjab) Pakistan. He is an Indian poet, critic, arts scholar, and curator.

Malik graduated from Amar Singh College in Srinagar, Kashmir in 1945. From 1947-48, he was a personal assistant to Jawaharlal Nehru. During the 1950s, Malik studied Renaissance art in Florence, French at the Sorbonne, and attended lectures at Columbia University.

From 1960-72, Malik was art critic for The Hindustan Times. During roughly the same period, he was literary editor of "Thoughts," an Indian journal of the arts. In 1973-74, Malik was curator for "The Human Condition," an exhibition of contemporary Indian art that traveled to Bulgaria, Poland, Belgium, and Yugoslavia. From 1978-2000, Malik was art critic for The Times of India.

Malik has published ten volumes of poetry, including "The Lake Surface and Other Poems", "Storm Warning," and "Between Nobodies and Stars." He has also edited six anthologies of English translations of Indian poetry, and is a frequent lecturer and seminar participant. He co-founded the Poetry Society of India and is currently president of the Poetry Club of India.

Malik was awarded the Padma Shri for literature in 1991. He is the brother of arts scholar Kapila Vatsyayan.

KIRAN DESAI

Kiran Desai was born in India in 1971, and educated in India, England and the United States. She is the daughter of Anita Desai, and now travels between the three countries, and says she feels 'no alienation or dislocation'. She spent four years writing her first novel, and says it is not at all autobiographical. An excerpt was featured in the New Yorker India Fiction issue, and in Mirrorwork, Salman Rushdie's controversial anthology of 50 years of Indian writing. She is currently a student in Columbia University's creative writing course.

Bibliography

The Inheritance of Loss

Atlantic Monthly Press, 2006

In a crumbling, isolated house at the foot of Mount Kanchenjunga in the Himalayas lives an embittered judge who wants only to retire in peace, when his orphaned granddaughter, Sai, arrives on his doorstep.

The judge's cook watches over her distractedly, for his thoughts are claimed by his son, Biju, who is hopscotching from one gritty New York restaurant to another. When an Indian-Nepali insurgency in the mountains interrupts Sai's exploration of the many incarnations and facets of a romance with her Nepali tutor, and causes their lives to descend into chaos, they are forced to consider their colliding interests.

In a generous vision, sometimes funny, sometimes sad, Desai presents the human quandaries facing a panoply of characters. This majestic novel of a busy, grasping time -- every moment holding out the possibility of hope or betrayal -- illuminates the consequences of colonialism and global conflicts of religion, race, and nationality. Sawnet Review by Champa Bilwakesh

Hullabaloo in the Guava Orchard

Faber and Faber, London. 1998.

KIRAN NAGARKAR

Kiran Nagarkar (b. 1942) was born in Mumbai and studied at the University of Bombay.

Kiran Nagar is a bilingual writer with a difference. He wrote his first novel in Marathi, though he had not written in it before. After that, he moved to writing in English, but translated his second novel Ravan and Eddie back into Marathi.

His creativity and storytelling come to the fore in Cuckold, a fictio-historical account of 15th century Mewar (Rajasthan). His pacy writing makes even profound philosophical concepts lucid.

KUNAL BASU

Kunal Basu was born in Calcutta. Educated in India and the United States, he has lived in many countries. A Professor of Marketing, he has taught at McGill University, Canada and at Oxford University, England. He is the author of three acclaimed novels: The Opium Clerk based on 19th century's opium trade, The Miniaturist set in Mughal India, and most recently, Racists , which delves into the world of Victorian racial science. He speaks frequently at literary festivals, and critical commentary of his work has appeared in Romancing the Strange: The Fiction of Kunal Basu , published by the Shakespeare Society of India. He is married with one daughter.

M. G. VASSANJI

M. G. Vassanji is not an author who is easily labelled. He is of South Asian descent and was born in Nairobi, Kenya where he lived until the death of his father. His family then moved to the community of Dar es Salaam, Tanzania. Vassanji left Dar es Salaam in 1970 to study at the Massachusetts Institute of Technology, investing many years in his career as a physicist. In 1978 he came to Canada and began work at the Chalk River power station. Two years later he became a research associate and lecturer at the University of Toronto. He was reluctant to take his passion for writing as a serious career alternative until he published his first novel, The Gunny Sack, in 1989 and won the 1990 Commonwealth Writers' Prize for best first book in the African region.

Vassanji's novels and short stories draw on his experiences and sense of community and are peopled with the old and young, traditional and modern, and the assimilated and displaced. Thematically, his fiction attempts to connect the past and the present, assimilate traditional and contemporary values, and balance a sense of community with an individual's struggle to belong.

Vassanji is the founder of the Toronto South Asian Review, a nonprofit organization that supports South Asian Canadian writers. He is the editor of their journal, The Toronto Review of Contemporary Writing Abroad (formerly The Toronto South Asian Review) and contributes his short stories to anthologies and other collections on behalf of the organization.

MANIL SURI

Manil Suri was born in July, 1959 in a city Mumbai. He spent several years of his life acquiring degrees in mathematics (B.Sc. (1979), University of Bombay; M.S. (1980) and Ph.D. (1983), Carnegie-Mellon University) followed by several years climbing the academic ladder as a mathematics professor at the University of Maryland, Baltimore County (assistant (1983-89), associate (1989-94), full professor (1994-present)).

In 1995, he did have his first story, "The Tyranny of Vegetables," published. Unfortunately, it was in a Bulgarian-language journal and he was only able to identify it by an author photograph next to the piece. He thinks the name of the journal is Orpheus , but as he is unable to read the title of the complimentary copy that came from Bulgaria, he cannot be sure.

He started The Death of Vishnu as a short story in 1995. It was inspired by the death of an actual man named Vishnu who had lived (and died) on the steps of the Bombay apartment building in which he grew up. By 1997, it had grown to three chapters, and he took it to a workshop at the Fine Arts Work Center in Provincetown, Massachusetts led by Michael Cunningham. Cunningham began his critique with the exhortation to "keep writing this at any cost" and ended it with "you must do whatever is necessary to finish this." That's when Suri realized that perhaps the time for dabbling had come to an end, perhaps he had stumbled onto the start of something more serious. Three years later, an excerpt, "The Seven Circles" appeared in The New Yorker, bringing in his first non-Bulgarian audience.

In addition to Michael Cunningham, Suri has taken writing workshops with two other wonderful teachers: authors Jane Bradley and Vikram Chandra. He has been a fellow at the Virginia Center for the Creative Arts and the MacDowell Colony, and was the winner of the 1998 Jenny McKean Moore Residency Fellowship awarded biannually by George Washington University.

MANOJ DAS

Manoj Das was Born in a coastal village of Orissa in 1934, Manoj Das grew up amidst Nature's splendour. But he also experienced its fury when a cyclone devastated his area, followed by a famine and an epidemic that killed thousands of people. Added to that, his affluent house was twice plundered by dacoits while Manoj, aged six then, looked on with disbelief. Such ups and downs in life probably enriched his creative mind at its formative stage. And by the time he was in high school, he had already published many works in his mother tongue, Oriya. He taught English in a college at Cuttack before he came over to Sri Aurobindo Ashram at Pondicherry in 1963, where he continues to be a professor at the Sri Aurobindo International Centre of Education. He started writing in English in the late 1950s and today he can probably be called the foremost bilingual writer in India. Why did he start writing in English? He said, "... At one stage, I felt inspired to write in English because I was haunted by the feeling that much of the Indian fiction in English that claimed to project the Indian life and situation was not doing justice to its claim. I thought born in a village just before Independence and hence living through the transition at an impressionable age, I could present through English, a chunk of genuine India".

He has received many awards including the Padma Shree, Sahitya Akademi Award and the Saraswati Samman. Some years ago, he was given the annual BAPASI Award by the Booksellers and Publishers Association of South India.Does he feel at home in Pondicherry? He feels he is an Indian first, wherever he is. He has lived in Pondicherry for more than four decades. He loves its ambience and has great regard for its people.Manoj Das is a formidable influence on contemporary Oriya literature. But outside Orissa, he is better known as an Indo-Anglian writer. Which of the two aspects of his literary personality would he wish to be remembered for? "That does not depend on my choice," he said and continued, "I have a wide readership in Orissa. In English I have a trusted and serious readership, but numerically smaller. If the quality of my writing matters, both the streams of my contribution should prove lasting in their own rights."

Through his nearly 300 short stories, Manoj Das had brought about an awareness about the rural Indian life. He has been a crusader against the invasion of India's intellectual climate by decadent values. He has stressed the divinity and psychic splendour inherent in man. No wonder, he has among his admirers celebrities such as Graham Greene, Keating, Dr. K.R.Srinivasa Iyengar and so many academics in the Western world.

MEENA ALEXANDER

Meena Alexander was born in Allahabad in India in 1951 to a family of Syrian Christians. As a very young child she moved back and forth between Allahabad in the North and Kerala on the South west coast, where her parents came from. When she was five, her father started to work in Sudan and she travelled by boat, with her mother, to join him.

As a girl in India, Alexander was often expected to conform to traditional ways. In the Sudan she received an English education, and went on to study English at Khartoum University aged only thirteen. There she wrote her first poems in English which were translated into Arabic and published in a local newspaper. At eighteen she travelled to England to study for a PhD and then returned to India to teach at universities.

She began to write and publish her poetry. She met and fell in love with an American and within three weeks of meeting they decided to marry. In 1979 she moved once again, this time to live and work in the United States with her husband. She's now a Professor, living in Manhattan and has two children. She's continued to write poetry and prose and was only forty two when she wrote Fault Lines, her autobiography, in which she traces her growth as a writer and a woman.

MEERA SYAL

Meera Syal was born in 1963 near Wolverhampton in the West Midlands and was educated at Manchester University where she read English and Drama. She co-wrote the script for 'My Sister Wife', a three-part BBC Television series, and wrote the film Bhaji on the Beach for Channel 4. She co-writes and is a cast member of the popular BBC Television comedy series 'Goodness Gracious Me' and The Kumars at No. 42'. She also works as a journalist and is a regular contributor to The Guardian.

Meera Syal's childhood experiences growing up in a small mining community provided the background to her first novel, Anita and Me (1996). The novel was shortlisted for the Guardian Fiction Prize and won a Betty Trask Award. It tells the story of Meena Kumar, a young Asian girl struggling to accommodate the opposing influences of her white schoolfriends and her traditional Punjabi background. Syal's second novel, Life Isn't All Ha Ha Hee Hee (1999), narrates the adventures of three young Asian women growing up in Britain.

Meera Syal was awarded an MBE in 1997 and won the 'Media Personality of the Year' award at the Commission for Racial Equality's annual 'Race in the Media' awards (2000), as well as the EMMA (BT Ethnic and Multicultural Media Award) for Media Personality of the Year in 2001.

Bibliography

- Six Plays by Black and Asian Women Writers (includes My Sister Wife by Meera Syal) Aurora Metro Publications, 1995
- Anita and Me Flamingo, 1996
- Life Isn't All Ha Ha Hee Hee Doubleday, 1999

Prizes and Awards

- 1996 Betty Trask Award Anita and Me
- 1996 Guardian Fiction Prize (shortlist) Anita and Me
- 1997 MBE

- 2000 Commission for Racial Equality Race in the Media Personality of the Year Award (Commission for Racial Equality 'Race in the Media' awards)
- 2001 EMMA (BT Ethnic and Multicultural Media Award) for Media Personality of the Year

MEIRA CHAND

Meira Chand was born and educated in London. Her mother is Swiss and her father is Indian. She trained as a textile designer and married an Indian businessman before moving to Japan in 1962.

MITRA PHUKAN

Mitra Phukan is a well-known Assamese writer and contributes regularly to prominent English dailies in Assam. She is the author of a number of books for children and has recently edited a collection of Assamese short stories. She is a committed member of the North East Writers' Forum and edites their journal, NEWFrontiers.

SUKUMAR ROY

Roy, Sukumar (1887-1923) children's writer, was born in Kolkata on 30 October 1887. His family was originally from Masua in Mymensingh. His father, Upendra Kishore Roychowdhury, who also wrote for children, was a musician and mechanic and his son was the Oscar-winning filmmaker Satyajit Roy.

After passing the Entrance examination from the City School, Sukumar Ray took his BSc (1911) in chemistry from Presidency College. He then went to England on the Guruprasanna Ghosh Scholarship to study photography and printing technology. Sukumar studied at the Manchester School of Technology, where he proved the effectiveness of photo printing in halftone invented by his father.

At the East and West Society, Sukumar Roy read an essay called 'Spirit of Rabindranath', which was later published in

The Quest magazine. This earned him the opportunity to speak at various meetings in England. He was selected fellow of the Royal Photographic Society; he was the second Indian to earn this distinction. Back home in 1913, he took over his father's enterprise called U Roy and Sons.

Sukumar Roy was a versatile genius. He used to compose rhymes at an early age. Along with photography he learnt painting. While at college, he used to write comedies and act in them. He also acted in a play called Goday Galad with Rabindranath Tagore and Abanindranath Tagore at Santiniketan. He composed some songs during the Swadeshi Movement and also sang the songs himself. After his father's death, he took over the Sandesh, a magazine published by his father. While in England, he sent stories, poems and paintings to be published in the magazine.

While studying at Presidency College, he set up an organisation called 'Nonsense Club' and published the magazine Sade-Batrish-Bhaja as its mouthpiece. On his return from England, he started the 'Monday Club' where he used to arrange discussions along with refreshments, which earned the club another name, Monda (Bangla for sweetmeat) Club.

Sukumar Roy was principally noted for his writings for young children. He mixed comic elements and subtle satire in all his works-poems, plays, stories or paintings. His satire is marked by his social consciousness. His prominent writings include, Ha-Ya-Ba-Ra-La (Topsy-Turvy, 1928), Pagla Dashu (1940), Bahurupi (The Jester, 1944), Khaikhai (I Want More, 1950), Abak Jalpan (Strange Drink), Shabdakalpadrum (The Tree of Words) and Jhalapala (Irritation). He also wrote some serious essays in Bangla and English. He wrote a collection of belles-lettres called Hesoramer Dairi, written in the form of a diary.

Sukumar Ray's finest work Abol-Tabol the nearest English translation of which can be 'nonsense' or 'gibberish,' was written in the last two and a half years of his life. He died in 1923, nine days before his best-loved book 'Abol Tabol' was published. Anyone who has had his early schooling in Bengal, has grown up with the delightfully crazy verses of Abol Tabol that children love to recite. The poems of Abol Tabol had been gathered out of various issues of the children's magazine, Sandesh, which Sukumar Ray had been editing. The comic fantasies of Abol Tabol display a special brand of anarchic madness which bears the distinctive stamp of Sukumar Ray. Among his fantastic characters is an old man who survives on boiled wood and can tell you the taste and smell of different kinds of wood ("Kaath Buro"). There is the old woman whose rickety house has been put together with spit. There is a singer whose voice echoes from Delhi to Burma and makes animals faint. Roy's artistry and genius is best portrayed in this collection of fine verses and if he had not written a single word elsewhere - Abol Tabol would have anyways made him what he is today.

Bibliography

Alice Walker's: *The Color Purple: A Reader's Companion,* New Delhi, Asia Book Club, 2002.

Allen, Ernst: *The English Novel: a Short Critical History,* London: Phoenix House, 1954.

Amitav Ghosh's: *The Shadow Lines: Critical Essays,* New Delhi, Atlantic, 2002.

Anita Desai: *Vision and Technique in Her Novels,* New Delhi, B.R., 2001.

Ball, M. J. : *Phonetics: The Science of Speech,* London, Arnold, 1999.

Barter, James: *The Ganges,* San Diego, Lucent Books, 2003.

Bennett, J. A. W.: *Middle English Literature,* Oxford, Clarendon Press, 1986.

Bentley, Eades: *The Jacobean and Caroline Stage,* Oxford, Clarendon Press, 1941.

Beyond Borders: *An Anthology of SAARC Poetry,* Noida, Rainbow, 2002.

Bhattacharyya, Nath: *Indian Religious Historiography,* New Delhi, Munshiram Manoharlal Publishers, 1996.

Brown, J. M.: *Ireland in Fiction; a Guide to Irish Novels, Tales, Romances, and Folk-lore,* London: Maunsel, 1919.

Bush, Douglas: *English Literature in the Earlier Seventeenth Century, **1600-1660**,* Oxford, Clarendon Press, 1962.

Cahalan, M.: *The Irish Novel: a Critical History,* Boston, Twayne Publishers, 1988.

Caidin, Martin: *The Tigers are Burning,* NY, Hawthorn Books, 1974.

Cavanagh, John: *British Theatre: a Bibliography, **1901** to **1985**,* Hampshire, Motley, 1989.

Christopher, A.: *Roll of Infamy*, Osceola, MBI, 1997.

Courthope, John: *A History of English Poetry*, London, MacMillan and Co., 1903.

Crystal, D.: *Prosodic Systems and Intonation in English*, Cambridge, Cambridge University Press, 1969.

Davis, Brian L. : *Uniforms and Insignia of the Luftwaffe*, London, Arms and Armor, 1999.

Davis, Gwenn: *Drama by Women to 1900: a Bibliography of American and British Writers*, London, Mansell, 1992.

Desai, A.: *Vision and Technique in Her Novels*, New Delhi, B.R., 2001.

Eades, B.: *The Jacobean and Caroline Stage*, Oxford, Clarendon Press, 1941.

Edmund Spenser: *A Critical Study*, New Delhi, Anmol Pub., 2005.

Ernst, A.: *The English Novel: a Short Critical History*, London: Phoenix House, 1954.

Ferrence, G.: *Deadly Fashion: the Rise and Fall of Cigarette Smoking in North America*, New York, Garland, 1989.

Florette, Henri: *Kings Mountain*, Garden City, Doubleday, 1950.

Francis, Russell: *The Scottish Novel: from Smollett to Spark*, Cambridge, Harvard University Press, 1978.

Gerald, Eades: *The Jacobean and Caroline Stage*, Oxford, Clarendon Press, 1941.

Gilmer, Moss: *The Patriots of Kings Mountain*, Blacksburg, Scotia-Hubernia, 1990.

Halliday, M. A. K.: *Intonation and Grammar in British English*, The Hague, Mouton, 1967.

Harivansh R.B.: *In the Afternoon of Time: An Autobiography*, New Delhi, Penguin, 2001.

Hart, Russell: *The Scottish Novel: from Smollett to Spark*, Cambridge, Harvard University Press, 1978.

Horsman, E. A.: *The Victorian Novel*, Oxford, Clarendon Press, 1990.

Ian Robert James: *English Literature, 1815-1832*, Oxford, Clarendon Press, 1963.

James, Ernest: *Principles of Textual Criticism*, San Marino, Huntington Library, 1972.

James, M.: *The Irish Novel: a Critical History*, Boston, Twayne Publishers, 1988.

Koehl, Lewis: *The Black Corps*, Madison, University of Wisconsin Press, 1983.

Laver, J.: *Principles of Phonetics*, Cambridge, Cambridge University Press, 1994.

Logan, P.: *The Later Jacobean and Caroline Dramatists*, Lincoln, University of Nebraska Press, 1978.

Moss, B.: *The Patriots of Kings Mountain*, Blacksburg, Scotia-Hubernia, 1990.

Naipaul, V.S. : *A House for Mr. Biswas: With an Introduction by Ian Buruma*, New Delhi, Penguin, 1992.

Neil Bissoondath: *Indo-Caribbean-Canadian Diaspora*, New Delhi, Rawat, 2005.

Pearsall, Albert: *Old English and Middle English Poetry*, London, Routledge & K. Paul, 1977.

Philip Roth: *A Novelist in Crisis*, New Delhi, Classical Publishing, 2001.

Rahilly, J.: *Phonetics: The Science of Speech*, London, Arnold, 1999.

Richard, L.: *A Microfiche Concordance to Old English*, Newark, University of Delaware, 1980.

Robert, Goode: *The Modern Irish Drama: a Documentary History*, NJ: Humanities Press, 1975.

Roberta, G.: *Deadly Fashion: the Rise and Fall of Cigarette Smoking in North America*, New York, Garland, 1989.

Royle, Trevor: *The Macmillan Companion to Scottish Literature*, London, MacMillan Reference Books, 1983.

Salman Rushdie: *New Critical Insights*, New Delhi, Atlantic Pub., 2003.

Seidlhofer, B.: *Pronunciation, Oxford*, Oxford University Press, 1994.

Stephen, J. M.: *Ireland in Fiction; a Guide to Irish Novels, Tales, Romances, and Folk-lore*, London: Maunsel, 1919.

Sutherland, John: *The Stanford Companion to Victorian Fiction*, Stanford, Stanford University Press, 1989.

Sydney, J.: *Brands, Consumers, Symbols and Research*, Thousand Oaks, Sage Publications, 1999.

Texts, Issues: *Essays on Indian Literature*, Delhi, Pencraft International, 2003.

Thorpe, Ernest: *Principles of Textual Criticism*, San Marino, Huntington Library, 1972.

Underhill, A.: *Sound Foundations*, London, Heineman, 1994.

Venezky, L.: *A Microfiche Concordance to Old English*, Newark, University of Delaware, 1980.

Vikram Seth: *Multiple Locations, Multiple Affiliation*, New Delhi, Rawat, 2001.

Walter, Ernst: *The English Novel: a Short Critical History*, London: Phoenix House, 1954.

Wearing, J. P.: *The London Stage, 1890-1899: a Calendar of Plays and Players*, NJ, Scarecrow Press, 1976.

Weathers, B.: *The Living Past of Cleveland County: A History*, Spartanburg, The Reprint Company, 1956.

Wickham, Gladstone: *Early English Stages, 1300 to 1660*, London, Routledge and Paul; 1959.

William Blake: *A Critical Study*, New Delhi, Anmol, 2005.

William, John: *A History of English Poetry*, London, MacMillan and Co., 1903.

Yeats, W.B. : *Poetry and Plays*, New Delhi, Atlantic, 2002.

Yonah, A.: *Combating Terrorism: Strategies of Ten Countries*, Mich., University of Michigan Press, 2002.

INDEX

D

E

F

G

I

J

❑❑❑